# Terrorism and the State

# Terrorism and the State

## A Critique of Domination Through Fear

### WILLIAM D. PERDUE

**PRAEGER**

New York
Westport, Connecticut
London

**Copyright Acknowledgments**

The author and publisher are grateful to the following for allowing the use of excerpts from:

"The Geneva Declaration on Terrorism." In *Terrorism and National Liberation*, edited by Hans Koechler, 307–13. New York: Peter Lang, 1988. Reproduced by permission.

William D. Perdue. "The Selling of International Terrorism." In *Terrorism and National Liberation*, edited by Hans Koechler, 217–33. New York: Peter Lang, 1988. Reproduced by permission.

William D. Perdue. *Sociological Theory: Explanation, Paradigm, and Ideology*. Palo Alto, Calif.: Mayfield, 1986. Reproduced by permission.

**Library of Congress Cataloging-in-Publication Data**

Perdue, William D., 1943–
    Terrorism and the state / William D. Perdue.
        p.    cm.
    Bibliography: p.
    Includes index.
    ISBN 0-275-93140-4 (alk. paper)
    1. Terrorism—Government policy.    I. Title.
HV6431.P46   1989
363.3'2—dc19        88-34029

Copyright © 1989 by William D. Perdue

All rights reserved. No portion of this book may be reproduced, by any process or technique, without the express written consent of the publisher.

Library of Congress Catalog Card Number: 88-34029
ISBN 0-275-93140-4

First published in 1989

Praeger Publishers, One Madison Avenue, New York, NY 10010
A division of Greenwood Press, Inc.

Printed in the United States of America

The paper used in this book complies with the Permanent Paper Standard issued by the National Information Standards Organization (Z39.48-1984).

10 9 8 7 6 5 4 3 2 1

# Contents

| | | |
|---|---|---|
| Preface | | ix |
| 1 | **The Ideology of Terrorism** | 1 |
| | International Terrorism in the 1980s: The Bush Report | 2 |
| | Power Relations | 3 |
| | Ideologies of Domination | 4 |
| | Total Ideology | 6 |
| |    *The Dominant Ideology of Terrorism* | 8 |
| |    *The Utopian Ideology of Terrorism* | 12 |
| | The Western Academic Construction of Terrorism | 14 |
| 2 | **Terrorism and the State** | 17 |
| | The Reification of the State | 17 |
| | Domination through Fear | 19 |
| |    *The Warfare State and the New Global Security Economy* | 20 |
| |    *Imperial Terror* | 23 |
| |    *The Imperial Legacy: Northern Ireland and the I.R.A* | 26 |
| | Global Market Disjunction and Regime Terror | 33 |
| |    *The French Revolution and the Jacobin Reign of Terror* | 33 |

|   |   |   |
|---|---|---|
|   | German Fascism and the Final Solution | 36 |
|   | Stalinism: Modernization and Purge | 38 |
|   | Toward Revisionist Definitions of Terrorism | 41 |
| 3 | **Mediaspeak: The Selling of International Terrorism** | 45 |
|   | Terror in the Skies: The Hijacking of T.W.A. Flight 847 | 45 |
|   | The Headline Story | 48 |
|   | *Mad Dogs and Presidents* | 50 |
|   | The Media Prism | 57 |
|   | *The Other Anti-Semitism: Stereotyping the Arab World* | 57 |
|   | *The Western* Weltanschauung | 60 |
|   | The International Information and Communication Order | 60 |
|   | *Commodification and Terrorism* | 61 |
|   | *The Means of Influence: The Networks* | 62 |
|   | Conclusion | 66 |
| 4 | **The Real Nuclear Terrorism** | 69 |
|   | Nuclear Renegades: The Official Story | 70 |
|   | Terrorism Unlimited | 71 |
|   | *The Heat, the Cold, and the Dark* | 72 |
|   | *Nuclear Legitimation: Bomber, Missile, and Other Sanity Gaps* | 77 |
|   | *The Ideology of Nuclear Deterrence* | 80 |
|   | *The Nuclear Warfare State* | 82 |
|   | *Weapons Immortality: Star Wars* | 83 |
|   | *The Doctrine of Discriminate Deterrence* | 84 |
|   | *Social Negation* | 85 |
|   | Summary: The World's Business | 87 |
| 5 | **Racial Terrorism: Apartheid in South Africa** | 89 |
|   | The Red Scare in Black Africa | 90 |
|   | The South African National Emergency State | 92 |
|   | Regional Domination | 94 |
|   | R.S.A. Institutional Terror | 96 |
|   | Internal Colonialism | 97 |
|   | *Settler Isolation and the Ideology of the "Chosen"* | 97 |

|   |   |   |
|---|---|---|
|   | *Ideological Permutations and Neo-Apartheid* | 98 |
|   | *Caste Capitalism* | 99 |
|   | Global Apartheid | 103 |
|   | Summary: The South Africa of Tomorrow | 107 |
| 6 | **"Terrornoia" and Zonal Revolution: The Case of Libya** | 111 |
|   | Libyan Terrorism: The Official Story | 113 |
|   | The Specter of Zonal Revolution | 118 |
|   | Libya and the Maghrib: Successive Colonization | 118 |
|   | *The Al Fatah Revolution* | 121 |
|   | *Authentic Independence* | 123 |
|   | *Ideological Synthesis* | 126 |
|   | *Material Transformation* | 127 |
|   | Summary | 131 |
| 7 | **Settler Terrorism: Israel and the P.L.O** | 133 |
|   | How the West Can Win | 135 |
|   | The P.L.O. and the Question of Terrorism | 137 |
|   | The Jewish State | 140 |
|   | Sacred Terrorism | 144 |
|   | Settler Terrorism | 150 |
|   | *Intifadah: The Revolution of Stones* | 151 |
|   | *Maximal Zionism and Apartheid* | 153 |
| 8 | **Holy Terror: Iran and Irangate** | 159 |
|   | Whom the Gods Would Destroy | 161 |
|   | The Great Satan | 163 |
|   | Theocratic Reaction | 166 |
|   | The Neoimperial Crucible | 169 |
|   | *Mossadeq, Nationalization, and Operation Ajax* | 172 |
|   | *Iranian Regime Terror: 1953–79* | 173 |
|   | Theoretical Conclusions | 176 |
| 9 | **Surrogate Terrorism: The United States and Nicaragua** | 181 |
|   | Manifest Destiny and Nicaragua: The Roots of Terror | 182 |
|   | *The Rogue and the Tycoon* | 183 |
|   | *Beachheads Old and New* | 184 |
|   | Sandino and Somoza | 186 |
|   | Sandinista National Liberation | 191 |
|   | Counterrevolution and Surrogate Terror | 193 |

*The United States and the World Court* 196
*The Doctrine of Low-Intensity Conflict* 198
*The Real Narcoterrorism* 200
The Nicaraguan Experiment and Hemispheric Hegemony 202

Bibliography 205

Index 221

# *Preface*

One man's terrorist is another man's freedom fighter.

This observation, now something of a cliché in international circles, puzzles many for whom the question of terrorism is not a question at all. Certainly, the issue is a popular one in the United States and the Western world today. Moreover, a conclusion has taken form (routinely expressed by political leadership and media personalities, as well as in most academic literature) that the nature of terrorism is unambiguous. The official view presents a study in international deviance on the part of outlaws and fanatics. Argued thus, the only question about terrorism is how to control it.

Perhaps the view that terrorism is a given stems from the consensus of images systematically disseminated through the United States and much of the Western world. Political language is a powerful device for the creation of such a consensus, but imagery does not rest on the spoken word alone. The international media also employ powerful visual technology. Thus the word *terrorism* is associated with scenes of outrageous violence such as hostage-taking, aircraft piracy, sabotage, assassination, and indiscriminate bombings and shootings. The victims are routinely described as innocents and noncombatants. And always, those officially labeled as terrorists are said to represent the forces of barbarism who threaten civilization and democratic order. Once the label is official, the term counterterrorism may be used to legitimate extraordinary sanctions directed toward offending parties; sanctions that might otherwise be rejected by many.

Yet while the implications of "one man's terrorist..." may challenge absolutist views, the argument of multiple meanings is itself narrowly framed. Even in this more pluralist thought-world, the focus is with the definition of behaviors, not with the real relations of domination and subjugation embodied in social structure. Thus, the liberal relativism of "one man's terrorist..." is not sufficient to prompt the critical thought by which the *institutionalized* forces of domination through fear can be analyzed. The premise of the work at hand stands apart from both the control and relativistic models. The issue of meaning remains crucial, but at a higher level definitions give way to the ideological *problematique* of terrorism. And at the base of these conflicting images of terrorism are real relationships; enduring structures of global dependency in which the forces of order clash with those of change.

From an institutional perspective, the means of domination through fear may be embodied in the modern nation-state. Ultimately, this entity represents the supreme organization of political power, whereby dominion and rule is concentrated in a single structure. It holds a monopoly on many forms of lethal force, including that exercised by the military and the police. There are clear differences among states bearing on formal organization and the legitimation of authority. However, there are two common properties that make the question of *state terrorism* one of the more vital of our time. On the one hand, the modern state is a system that provides for the efficient, routinely bureaucratic marshaling of human and material resources. Accordingly, it confers upon those who control it, whether directly or indirectly, the power to intimidate or coerce both domestic and international opponents and to do so efficiently and continuously over time. On the other hand, the state quite frequently enjoys a legitimacy born of political socialization and the power of ideology. Therefore, that which is done in the name of protecting the state, the country, or the leadership may be held up to a different measure. This implies a double standard of terrorism, one for the state and the other for its opponents. Yet even state power cannot be understood in isolation.

The clarification of institutional forces is at the base of the political economy of terrorism. From this critical and holistic perspective, the relevant literature must logically include works on ideology, colonialism, imperialism, dependency, models of development, state organization, and social change. With a few sterling exceptions, such topics are routinely absent from the specialized literature on terrorism. But it is not enough to remain formally academic. Throughout this work, some attempt will be made to give fair hearing to certain of the victims and resisters of institutional terror. By this device, it may be possible to fashion something of an ideological breakout.

Early on, the terrorism debate will be reframed. In Chapter 1 on the ideology of terrorism, the different prisms for understanding and defining political violence are explored. In Chapter 2 on state terrorism, a succinct historical review supports a revisionist position, that places the issue in the context of global relations. From *the Terror* of the French Revolution to the *Great Purge* of the Stalinist era, from the *Imperial Terror* in the British relationship with Ireland to the *Death Squads* of El Salvador, from the *Final Solution* of the Nazi death camps to the grim arsenals of the *Modern Warfare State*, regime terror is shown to reflect transnational forces. In Chapter 3, attention is given to the vital role of the media in the selling of international terrorism. It is often argued that the media contribute to terrorism through giving its practitioners a world platform. More complex is the contention that the media are selective in the definition and coverage of this question, specifically ignoring or understating its institutional forms.

Chapters 4 through 9 are historically grounded cases, in which the framework established in the first three chapters is employed in a systematic analysis of state terrorism. In Chapter 4 on the real nuclear terrorism, the specter of outlaw organizations acquiring a nuclear device is juxtaposed with the coercive power of today's nuclear weapons states. In Chapter 5, the question of state terrorism is explored in the context of the apartheid system of the Republic of South Africa. The inquiry first explores a modern form of regime terror, embodied in torture, mass arrests, surveillance, false charges, show trials, and the silencing of critical media. Yet, R.S.A. repression is not to be conceived simply in terms of race relations within the boundaries of a modern nation-state. What is at issue here are the relations of power that mark a *global apartheid*.

The question of state-sponsored terrorism is contrasted with the cultivation of *terrornoia* as a geopolitical weapon in Chapter 6 on Libya. The internal war between Israel and the Palestine Liberation Organization is the focus of Chapter 7 on *settler terrorism*. In Chapter 8, the strange saga of *Iran and Irangate* is explored in a study of "holy terror," a chapter that bridges the final inquiry into *surrogate* terrorism. Here, official charges of Central American totalitarianism are contrasted with the history of hemispheric hegemony and the role of the U.S. Central Intelligence Agency and National Security Council in Nicaragua.

This book offers no conspiratorial view of "terror networks," no simple conceptions of civilization and barbarism, and no call for the development of new forms of security and conflict designed to control the terrorist threat. Indeed, it shall be argued that the more insidious forms of terrorism may visit the world in the guise of antiterrorism. This book does not argue that to explain reactive political violence is to excuse it, nor that all politically inspired acts of resistance are legitimate, nor that terrorism is an overblown issue. Properly conceived, institutional terrorism in all its forms (together with the vendetta reactions it breeds), threatens the legitimate aspirations of the world's peoples to a life of dignity and purpose. Whether manifested in the grinding fear of privation, in the dread of the instrumentalities of the state, or in the caprice of random violence, terrorism stands as the negation of social being. As such, it is an offense against humanity, against history, and against the human future.

# Terrorism and the State

# 1

# The Ideology of Terrorism

> The United States must be able to deal with terrorists as brutally and as deviously as they deal with it.
> Raymond Price, former member of the Nixon administration, quoted in the *International Herald Tribune*, November 9, 1985

Calling for terror to oppose terror represents well the polemic that dominated U.S. international policy during the 1980s. Yet the question of terrorism, both in terms of events and ideology, is clearly not the invention of one nation, one administration, or one decade. As shall be demonstrated, its dilemmas and controversies have a history, and one fears, a future. It is the nature of our time, however, that some appear ready to yield to barbarism in the name of antibarbarism. Yet, the *problematique* of terrorism transcends the political, tactical, and philosophical questions of how to respond. Even those who wish to take the "high moral ground" (by opposing the position exemplified by Raymond Price), still assume that a "civilized" nation must not stoop to "brutal and devious" measures. So framed, the terrorism debate in Western nations is often over tactics of international social control. Such a focus pits the moralists, who favor diplomatic and other political approaches, against the realists, who opt for forms of coercion ranging from economic sanctions to military action.

Realism is a much abused term, but as a kind of "statespeak," it means that holders of power must deal with the world as it is, not as "we" might wish it to be. This position assumes, of course, that "we" are not part of the problem. C. Wright Mills (1959: 356) unkindly referred to this blindness, which emanates from the elite but that spreads through the lower echelons of power, as "crackpot realism." Ironically, whatever their differences on means, tacticians agree on ends. Both hold to the rightness of their position while attributing brutality to the other side. To assume the superiority of one's own political culture is perhaps a simple modification of a more general ethnocentrism, and such influences are clearly evident in many pronouncements on terrorism. Still, there is more to the terrorism debate than the brutality of tactics or the phenomenon of culturally induced blindness.

## INTERNATIONAL TERRORISM IN THE 1980s: THE BUSH REPORT

Terrorism for most people is captured more in images than in words. In the West, high-impact media portrayals feature personal and dramatic accounts of victims and their families, with the signature of the terrorist written in blood. In the 1980s, a cornerstone of U.S. foreign policy became its "low-intensity" war on terror, legitimated by the imagery of senseless, brutal, and random violence. It is in this spirit that the *Public Report of the Vice President's Task Force on Combatting Terrorism* proclaimed in 1986 that "terrorism is a phenomenon that is easier to describe than define." Undeterred, the Bush report cites: "the unlawful use or threat of violence against persons or property to further political or social objectives. It is generally intended to intimidate or coerce a government, individuals, or groups to modify their behavior or policies." This cabinet-level attempt at definition also specified the methods of terrorism, including "hostage-taking, aircraft piracy or sabotage, assassination, threats, hoaxes, indiscriminate bombings or shootings." And finally, the document portrayed the targets of terrorism as innocent, noting that "most victims of terrorism seldom have a role in either causing or affecting the terrorist's grievances." (1986: 1)

Having defined the undefinable, the vice-president's task force constructed a profile of the terrorist, followed by a listing of likely targets.

The motivations of those who engage in terrorism are many and varied, with activities spanning industrial societies to underdeveloped regions. Fully 60 percent of the Third World population is under 20 years of age; half are 15 years or less. These population pressures create a volatile mixture of youthful aspirations that when coupled with economic and political frustrations help form a large pool of potential terrorists. Many terrorists have a deep belief in the justice of their cause. They are tough and vicious and may have little regard for their own lives or those of their victims in attempting to achieve their goals. Others may even be hired assassins.... Middle East terrorist groups have three main targets: Israel; Western governments and citizens... and moderate Arab governments and officials. (1986:1–2)

These targets were allegedly at risk from several sources. While European organizations (such as the Italian Red Brigade, French Direct Action, German Red

Army Faction, and the Provisional Irish Republican Army) were duly noted, the report held that: "the most deadly terrorists continue to operate in and from the Middle East. In 1985, they were involved in roughly 50 percent of the total worldwide terrorist incidents. The two main sources are militant Shi'ites from various Middle Eastern countries, especially Lebanon, supported to varying degrees by Iran or Syria; and radical Palestinian elements, principally offshoots of the Palestine Liberation Organization (PLO), often with direct support from Libya, Syria or Iran." In Latin America, the document declares, "Nicaragua and Cuba have been implicated in terrorist activity . . . " (1986: 1–3).

Taken as a whole, the excerpts convey the official story of terrorism. The statist standing of the document and the extent to which its themes have entered public perception qualifies it as an exemplar of the dominant ideology of terrorism. By this set of interrelated ideas, the legitimation of a particular view of world order is constructed through claims made about the nature of terrorism. This idea-system identifies what terrorism is, which methods terrorists employ, and who the terrorists and their victims are. From this viewpoint, terrorism (whether employing action or threat) is unlawful, intended to advance a political or social agenda, and its first targets are Western and other friendly governments.[1]

## POWER RELATIONS

To begin to demystify terrorism then, is to raise the question of power relations. One might begin simply by noting that powerless groups often employ guerrilla methods to compensate for their military disadvantage; tactics ordinarily decried by powerful forces as uncivilized. The hit and run tactics of native tribes in North America were called "savage" by European colonials, who then used them later against the British in the American Revolution. The guerrilla forces of Pancho Villa and Emiliano Zapata were similarly denounced by the privileged patrons during the Mexican revolution. Today, the African National Congress, a resistance movement that advocates armed struggle against white minority rule, is termed "terrorist" by the South African government. (Perhaps the ANC would prefer to use air and naval forces against the apartheid government of South Africa if they were available.) All of this is not to argue that powerless groups are incapable of acts of violence that betray whatever cause they claim. The point is that the guerrilla tactics of the powerless are more apt to be labeled terrorist than martial force on the part of an established state.

Second, a focus on power relations goes beyond tactics to ask why some forms of political violence are described as terrorist, while others that bring greater human loss do not invite that label. If parties in conflict do not have equal standing, a double standard of terrorism may be expected to emerge. Thus the definitions of terrorism that prevail reflect such forces as the influence of office, access to the highly sophisticated and pervasive international media, and the "audience appeal" of common values, stereotypes, and symbols. A presidential address on terrorism will have a vast media audience, many of whom are predisposed to respond favorably to the symbols of office, the appeals to nationalistic imagery and the attribution of terrorism to ethnic, ideological and religious forces that already carry negative stereotypes.

Finally, differences in power on the international stage often obscure the reality of institutional terror. To focus on institutional terror means to critically analyze violent and coercive patterns that coalesce around fundamental human purposes, such as meeting material needs and resolving the questions of political rule. It poses the plausible yet disturbing thesis that people face grinding conditions of fear rooted in the very arrangements that promise to safeguard and better their lives. These arrangements are not confined to the societal level, nor do they recognize lines drawn on maps.

To this point, an international economic order may quite "normally" reproduce inequality on a world scale, quite efficiently and systematically transferring wealth from the southern to the northern hemispheres. In the lives of ordinary people, this means 450 million severely malnourished people, the deaths of 15 million children yearly from hunger or hunger-related illness (George, 1984: 3), and in the poorest countries, the death of one child in four before the age of five (Brandt Commission, 1980: 32). On another level, the political organization known as the modern state may be used alone or in alliance with others to advance or protect that order. In the name of security, it offers missiles; in the name of freedom, war; in the name of antiterrorism, terrorism. In the lives of ordinary people, the corruption of state power may be expressed in the knock on the door, mass arrests, disappearances, and summary execution. It may be a device for diverting water, occupying land, and sponsoring its settlement. It may mean capital punishment for those "without the capital," especially if the victims are of some ethnic or racial minority group.

## IDEOLOGIES OF DOMINATION

Ultimately, terrorism is a label of defamation, a means of excluding those so branded from human standing. When applied in a one-sided fashion to those who struggle against established political structures, it is a means of organizing both the perceptions and reactions of others in the world community. Once so defined, those affected may become international lepers. Hence the nature of their movement; its objectives, ideology, and historical reason for being will be dismissed out of hand. Paradoxically then, the very label of terrorism has of itself assumed a terrifying power.

Those ideas that interpret the nature and dimensions of human behavior do not arise in a historical vacuum. They are created, formed, and shaped in the minds of people who participate in and respond to the conditions of their age. Yet not all who would define the nature of terrorism exist as equal contributors to the debate. For the ideological construction of terrorism is a function of power; of the ability to control events and to impose one's ways upon others against their will. It follows from the preliminary and sensitizing argument to this point, that power consists of more than overt force and coercion. Within its nature must be found an ability to define events, and to broadly disseminate the official view.

Historically, colonial powers plundered the human and natural resources of their territories. The great plantations of the new world were built by the Africans, wrested from their native land, stacked like timber in the holds of slave ships, then broken from tribe and family and sold into bondage. This conversion to chattel meant more than the death of millions in passage; it also meant that survivors and their descendants would know the negation of their humanity, while the African continent would suffer the devastation of its labor force and thus of its productive future. Even with the decline of the slave trade, the nations of the northern hemisphere continued to transform the vast riches of the south into finished products the original providers of primary resources still find difficult to purchase.[2] And the labor in the north was provided by workers who owned neither factory nor mill, their tools nor their machines, their time nor their jobs.

No doubt, had they been asked, victims then and now would define such conditions as those of constant dread and fear. However, the ideologies that prevailed proved to be those of the master not the slave, of the colonizer not the colonized, of the owning class, not those who sold their labor for a wage. Hence the ideas of racism legitimated the conversion of human beings into chattel, those of colonialism portrayed the native as primitive, and those of social Darwinism argued that the class system was a form of merited inequality. These ideologies of domination were routinely offered academic legitimation. For example, William Graham Sumner joined the faculty of Yale in 1872 and three years later offered one of the first sociology courses on the continent. Drawing from the "principle of noninterference" (social, political, economic *laissez-faire*) of Britain's Herbert Spencer, he reproduced the darker side of the age of imperialism. In this context, the social world, as the natural, was an orderly creation obeying the prime directive of all life: a struggle in which the fit survive and the unfit perish.

The sociologist is often asked if he wants to kill off certain classes of troublesome and bewildered persons. No such inference follows from any sound sociological doctrine, but it is allowed to infer, as to a great many persons and classes, that it would have been better for society and would have involved no pain to them, if they had never been born. (Sumner, 1963: 25)

The Aryan myth was nurtured in the works of Arthur de Gobineau (1816–82) and H. S. Chamberlain (1885–1926) and others. It remained for Karl Pearson (a turn-of-the-century mathematician who pioneered in the area of correlation) to succinctly demonstrate the power of racism as an ideological tool for political and economic domination. In one paragraph, he offered a defense of the colonization of Africa, the superiority of the white race, and the survival of the fittest component of social Darwinism.

How many centuries, how many thousands of years, have the Kaffir or the negro held large districts in Africa undisturbed by the white man? Yet their intertribal struggles have not yet produced a civilization in the least comparable with the Aryan. Educate and mature them as you will, I do not believe that you will succeed in modifying the stock. History shows me one way, and one way only, in which a high state of civilization has been produced, namely in the struggle of race with race, and the survival of the physically and mentally fitter race. (Quoted in Sorokin, 1964: 260)

Supremacist thought from the age of imperialism served only to disguise and legitimate the institutional terror of slavery, forced labor among the colonized, the exploitation of the industrial working class, child labor, and ultimately, patterns of genocide. The historical functions of such myths are clearer today. But the contemporary question is whether new or reformulated patterns of inequality have given rise to modern myths of legitimation and defamation.

## TOTAL IDEOLOGY

Among liberal philosophers of the French Revolution, the term ideology referred to specific solutions to the problems of society. As a "science of ideas," it was to conform to the scientific knowledge of the day, offering an alternative world view to that advanced by the dominant ideological institution of the age, the Catholic church (Drucker, 1974: 3–10). Now the conflict between religion and science is important because of differing methods for discerning truth. But there is more to this and other kinds of conflicts involving ideas. The making of truth concerns more than method, evidence and law. It also reflects a struggle between traditional and alternative orders. What if "God's laws" are restricted to the supernatural realm, to be replaced in the natural order by scientific laws? It can only follow that the custodians of the revealed word must find their influence on matters pertaining to "this world" diminished. The differences in ideas and ideologies thus in part embody a struggle over real influence and material power.

Perhaps it is time to systematically explore the properties of ideology and ideological analysis. To begin, an ideology constitutes a *system* of thought. As such, each element of that system cannot be understood in isolation but is rather interlocked with the other ideas that constitute the whole. Although the term may be used to represent the views of certain individuals, or the guiding principles of certain political parties, it is more useful to understand ideology in a structural sense. Idea systems do not emerge in a vacuum, nor do they originate wholecloth in the minds of men and women. Instead, ideologies have a history. They embody the events of an age, and they arise from struggles for power.

It can be further argued that in a divided or segmented society or world the privileged groups who benefit from that hierarchical order will see the world somewhat differently from those on the bottom. This argument need not hold for every member in a specified category of persons but rather for the category or group in general. Thus ideology is a collective phenomenon that cannot be reduced to the level of the attitudes of individual group members. It is made and remade by people who share a common position in the hierarchy, but it is that structural position that must be understood, not the personalities of social actors. What is more to the point, the means available to those in more powerful positions include greater access to the modern forms of ideological institutions (education, media, and religion) that disseminate the ideas and ideals of the existing order. Thus whether on a societal or world scale, thought systems that justify the existing order will be advanced more systematically than those that justify change (Perdue, 1986: 325–27, 388–93).

Although Marx and Engels explored the uses of dominant modes of thought to demystify ideological coercion on the part of a capitalist ruling class (1967, originally published 1845–46), it was Karl Mannheim who advanced the modern field. Mannheim made a number of contributions, several of which are important to this inquiry. First, he held that politics is not merely a "struggle for power" but is first and foremost a "political conception of the world" (1968: 36, originally published in 1936). Put descriptively, it is a struggle for the hearts and minds of human beings. Further, Mannheim distinguished between two conceptions of ideology: the *particular and the total* (1968: 55–59). Those who conceptualize ideology as particular are interested in whether or not a specific view is demonstrably false. Hence, at this purely psychological level, particular forms of ideology range in meaning from a conscious attempt to manipulate others, to simple self-deception that may be passed on in good faith. Whatever the case, the particular conception of ideology holds that contending parties share the same standards for judging truth. However, Mannheim's total conception of ideology lifts the analysis to a higher plane, and in the process raises the political stakes.

When Mannheim identified the total conception of ideology, he advanced a form of analysis based on opposing world views. These differences in world views mean that parties in conflict represent different intellectual universes, each with distinctive criteria by which truth may be discovered. The total conception of ideology also holds that thought systems are associated with specific sociohistorical groups (such as a class). Thus the total conception of ideology is not concerned with motivations (or self-serving falsehoods) but with the relationship between social forces and world view. More specifically, the interests reflected in ideas are those of contending parties in history. Thought systems can thus be divided into two ideal types: those that favor the existing order and those that favor change.

Mannheim reserved the term *ideology* to refer to those total systems of thought held by society's ruling groups that obscure real conditions and thereby preserve the status quo. Or, in his words, "ruling groups can in their thinking become so intensively interest-bound to a situation that they are simply no longer able to see certain facts which would undermine their sense of domination" (1968: 40). "Utopian" thinking for Mannheim represented an opposing constellation. Here total systems of thought are forged by oppressed groups interested in the transformation of social or global orders. From the utopian side, the purpose of social thought is not simply to diagnose (much less legitimate) existing reality. It is rather to provide a rationally justifiable system of ideas to legitimate and direct change. *Utopian* thought thus means that oppressed groups selectively perceive "only those elements in the situation which tend to negate it" (1968: 40).

The subject at hand is not ideology in general but a more narrowly drawn thought-system on the nature of terrorism. But to comprehend the ideological factor in terrorism requires a coming to terms with important distinctions. First, this approach is more an inquiry into domination and its responses than it is a study of social control. While there are bands of nihilists, given to random acts of violence and representing no popular constituency, it is abundantly clear that they are not the real ideological targets of state wars on terror. Instead, the delegitimating label of terrorism has been reserved for far more significant adversaries.

Second, the ideological battle over the nature of terrorism both embodies and alters relations of power, with implications for the direction of social change. To illustrate, deciding on what constitutes "real terrorism" may mean that authentic movements of national liberation will come to limit vendetta in their ranks and thereby gain global support. At the level of the nation-state, it is also plausible that a Habermas-style "legitimation crisis" (1975) may result if and when forms of state violence are redefined as institutional terrorism. Stated simply, broad-scale rejection of that state violence masquerading as "counter-terrorism" may push states into new modes of conflict resolution.

## The Dominant Ideology of Terrorism

The dominant ideology of terrorism refers to a specific thought-system held by an institutional elite; the higher circles of political, economic, and military power committed to the preservation of an existing material and superstructural order. From the dominant side, terrorism is a form of international deviance; a set of behaviors that violate a collective consensus supposedly held by a "civilized people" on acceptable forms of violence. When defined in more general political terms, terrorism is an attack on legitimate transnational order. Viewed through a Western prism, that order includes not only loosely defined democratic governments but world-class corporations, international banks, and the indigenous institutions in those developing societies that are extensions of the Western model of development. Specifically, these are countries in alignment with the international market economy. This alignment is demonstrated by the welcoming of foreign capital or (in rare instances where resources may bring substantial return in the world market) a willingness to spend national income on the import of infrastructure and finished goods; acceptance of conditional loans; openness to corporation subsidiaries, and participation in a system of world market trade.

In the dominant view, those who perpetrate outsider violence are often portrayed as irrational or crazed, exercising a twisted thirst for blood. For example, Claire Sterling writes in her prologue to *The Terror Network*: "My own conclusion was that, Black or Red, right or left, there are no good killers and bad killers—only killers" (1981b: 2). This conclusion effectively magnifies, depoliticizes, and delegitimates all violence on the part of outsiders. And from a somewhat less polemical author:

> It is clear that those who attempt bizarre, ostensibly political actions with uncertain or irrational outward motivations do so for what are internal, personal reasons.... Those who act out their fantasies by murdering the mighty are only one variant in the pool of psychotics whose acts can threaten transnational order. (Bell, 1975: 10)

The dominant ideology of terrorism as known in the West is more than content, it also reflects a particular style. Specifically, the nature of terrorism is privatized as are attempts to explain it. History is reduced to the behavior of notorious persons (whether good or evil) locked in an international morality play. Institutions (such as the state) and movements that oppose those institutions are downplayed or ignored as social forces respectively committed to order and change. There is instead an emphasis on enemy ideologies, conspiracies, and shadowy organizations. Expressed polemically, the good guys are free enterprisers, democratic, Christian, and civilized. The bad guys are communists, Marxists, Islamic fundamentalists, and assorted crazies.

## Demonology and Solidarity

Questions of content and style should not obscure the consequences of ideological imagery. Human beings live in a symbolic universe, and symbols represent the medium of social interaction. The most intricate of symbolic systems is language, and the use of complex and highly expressive languages distinguishes the human species. Of course, all words represent some level of symbolism, but in considering the properties of political language certain words are more equal than others. This is not simply because of the precise definitional content (what the word denotes) but also because of the inherent emotional impact (what the word connotes). The argument again is that the term terrorism unleashes powerful imagery with clear societal and intellectual consequences.

Symbolism and allegory are ideological devices that intensify what the Arab social philosopher Ibn Khaldun termed solidarity: a collective sense of oneness or cohesion among the members of a given social order. Through imagery and intricate political fables, those who have alternative visions of society or a changed international order are defined as irrational. Combined with appeals to nationalism, faith, and other traditional symbols, the war on terror unites the social audience against the forces of barbarism and heresy. However, from the standpoint of the state, it is useful to magnify the threat and to weave a pattern of conspiratorial power in order to make a credible foe. This pattern will necessarily involve the identification of a cast of higher demons. The following quotation features the magnification of the threat, the use of imagery (ironically drawn from the history of crime in the speaker's nation), and an appeal to grandeur and unmerited persecution.

So, there we have it: Iran, Libya, North Korea, Cuba, Nicaragua—continents away, tens of thousands of miles apart, but the same goals and objectives. I submit to you that the growth in terrorism in recent years results from the increasing involvement of these states in terrorism in every region of the world. This is terrorism that is part of a pattern, the work of a confederation of terrorist states. Most of the terrorists who are kidnaping and murdering American citizens and attacking American installations are being trained, financed, and directly or indirectly controlled by a core group of radical and totalitarian governments—a new international version of "Murder Incorporated." And all of these states are united by one, simple, criminal phenomenon—their fanatical hatred of the United States, our people, our way of life, our international stature." (From Ronald Reagan, "The New Network of Terrorist States," an address to the American Bar Association, Washington, D.C., July 8, 1985)

The use of the term *terrorism* to delegitimate those who oppose the West is not an invention of the 1980s. During the post–World War II period of political decolonization in Africa, various national liberation movements were described as terrorist by the affected European states. Only a few examples include the Mau-Mau uprising against the British in Kenya; the FLN (Front de Libération Nationale) opposed to French colonial rule in Algeria (Hutchinson, 1978) and the Simba forces that battled the Belgians in the Congo (Waggoner, 1980). More recently, ZANU (Zimbabwe African National Union) and ZAPU (Zimbabwe African People's Union), which ended white settler rule in Zimbabwe, and the African National Congress, which battles the RSA, were labeled "terrorist" by Ronald Reagan (Danaher, 1984: 61). Of course, the use of the term to delegitimate national liberation movements has not been confined to Africa. Predictably, as the United States became increasingly mired in Southeast Asia in the 1960s, its leader sought to rally public support by denouncing "Viet Cong terror tactics in South Vietnam."

Look for a moment at the record of the other side. Any civilian casualties that result from our operations are inadvertent, in stark contrast to the calculated Viet Cong policy of systematic terror. Tens of thousands of innocent Vietnamese civilians have been killed, tortured, and kidnapped by the Viet Cong. There is no doubt about the deliberate nature of the Viet Cong program. One need only note the frequency with which Viet Cong victims are village leaders, teachers, health workers, and others who are trying to carry out constructive programs for their people. Yet the deeds of the Viet Cong go largely unnoted in the public debate. (Lyndon B. Johnson, quoted in United States Department of State, 1968)[3]

It is clear that the war on "Viet Cong terror" reflected not simply opposition to national liberation movements but a continuing obsession with the threat of communism. The paradox is that the decline and fall of the Johnson presidency, as well as the U.S. defeat in Vietnam, was not a consequence of communism, but a paranoid style of anticommunism projected on a world scale. Of course, this record is not confined to a single presidency or to the executive branch. For example, the House Committee on Internal Security (charged with the control of "Communist and other subversive activities affecting the internal security of the United States") (U.S. Congress, Committee on Internal Security, 1974, Part 3: v) held hearings in 1974. These focused on the threat of domestic terrorism and supposed links to "foreign communist terrorists" (1974a: 3915).

However, in the recent past, terrorism has taken on a new and, I think, a more sinister complexion. This new terrorist phenomenon, particularly as applied to organized groups, poses extremely serious problems to our law enforcement agencies and also to our national security. From the testimony and evidence... it has become more and more apparent that Marxist, Leninist, and Maoist forces operating within worldwide networks do play a dominant role in promoting international terrorist incidents. (House Committee on Internal Security, 1974 (2): 3085)

That the ideological war on terrorism has been historically linked with the war on communism is further evidenced in hearings conducted by the Senate Internal Security Subcommittee of the Senate Committee of the Judiciary on the "Trotskyite Terrorist International."

In previous hearings, it has been established that the Communists, despite their repeated declarations that they do not engage in terrorist activities, do in fact provide training and logistical and financial support for terrorist groups.... This is true of the Moscow Communists, the Maoists, the Trotskyists and the Castro Communists. Indeed, a majority of those groups which are actively engaged in terrorism consider themselves Marxist-Leninists of some kind. (United States Senate, 1975: 1)

The process of constructing the greater meaning of terrorism is further evidenced in more recent congressional hearings on *narcoterrorism*. The argument follows a familiar conspiratorial theme, with a familiar demon.

Then, in the early 70's, the international terrorist community struck on a brilliant, new quick-buck scheme. Drug sales. It was a natural. As terrorism expert, Michael Ledeen of the Georgetown Center for Strategic and International Studies said in a recent article: "Running drugs is one sure way to make big money in a hurry. Moreover, the directions of the flow are ideologically attractive. Drugs go to the bourgeois countries where they corrupt and where they kill, while the arms go to pro-Communist terrorist groups in the Third World." It has worked like a charm. (U.S. Congress, Senate Committee on Labor and Human Resources, 1984: 2)

The statement of former Senator Paula Hawkins of Florida went on to name various "terrorist" groups in Latin America, Malaysia, Burma, while implicating Bulgaria in the use of narcotics to "destabilizing NATO's easternmost flank," and accusing the Vietnamese government of selling opium to resolve that nation's economic problems. The effect of this argument is to blame the huge U.S. narcotics market on an international communist conspiracy that employs terrorism to realize its objectives. (Such a position implicitly denies that the appetite for drugs reflects problems *within* the demand society, while ignoring the historical role of U.S. government agencies and/or allies in narcotics trafficking originating in Southeast Asia (McCoy, 1972: 149–217), and Latin America (see Chapter 9).

Perhaps most revealing in a context of continuing anticolonial struggle is the conceptual (as opposed to polemical) linkage of terrorism and revolutionary movements. To wit:

1. Terrorism is a systematic and purposeful method used by a revolutionary organization to seize political power from the incumbent government of a state.
2. Terrorism is manifested in a series of individual acts of extraordinary and intolerable violence.
3. Terrorism involves a consistent pattern of symbolic or representative selection of its physical victims or objects.

Terrorism is deliberately intended to create a psychological effect on specific groups of people . . . in order to change political behavior and attitudes in a manner consonant with the achievement of revolutionary objectives. (Hutchinson, 1978: 21)

Considering this definitional attempt, it is evident that the term *revolutionary* when added to *terrorism* once again expands the scope of the problem and makes evident its political direction. It is also clear that this aspect of the dominant ideology of terrorism ignores the role of the state. It is certainly plausible that incumbent governments may be implicated both in the conduct of terrorism and in the creation of those conditions that give rise to a reactive form of "extraordinary and intolerable violence." Also ignored or understated in this fear of the left is the terrorism of the right, whether on the part of friendly regimes that may support the interests of "national security" or on the part of counterrevolutionaries seeking to restore a lost order.

## The Utopian Ideology of Terrorism

Both dominant and utopian ideologies emphasize the role of fear, and the victimization of innocents. However, the nature of both are again interpreted through a different prism. In opposition to the dominant view of the *episodic* terror associated with the random and unpredictable nature of violence, the liberation conception centers on structural forms of persecution. These are not episodic but constant, not random and unpredictable but *systemic*. Hence, the utopian conception of terrorism focuses on institutionally founded horror that permeates the day-to-day existence of whole populations. This is the sense in which the African revolutionary Franz Fanon defined colonialism as "violence in its natural state" (1963, originally published in 1961). From the dominant view, the innocents are the few who die dramatically at the hands of primitive deviants. From the liberation view, the innocents are the many who die quietly at the hands of primitive systems.

## Solidarity and the Imagery of Betrayal

The utopian view gives evidence of a sense of betrayal directed toward powerful persons, groups, and states and an appeal to a sense of lost dignity on the part of the subjugated. Terms like imperialism, colonialism, and militarism carry an historical and emotional meaning not well understood by those who live in dominant states. So understood, the denunciation of imperialism as a form of official violence is intended to delegitimate state policy and to critique world patterns of domination. The utopian ideology of terrorism is part of a larger ideological struggle, designed to develop a political consciousness within a political audience. However, the audience in this case is an underclass and utopian ideology is intended to transform that class into a material force for the alteration of human history.

In addition to the creation of solidarity and a consciousness of resistance, there is the issue of selective perception. From the utopian view, terrorism is purely institutional and official, just as in the dominant view terrorism is purely the work of deviant outsiders and enemies of civilization. In particular, those who define themselves as members of a national liberation movement believe that the terrorist label is used to deny them human standing and a reason for historical being. They are also aware that armed violence directed against them is seldom called terrorism in dominant political and media circles, while their own recourse to armed struggle (often slow to develop) does not so easily escape the label. However, the utopian emphasis on the institutional roots of terror and the legitimacy of armed resistance may give rise to a certain blindness. This is expressed ideologically in an unwillingness to raise the issue of *vendetta terror*.

## Vendetta and Subterranean Terror

*Vendetta* is from the Latin *vindicta*, "vengeance." Formerly in Corsica and parts of Italy, the term referred to a blood feud in which the relatives of one who was murdered sought to kill the responsible person or members of that person's family. Thus those who were individually innocent were collectively guilty by virtue of blood kinship. It is clear that it is possible to define "collective guilt" to include other than blood kin. In a bloody raid carried out at the Rome and Vienna airports on December 27, 1985, innocent people were slaughtered because they happened to be in the area of the Israeli national airline (El Al).

The raid was attributed to the direction of the renegade Abu Nidal, but the youthful commandos who undertook this suicidal act of rage had been recruited from the Palestinian refugee camps of Sabra and Shatila (outside Beirut, Lebanon) (Ahmad, 1986). These camps have a long and tragic history, and it was in them that a slaughter was carried out by Lebanese allies of the Israeli army in September of 1982 (see Chapter 7 and Chomsky, 1983: 364–87). Despite such roots, the ideological point is that the utopian conception of terror will tend to understate or ignore vendetta. In part this is because the concept is not central to the negation of the existing order of institutional terror.

Yet the principle of collective guilt, and hence vendetta, cannot be applied in one-sided fashion. State officials may declare a "willingness to accept" civilian casualties in service of state objectives. Although a distinction can be made between the intentional targeting of innocents, and a willingness to inflict civilian deaths to strike at other targets, this very *caveat* is subject to abuse. Also to the point, within the context of state and other institutional terror, unauthorized actions by subterranean forces may also be carried out in the name of vengeance. Subterranean forces may hold ideological views that are called extremist, but by inference such views are often pure or exaggerated derivations of dominant ideals. As with other forms of "terror from the right," these episodes do not receive a prominent place in the dominant ideology of terrorism.

## THE WESTERN ACADEMIC CONSTRUCTION OF TERRORISM

Most Western academic contributions to the terrorism debate evade the question of institutional domination through fear. Mention has already been made of some intellectually dubious efforts dealing in sensationalism and conspiracy. Other work in what might be called an order paradigm of terrorism is clearly committed to a control perspective. The Rand Corporation, routinely supported by funding from the U.S. government, has generated a great deal of literature dealing with such topics as the terrorist environment, terrorist "mindsets," government responses, and the future of terrorism (Jenkins, 1982). Similar approaches view terrorism as a challenge to the state, or a weapon of political agitation (Lodge, 1981; Thornton, 1964). Whether or not by explicit design, these works (and many others) are rooted in the assumption that the Western state is the political expression of a societal consensus, and that terrorism is primarily (if not exclusively) the practice or threat of nongovernmental public violence (see Krieger, 1977).

Other less "tactical" works consider how terrorism represents a threat to democratic or liberal states, while probing how counterterrorism can be balanced with civil liberties (Wardlaw, 1982: Wilkinson, 1977). One well-known historical study (Laqueur, 1987) finds "different terrorisms" (p. 9) and while not disputing that "crimes committed by governments" (p. 11) have been historically more deadly, continues to focus on "terrorism from below" (p. 11). Ironically, in centering on "movements that have used systematic terrorism as their main weapon" (p. 12), this inquiry transfers the emphasis on "system" from its acknowledged historical connection with the Jacobin *régime de la terreur*, to outsiders who threaten existing orders.

A recent and more conceptually sophisticated comparative inquiry provides some sense of proportionality on the scope and effectiveness of outsider violence, while casting serious doubts on the question of an "international revolutionary terrorism" (Gurr, 1988). Another distinguishes between legitimate guerilla warfare and the generalized terror directed toward innocents (Wilkinson, 1977: 52). *Caveats* notwithstanding, the prime focus of these and more historically oriented orderist literature on terrorism remains with antistate forces.

Certainly, some of the literature goes beyond the tacit admission of state coercion through fear, seeking to analyze regime terror (Parry, 1976: 187–243, passim). However, there is a recurring tendency to specify notorious regimes, such as the Jacobins, the Nazis, the Stalinist, and so on, and to avoid placing such regimes in historical and global context. One effort to study a regime of terror (as opposed to a "siege" of terror by outcasts) ties terrorism to fear induced by government violence and even includes certain acts of war (Walter, 1969: 6). However, the thesis of this book is explored through a study of what the author terms "primitive" African communities, with the exemplar of the terrorist regime being the early 19th-century Zulu state under Shaka. (To the ideological point, no mention is made of the British armies who were involved in perhaps 50 major colonial wars in the same century (Giddens, 1985: 223). Absent from this entire type of inquiry is an analysis of Western state violence, much less the global relations that give it form.

The more critical literature on terrorism is sparse and often suffers from mechanical and instrumental conceptions of the nation-state. However, the argument has been made that regime terror is a means of insuring the social "stability" required to secure loans from Western-dominated "multilateral" lending institutions (such as the International Monetary Fund) (Pion-Berlin, 1984), and to attract multinational corporate investment (Chomsky and Herman, 1977). Thus, regime terror is driven by more than Caesaristic ambition. It is routinely directed at opposition movements and leaders who threaten the maintenance of systemic inequality, between nations and more specifically between classes (Carleton, 1988). And it is frequently the result of training and financing provided by core states, who otherwise may resort to both overt and covert programs of intervention and counterrevolution. To this specific point is a study of the sponsorship and support of "National Security States" by the United States (Herman, 1982: 119–37; McClintock, 1985).

That the definition of terrorism by U.S. officials and the mainstream media routinely masks state (wholesale) terrorism has been argued eloquently by some (see especially Chomsky, 1986a). St. Augustine's morality tale (in which the emperor that uses a fleet to intimidate and plunder is judged by different standards than a pirate with a single ship) is heuristic. Also instructive is an examination of terrorism, the "Red menace," and the legitimation of the post-World-War II Truman Doctrine of "containment" in the United States. The case that real terror involves land-owners, death squads, and malnutrition tied to a developmental model structurally designed for permanent peripheral dependency has been made well, if only rarely (Herman, 1982).

A political economy of terrorism must take note of such efforts, probing theoretically the structure of ideological systems, and placing these in a material context. Beyond this, a political economy of terrorism must place statist behavior in a world system context. However, terror is not confined to purely instrumental linkages between specific nation states and the misdeveloping world. The internal dynamics of the national security economy, with its expression in nuclear and other forms of warfare misproduction, cannot be separated from the New Global Security Economy. This misproductive system is marked by its traffic in arms and military sales and its needs for strategic resources. It is also an employer, not only of national and military support personnel but of an indigenous workforce to help maintain worldwide bases, to provide local "security" and to manufacture weapons systems and military supplies.

And finally, the dominant ideology of terrorism has arisen dialectically in conflict with rival visions of societal transformation and alternative development. It is not enough to document and critique abuses of world market power. It is also necessary to examine fledgling movements and new attempts at institutional formation to further understand why they have been targeted for negation by core powers. Such questions will guide the exploration of the higher terrorism in the chapters to come.

**NOTES**

1. The actual loss to life and property for U.S. citizens does not appear to match the publicity surrounding the issue throughout the 1980s. To illustrate, by the reckoning of the Task Force, 23 U.S. citizens lost their lives to international terrorism in 1985, and 2 were victims of the domestic variety. This compares with 18,980 domestic homicides in the same year (*World Almanac*, 1987: 786).

2. This phenomenon of declining terms of trade reveals the permanence of "unequal exchange." When a country's terms of trade decline, which is the case for many in Africa, Latin America, and Asia, the value of exports (routinely raw materials) is artificially low compared to the cost of manufactured or finished imports. The exchange gap widens, ever exacerbating the relations of dependency (Debt Crisis Network, 1985: 19–20).

3. Of course, as was to become distressingly clear to the American people, U.S.-trained allies in Vietnam were no strangers to the practice of state torture. And the tactics of that war of terror, with its saturation bombings, napalm, white phosphorous, search and destroy missions, free-fire zones, and ecocidal chemicals, were not lacking in terror.

# 2

# *Terrorism and the State*

> No beast so fierce that knows some touch of pity—But I know none—and therefore am no beast.
> 
> William Shakespeare (*Richard III*)

In answering the question of terrorism, it is tempting to reduce the formal organization of the modern state to the level of political behavior, and approach its workings through a probe of personality style or individual motives. Yet an historically bound elite do not spontaneously reinvent the structural relations of power from moment to moment. They do not form by act of will the transinstitutional linkages, the imperatives for maintaining systems, the network of roles, the bureaucratic instrumentation, the web of laws, and the legitimations by which the right to command is organized and claimed. And it is precisely these higher forces that shape the enigma of state domination through fear.

## THE REIFICATION OF THE STATE

In *Richard III*, the absence of pity emerges as an idiosyncratic flaw in character. From a Weberian framework, such symbolism reflects an exemplary crisis of traditional authority where rule is personal and subject to abuse by the weak or unscrupulous. But for Weber, the legitimation of modern state authority is rooted neither in royal descent and *noblesse oblige* or in the even more temporal forms of charisma. Instead, legitimation is founded in a rational-legal basis for rule, exemplified by a system of laws and embodied in bureaucratic forms of administration (Weber, 1957: 324–65; originally published in 1922). Thus government is understood to be one of "laws not men" in which the force of law supplants the law of force.

Yet while Weberian thought is an alternative to character analysis, it is within a *critique* of his rational-legal authority that we may discern the relationship between terrorism and the modern state. Under legal authority, those who rule retain legitimacy insofar as they function politically in a lawful manner. Much of the controversy surrounding the Iran-Contra affair (see Chapters 8 and 9) in the United States during the last years of the Reagan administration, focused on whether government officials had circumvented the checks and balances of the Constitution. While such questions are a logical extension of Weberian dilemmas of power, they also narrow the focus of inquiry. Conceived more holistically, the relations between the United States and Iran, as between the United States and Nicaragua, have a history, a dialectical history of multidimensional intervention and response. The Iran-Contra affair represents but a moment in this ongoing clash between higher forces of order and change.

Thus a critique of rational-legal authority transcends technical questions of law and legalism to consider the domination of weaker states by the stronger. Whatever their utility, terms like "unlawful," "rational," and "official" offer legitimation for a system of rule. Such descriptions may camouflage the real nature of state power and mystify its functions. Moreover, the limited parameters of a procedural debate rests on the assumption that the machinery of state power is self-correcting, provided its rules are not abused. These appeals to law and process, when combined with symbolic references to democracy, are powerful mystifications. So described, the state appears as fair and neutral and the servant of the common good. Such symbolism has the clear potential to disguise patterns of intimidation and intervention, designed to keep the world safe from change. It may distort an ongoing struggle between conflicting strata, positioned in a hierarchical international order of production, transfer, and concentration.

To people accustomed to having the conditions of their material existence controlled by others, the state is *reified* (Lukács, 1971: 83–92 passim, originally published 1923); appearing as a rational, all-embracing, and autonomous structure. Its masters, rules, procedures, and official functions acquire a life of their own: the law becomes Justice; the president becomes the Office of the Presidency: the state becomes the State. Under these circumstances the real people who hold official power find their personalities merged with the office they hold and evade personal responsibility by *raison d'etat*. As human beings they may or may not agonize over decisions, but in the final analysis they endure a numbing born of expediency and the grandeur of overriding ends. From Machiavelli to Weber, the questions of innocence and compassion are not preeminent in the practice of statecraft. They contradict the imagery of the rational state, seeking always the security of control.

Putting aside the questions of administration, territoriality, and the legitimacy (or ideological legitimation) of authority, the *problematique* of the state is rooted in its monopoly on violence. That it is rational and systematic is not at issue. The modern state may be quite "rational" in its projection of national power on a world scale through military force, covert intelligence operations, and economic sanctions. State power may be used quite "systematically" to maintain an order of inequality with both global and domestic dimensions. And all of this may be done in the name of national sovereignty and international law. Indeed, it may be a function of lawyers working for the state to find "lawful" reasons for policies of international and national intimidation.

Thus to dereify the state is to question its neutrality and the legitimating assumption that it is the product of political consensus. It is to consider that the state is neither autonomous nor a mechanical instrument, but that it both reflects and reproduces the social divisions within a society. It is to understand that means of deadly force are at the ready disposal of its masters; force that may be deployed in the context of the shifting definitions that power may impose on behavior and events. What may be defined as the terrorism of the state, as with all other institutional forms, is rooted in systematic and recurring patterns. Once institutionalized, these patterns are not peculiar to specific rulers or parties, although the techniques of terror may vary with different agents over time.

## DOMINATION THROUGH FEAR

An analysis of state terrorism must be carried out at different levels. At the national level, the state may become an instrument designed to control through fear its subject population. *Regime* terror involves the systematic use of torture and the rise of military and police forces engaged in an internal war against a subject population. This form of state terrorism may also be waged through shadow organizations, death squads, and the like that have no official power but that are clearly linked with the national elite. However, to focus on regime terror is often deceptive. To cast the issue of terrorism as the abuse of state power by political deviants may be to ignore the more endemic, taken-for-granted, higher forms of sanctioned violence that avoid the terrorist label. It may also ignore state structural imperatives (expressed in policy and action, including the threat or use of force) designed to preserve a transnational market system.

At the international level, the higher terrorism takes different forms. It is ironic that in the political lexicon of terrorism, war between states is routinely omitted. Indeed, the architects of the state may subscribe to humanitarian codes intended to govern the conduct of war. Although the concept of "war crimes" is important, the unintended message of criminality within the context of war is that war can be made more civilized, more palatable through international legal conventions. This is not to debunk such efforts, but to enter the debate at this level may reproduce the fiction that war can somehow to honorable. However, the issue can be cast in other terms. Perhaps the conduct of warfare can represent only shades of dishonor. Perhaps the issue of war crimes is superseded by that of the crime of war. Perhaps in addition to the waging of war, the preparation and planning for mass destruction in the nuclear age should be redefined as the ultimate form of terrorism.

## The Warfare State and the New Global Security Economy

Dulce et Decorum Est Pro Patria Mori

In the statespeak of the modern era, the meaning of "national security" is also obscured. For in the National Security State, an ideological monopoly has taken form. The root of *security* is in the Latin *securus*, which means freedom from care, or more broadly, freedom from fear, anxiety, and danger. The National Security State turns this definition on end, promoting conceptions of safety rooted in its organized ability to inflict fear, anxiety, and danger. Nowhere is this more evidenced than in the modernization of systems of mass destruction in the name of survival. State security has come to mean "preemptive" or "anticipatory" air strikes and raids in the name of self-defense. It means planning for the annihilation of life on a world scale in order to preserve a "way of life." It means the support of dictatorial regimes in the name of democracy. In George Orwell's *1984*, war was redefined as peace. In the world's ranking military superpower, the motto of the U.S. Strategic Air Command is "Peace is our Profession."

Given the focus developed thus far, the rituals of the war-making system, from research to development to deployment to use of deadly force, invite redefinition. However, it is not enough to identify the symbolic forms of legitimation that provide some measure of popular support for the ways of war. Thought-systems cannot be isolated from the material base by which security is commodified. If the terrorism of war (hot and cold) is not the product of a conspiracy of powerful individuals, if the warfare state is more than the expression of national chauvinism, then those specific forces (both national and transnational) that drive the warfare state must be identified. In the process comes the ability to distinguish more clearly the real threats to human security.

While some defenders of military spending cite the "spin-offs" to the civilian economy, it is clear that other forms of public investment have similar potential. Investment in public infrastructure (such as a modern rail system, highways, bridges, sewer systems, and so forth) also stimulate the economy and create jobs, while avoiding the nonproductive use of resources represented on the military side. If, as is officially claimed, one purpose of military spending is to stimulate new technology in the civilian economy, then it is simply logical to spend resources directly for these purposes, rather than to wait for the accidental by-products of military research and development.

The investment of national treasuries and human resources for the ultimate purposes of intimidation and destruction compounds the problem of economic waste by adding an ethical dilemma. Yet ethics and reason play little role in the broader economic dimensions of the warfare state. In 1970, only 8 percent of the military hardware produced throughout the world entered into international trade. By 1980, that percentage had grown to 12, with a projected growth to 16 percent for the year 2000. The ten world regions outside those representing the superpowers and their orbits import over 70 percent of the traffic in military goods. One of the consequences of this global traffic in arms is a redistribution of resources from poor nations, a process that bankrupts their developmental future (Leontief and Duchin, 1983: 56–57).

Thus, in addition to the clear forms of terror associated with the uses of military hardware, there is the collateral economic violence that follows military spending. Such violence is especially severe for poorer countries. However, it is not without implications for arms exporting states and the militarized economies they represent. Simply stated, massive investment in the warfare economy drains resources from the civilian side. Conversely, those national economies with a lighter military burden (such as Japan and West Germany) can be expected to advance more rapidly in the development of other economic sectors.

In contrast, toward the end of the Reagan administration's arms buildup, the United States had spent $10 trillion (in 1987 dollars) since World War II on its warfare state (Sagan, 1987: 9). The defense department budget in fiscal 1988 was 292 billion dollars. According to the Department of Defense, total military spending (including the military segments of the Department of Energy[1] and NASA budgets, foreign military aid, veterans' benefits, and the military's share of interest on the national debt) totaled 388 billion. Thus in seven years, total military spending in the United States increased by 134 billion annually (U.S. Department of Defense, 1988). This figure is conservative. One well-regarded critic put the *FY87* total military expenditures at 492 billion, assigning a much greater share of interest on the national debt to the warfare state (Bowman, 1987: 18).

In the United States, massive increases in military spending during the Reagan years, in conjunction with tax "reforms" that reduced tax revenues, yielded record deficits reaching over 200 billion dollars in 1985 (*World Almanac*, 1987: 116). In the summer of 1985, the United States had become a net debtor nation, poised to surpass the total debt of the developing world (Dumas, 1986: 22). The national debt almost tripled from 907.7 billion in 1980 to 2.643 trillion by the end of the Reagan era (U.S. Dept. of Treasury 1988: 1). In another relevant economic sphere, by 1987 the United States balance of trade deficit (value of imports over exports) had reached an annual level of 170 billion dollars (*World Almanac*, 1987: 118; *Spokane Spokesman-Review*, 1987: A–3). Although this deficit fluctuates with rates of currency exchange (which in turn impact the cost of imports and exports), the currency market is neither the origin nor the solution for the U.S. imbalance of trade. Factoring in the takeover frenzy (often financed through leveraged buy-outs), and the grave state of the thrift industry, the sobering portrait is one of a military superpower, beset by a declining position in the world economy, and increasingly dependent on the infusion of external investment to fund its debt. The ongoing temptation to play the military card in a context of economic crisis should not be minimized.

At the national level, the various constituencies that comprise the permanent war economy need only a brief review. The conception of a military-industrial complex portrays the structural integration of the pentagon and war contractors. In fiscal year 1985, the top 100 contractors received almost 106 billion of the 151 billion of prime contract awards, over 70 percent of the total. The top five alone (McDonnell Douglas, General Dynamics, Rockwell, G.E., and Boeing) accounted for 22.51 percent of total awards (U.S. Department of Defense, 1985: 9–10). On the supply side, today's arms merchants are intimately tied with arms procurers working for the state. There is a "revolving door" linking the personnel employed by the war contractors and U.S. government agencies that are a part of the military structure of the modern state. To wit, during the 1970s, the eight top military contractors employed 1,642 persons who had worked for the Department of Defense (1971–79) and NASA (1974–79) (Adams and Quinn, 1981: 3).

In May of 1986, total federal employment in the United States numbered over 2.9 million. Approximately one-third of these (987,000) worked for the Department of Defense (*World Almanac*, 1987: 120). Despite the general de-industrialization of the United States, over 2 million industrial jobs are dependent on military spending (McFadden and Wake, 1983: 6). Taken together, profits and jobs provide a powerful political incentive as every war plant, every new weapons-system, and every military base acquires a constituency. Chambers of commerce are quick to site the stimulus and the ripple effect provided the community's overall economy by military spending. Even the halls of ivy are not exempt. Pentagon-funded grants are eagerly sought by most leading universities, with 228 educational institutions receiving grants totaling 1.416 billion in *FY86*. M.I.T. was awarded just under $364 million, and John Hopkins, almost $317 million (U.S. Department of Defense, D.I.O.R. 1986: 1, 6).

The irrational nature of the U.S. version of the permanent warfare state can be presented in stark economic terms.[2] Military contracts are plagued by an absence of truly competitive bidding and cost-overruns; the military economy is capital intensive meaning that more jobs are created for less investment in other sectors; weapons systems are routinely gold-plated, unreliable, and subject to remarkable inflationary increases; interservice rivalry means a duplication of weapons-systems among the branches; and an obsession with high-tech destruction combined with the projection of grandiose power into the world's "hot spots" can only invite tragedy. (See Chapter 8 on the U.S. role in the Persian Gulf.)

The warfare state has both national and international reasons for being. On the national level, its reduction in the short-term would result in serious economic dislocation. Planning for demilitarization would absorb these shockwaves through the systematic retraining of workers and the conversion of war plants for civilian production. However, the United States approaches the last decade of the twentieth century as an example *par excellence* of the privatization (and it follows, the fragmentation) of its economic and institutional life. At the national level, it has in place no industrial plan, no agricultural plan, no educational plan, no health-care plan, and no environmental plan. And it has no plan for the conversion of the permanent warfare economy.

However, it is at the level of the New Global Security Economy that the most formidable obstacles to demilitarization must be found. The twentieth-century supercedure of Great Britain by the United States as the lead economy in the modern world system signalled the expansion of transnational military responsibilities for the new core state. As old colonial forms were supplanted, old formal colonial powers lost direct political control of their possessions. However, new forms of dependency gave rise to new forms of influence. Already a hemispheric power, U.S. military and other state functions were to be designed (especially in the post–World War II era) to expand and defend the new institutions of global reach including the multinational corporation.

The establishment of 3,000 military bases (Herman, 1982: 44) meant the deployment of a global strike force, while lease payments and local employment contributed to the further dependency of those societies that became military outposts. Since the Vietnam era, renewed support for counterrevolution has led to the development of new doctrines of war, including those of discriminate deterrence and low-intensity conflict (see Chapters 4 and 9). The New Global Security Economy offers direct employment for military and paramilitary surrogates, to effect a defense of capital accumulation on a world scale. In the same context, new forms of settler-states faced with internal insurrection have developed (with the support of the West) weapons systems for population control, regional invasion, and the international arms trade.

Economic, political, and general systemic arguments notwithstanding, it is in the name of national security that support for the warfare state is created. Within the United States, the modern-day "selling of the Pentagon" is geared to constant exhortations on the nature of the Soviet threat, the communist threat, the Marxist-Leninist threat, and of course, the terrorist threat. However, it is not enough to demonstrate that such arguments are self-serving for those who benefit from the Pentagon enterprise. Nor is it enough to note that political careers have been fashioned from this form of demonology. The national defense ideology is rooted in a real developmental stage in productive forces; a stage not confined by national boundaries. And it is within the social relations of conflict born of these global forces, embodied and regenerated within the political formations of the modern state, that we find the reality of terrorism.

## Imperial Terror

> This great continent could not have been kept as nothing but a game preserve for squalid savages.
> 
> Theodore Roosevelet, *The Winning of the West*

To comprehend the higher terrorism requires consideration of the real history of imperialism. The root of the word is from the Latin *imperare*, which means to command. Yet the structures of command vary in their nature. Wallerstein (1979) distinguishes between traditional conceptions of empire based on conquest and political tyranny, and a "modern world-system" based on economic subjugation. Examples of world empires included those of China, Egypt, and Rome, while the world-system refers to a number of "nation-states with colonial appendages operating within the framework of a world-economy" (Wallerstein, 1979 6).

One may trace the beginnings of this global economy to the emergence of a system of world market trade in northwestern Europe in the sixteenth century. Its nature is that of a one-sided international division of labor, rooted in hierarchical relations among zones of interdependent and uneven development. The history of the *core* is one of commercial, trade, financial, industrial, and technological domination on the part of its national societies. The history of the *periphery* is one of labor and resource exploitation by means of dependency formations ranging from slavery to colonization in its modern guise. Between the two, is the *semiperiphery* where intermediary societies rise and fall (Perdue, 1986: 340–43).

The national societies of the core, representing the metropole of the colonial system, were thus impelled by inherent structural forces to establish outpost territories that represented new sources of raw materials, cheap labor, new markets, and (in a restricted sense) outlets for investment capital. This process was accelerated by the coming of the industrial revolution, and routinely featured the establishment of European settlements, whose members sought to recreate in the colonies the social worlds they left behind. However, the colonization process did not hinge on substantial numbers of European settlers but rather on the development of new social institutions. This meant the transformation of native economies, the creation of colonial administrations, the imposition of Western laws and customs, and the education and training of a labor force to fit the needs of the colonial economy.

The nature of imperial terror is perhaps starkest under the historical conditions of formal colonialism. However, referring to more savage cases (such as Belgian atrocities in the Congo) or to countless other Third World examples of Franz Fanon's "dying colonialism" is to miss the contemporary variations of entrenched and one-sided development. To this point, a revisionist social history will prove vital for uncovering the evolving relations of dependency that give meaning to the political economy of terrorism. The formal colonial state was controlled directly by the metropole, which bore clear responsibility for policies of intimidation through fear. However, the role of settlers (whether descendants or new arrivals) and surrogates are conceptually basic to the comprehension of new forms of imperial terror.

Modern settlers, the historical heirs of European expansion, retain privilege through the subjugation (often predicated on violent fear) of a native population.

The latter brings to mind an indigenous elite who "stand in" for externally based leading players. This is not to make such an elite mere instruments of foreign domination. The absorption of economies into the global market system can be expected to reproduce its class formations in affected societies, which are in turn embodied in the political relations of the state. New class formations do not bring an end to traditional structures of conflict, however, which may strengthen a regime that relies on terror (see the case of the Zulu in modern South Africa, Chapter 5).

Participation in the modern world-system, and especially the competition for a place in its core, has other global implications. A concern for the expansion and defense of the world market (and a favored place for the nation-state within it) means that imperialism has a strategic-geographic dimension. Some colonial territories were acquired historically just to insure control of vital sea lanes and trade routes or to protect other more vital territories. So impelled, France took much of Equatorial and West Africa to protect its coastal possessions, while Great Britain dominated Malta, Cyprus, and Gibralter to extend its control to the Mediterranean. (Of course in the modern era, this sea has been a theater of operations for U.S. naval power, as the imperial debate continues over time with a different cast of historical players.)

On the ideological side, permutations of imperialism mirror, legitimate, and recreate the forces of national expansion and absorption through settlement. As evidenced in the earlier citation from Theodore Roosevelt, the conception of winning and losing, as well as the "advancement of civilization" from a "savage" or "primitive" state, offered justification for the taking of a continent by force of arms. Such ideas also by implication supported historical forms of state terrorism: military conquest, forced relocation of tribes from traditional lands, internment of a native population in reservations and prisons, the destruction of the tribal economic base (as with the buffalo on which the peoples of the plains depended), and subsequent starvation. Also destroyed were the cultural and social systems that offered identity, purpose, and dignity. By the end of the nineteenth century, the native population (Roosevelt's "squalid savages") had been decimated to the level of some 200,000 persons.[3]

Also on the ideological side, imperialism hinges on the projection of national chauvinism on a global scale. The French *chauvinism* is derived from the name of Nicolas Chauvin, a soldier notorious for his attachment to the lost imperial cause of Napoleon Bonaparte. It is instructive to recall the historical context within which this addition to political vocabulary took form, as belicose patriotism often legitimates the projection of imperial power on the international stage. The case for intervention routinely holds that the safety and position of one's own nation comes first in a dangerous and competitive world. Such an argument evades the possibility that intervention flows from, and reproduces the imperial relations that are at the root of danger. National chauvinism retards the development of an international consciousness, denies the basic equality of nations and peoples, and defines patriotism in terms of superiority. More to the point, it offers the myth of national unity as a means of mystifying real social divisions.

When the colonized peoples of the earth began to rise in the nineteenth and twentieth centuries to demand independence, they faced a series of problems that continue to intersect issues of terrorism. First, some nation-states were not so ready to quit their possessions. The resulting violence has not been forgotten among new nations for which anti-imperialism is today a political norm. When such new states provide aid and support for current national liberation movements (which frequently employ guerrilla tactics) they may be labeled terrorist by dominant states (see Chapter 3). Further, despite an end to formal political control, new states have not routinely escaped from the periphery of the modern world-system. Thus politically independent states often remain economically dependent.

There are of course two sides to a dependency relationship. Even successful national liberation movements have routinely failed to create new institutions. The new indigenous elite (often educated in the metropole and not infrequently from more privileged backgrounds) may find themselves in nominal control of domestic institutions that have been created by colonizers. Thus new nation-states may be institutionally equipped for continuing dependency. It follows that when new revolutionary societies seek alternative institutions in an effort to negate that dependency, they may be deemed terrorist, especially when there is danger of the spread of such alternatives to other countries. And finally, there are contemporary movements against state order in a number of places in the world today, movements that cannot be understood apart from the continued legacy of direct imperial rule. One such case is quite instructive, as we shall see.

## The Imperial Legacy: Northern Ireland and the I.R.A.

> All changed, changed utterly: A terrible beauty is born.
> William Butler Yeats, "Easter, 1916"

The war of children in Northern Ireland offers a particularly poignant portrait of those forced to live with terror. The troubled city of Belfast, as the country itself, is divided into the Orange and the Green, between those who swear allegiance to the British crown and those seeking unification with Ireland. For those who view the conflict in terms of its threat to civilized order (routinely symbolized by the British state), Irish resistance reflects a tradition of violence that supplants the political process. Thus argued, "the commitment of the physical force party to armed struggle, amounting at times to obsession, cannot be construed as a rational response to British domination, physical or cultural"

(Townshend, 1983: viii). (This position of course ignores the question of whether British domination is rational.)

For other orderists, conflict in Northern Ireland may be presented in religious guise, as a kind of holy war between the Protestant Loyalists and the Catholic Nationalists. Indeed, the violence of Irish resistance has at times been undisciplined and unfocused, too often emerging as vendetta terror that betrays the movement. And it is true that religious chauvinism is often an ideological weapon used to exacerbate and legitimate much deeper divisions. But these divisions are rooted, as always, in the larger forces of history.

In 1172, Henry II of England claimed Ireland, marking the beginning of a period of British intervention in the Emerald Isle now exceeding eight centuries. Under the reign of Henry VIII (1509–47), the Anglican church separated from Rome, and as a weak newcomer on the stage of history became a servant of the British crown. The Irish took solace in their traditional faith, and the pattern of domination thus took on a religious appearance. Under Elizabeth I (1558–1603), the English subjugated the Irish chieftains through starvation and the sword (FitzGibbon, 1983: 8–13). For many throughout Ireland today, the history of British imperial rule is one of state terror. However, these views are especially pronounced for the minority in that part of Ireland that still remains as a division of the United Kingdom.

In the first decade of the seventeenth century, the Tudors took much of the province of Ulster in the North. However, these lands for settlement (appropriately called plantations) were confiscated from native Roman Catholics. Between 1641 and 1649, the Catholic peasants responded to the British imperial policy of religious divide and rule with "rising" to regain lost lands that took the lives of many Protestant settlers. The rebellion was ultimately crushed by Oliver Cromwell's English army, which resorted to the systematic massacre of the inhabitants of Drogheda and Wexford. Cromwell, quite predictably, justified such terror as the will of God (Fitzgibbon, 1983: 26–37). By 1652, over half of the Irish people (750,000), Catholic and Protestant, had been killed, starved, lost to disease, or forced to emigrate (Lee, 1983: 46).

The tragic history of Ireland contains other watershed events. In 1690, the Protestant William of Orange defeated James II (the dethroned Catholic) at the Battle of the Boyne River, an event still at the center of loyalist ideology. However, the great fears of the eighteenth and nineteenth centuries were to center on simple survival. Between 1726 and 1879, sixteen years of potato crop failures devastated the peasantry, which had become dependent on it to survive. However, as is often the case with the politics of food, the problem was not one of availability but structural inequality. The destitute among the Irish simply did not have enough money to buy food, even though in each year of the Great Famine of 1845–48 Ireland shipped grain to England. During this particular holocaust, Ireland lost a quarter of its population primarily to out-migration. From the late eighteenth through the subsequent century, organizations of poor peasants and laborers from both Protestant and Catholic backgrounds formed local or regional organizations. One of these was the Orange Society (dating from 1795), controlled by more affluent Protestants who were successful in defusing potential class conflict through appeals to religious chauvinism.

In 1858, what was to be later termed the Irish Republican Brotherhood was organized in Dublin, and the Fenian Brotherhood began in New York City. The Fenians recognized the supreme council of the Irish Republican government as the provisional government of a yet-to-be born Republic of Ireland. Also in the nineteenth century, Daniel O'Connell and the Catholic clergy led a vast popular movement, unsuccessful in securing an independent legislative body for Ireland, but successful in raising nationalist consciousness. Charles Stewart Parnell employed the nonviolent tactic of the boycott to realize a measure of land ownership. Building on this tradition, the labor organizer James Connolly became a leader of the nationalist forces in Dublin and was executed by the British after the failure of the 1916 Easter Rising against British control. His words, uttered before the partition of the island, and the establishment of the Republic of Ireland, symbolize one form of utopian ideology still very much alive in the North.

> If you remove the English army tomorrow and hoist the green flag over Dublin Castle, unless you set about the organization of the Socialist Republic your efforts would be in vain. England would still rule you. She would rule you through her capitalists, through her landlords, through her financiers, through the whole array of commercial and individualist institutions she has planted in this country and watered with the tears of our mothers and the blood of our martyrs. (Quoted in Lee, 1983: 50).

Now fully embroiled in World War I, the British government increased conscription of the Irish into the military and began to rely increasingly on force to maintain internal control. Against the background of the executions of the leaders of the Easter Rising, and the brutality of the "blacks and tans" (occupation forces recruited from the British underclass), the proindependence Sinn Fein party used the occasion of the 1918 elections to organize a move for an independent Ireland. They called for the withdrawal of Irish representatives from the British parliament and the establishment of a new assembly and an independent nation. Sinn Fein won 73 of 105 seats, with the unionists (aligned with the British) gaining majorities only in four northern counties. Those of the winning Sinn Fein party not in jail formed an Irish Constituent Assembly (Dail Eireann), with the Irish Republican Army as its military arm. The British, with their unionist allies in the North, now faced a *de facto* provisional government.

In 1920, the British had passed a Government of Ireland Act, which authorized two dependent governments. Ignored by the popular Irish provisional government in the South, it was embraced in the North even in the context of guerrilla warfare throughout the island. When George V formally opened Northern Ireland's first parliament in June of 1921, it signified further institutionalization of the British imperial legacy, as well as political grounds for the continuing division of Ireland.

In December of 1921, a treaty was signed by the British and the Irish Provisional Government that created the Irish Free State. The parliament of Northern Ireland, which came into existence through British law, was to staunchly oppose the Free State or any form of reunification. For the Irish of the South, the form of nationhood took firm shape over time with a new constitution adopted in 1937. In 1948, the country became a republic (rather than a dominion) and withdrew from the British Commonwealth. For the Irish of the North, six of the nine counties of Ulster remained the "Orange State" where protestants outnumbered Catholics two to one. Hence today, what is sometimes called Great Britain is more formally (and symbolically) known as the United Kingdom of Great Britain and Northern Ireland (Lee, 1983: 43–58).

Taken as a whole, the historical "troubles" of Ireland thus implicate the forces of imperial rule, mystified perhaps by the religious designations employed simply to describe the combatants. Certainly it is possible for the ardor of faith to strongly fuel forces of order and change. These are certainly evident in more recent rhetoric. The Free Presbyterians (whose members include Reverend Ian Paisley) hold that Rome is the source of fascism, communism, and a continuation of Babylon (Bruce, 1986: 224–25). Yet the roots of conspiratorial theories of religion go deeper. They reach to the reproduction of the British class system in Northern Ireland. To this point, the first government of the Orange State (announced in 1921) was comprised of Protestants, yet they were also wholly of the industrial, commercial, and landowning elite. Thus began a modern system of state privilege offering advantages to Protestants of the lower classes at the expense of their Catholic "competitors."

In the decade of the 1950s, agricultural and industrial unemployment worsened in a continuing context of unfettered police power. The Irish Republican Army accelerated its guerrilla war, primarily on the border area. But the loss of life (19 between 1957 and 1959) was slight in comparison to the carnage to come. In fact, during the 1960s both the I.R.A. and Sinn Fein were undergoing internal change. By the end of the decade, a provisional wing had developed in opposition to the socialist leadership of the official I.R.A.

The official I.R.A. called for an end to the campaign of armed resistance and endorsed political strategies. The Provisional I.R.A. justified the break by claiming that leaders of the official I.R.A. had become ideologues only, failing to provide protection for nationalist areas in the north. Many Catholics in the wake of the violence directed toward them in the summer of 1969 bitterly observed that I.R.A. stood for "I Ran Away" (Bruce, 1986: 99). The Provisional I.R.A. thus became the symbol for armed struggle in Northern Ireland and sought to construct new ideologies of national liberation. However, its popularity is not to be explained in romantic or ideological terms. The rise of the provisionals cannot be isolated from the larger events of the decade.

The post–1969 phase of the *troubles* in Northern Ireland must be seen in a more complex context than that provided by a focus on the divisions within the I.R.A. or Sinn Fein. To no small extent, it was the emergence of, and response to, a nonviolent movement (inspired in part by the civil rights struggles in the United States) that led to the more recent tidal wave of violence in Northern Ireland. This movement featured organizations such as the Campaign for Social Justice and the Northern Ireland Civil Rights Association. It was led by a middle class (predominantly Catholic but with some Protestant support) intent on reforms taken for granted in Great Britain and much of the West. Its early marches even drew nonviolent participation from some of the I.R.A. The movement also gained support from many British members of Parliament, and predictably galvanized the opposition of the official Orange as well as loyalist extremists in the North. In 1968–69, large demonstrations demanded abolitions of property requirements for voting in local elections, called for an end to discriminatory practices in employment and housing, and opposed the Special Powers Act. The response by authorities and vigilantes was further repression, repression that opened a new and bloody chapter of revolt.

On August 24, 1968, a civil rights march in Dungannon drew 2,500 participants and remained peaceful. On October 5, a march in Derry drew 2,000 and was met by riot police with batons and water hoses. Other demonstrations, including one in November of 1968 that drew 15,000 marchers, remained nonviolent despite the presence of increasing numbers of police. However, on November 30, new events were to signal the shape of things to come. The Reverend Ian Paisley led a crowd of loyalists who turned back a march in Armagh. A group of loyalists extremists representing the "Loyal Citizens of Ulster" then dogged a four-day march sponsored by the Northern Ireland Civil Rights Association in January of 1969. At Burntollet Bridge on January 4, the marchers were attacked by representatives of the Orange order with the support of the police on duty (Bruce, 1986: 94–95). (The Northern Ireland police, predominantly loyalists, consisted of the Royal Ulster Constabulary and the Ulster Special Constabulary.)

In April of 1969, Terence O'Neill resigned, with the leadership of the Unionist Parliamentary party and, hence the position of prime minister, going to Major James Chichester-Clark. O'Neill's reformist gestures (Utley, 1975: 41) (cosmetic in essence) had only infuriated Paisley Protestants, who were not worried about Northern Ireland's image but wanted the full power of the state used against the People's Democracy movement and the I.R.A. Traditional celebrations by loyalists of their political history in July were then to occur in a changed political climate. They were now more provocative than ever in the minds of Catholic (and some Protestant) supporters of civil rights, who were convinced of the institutional bias of the state. In August, civil disturbances escalated to riot stage in Londonderry, and on the 14th police acted on the view that an armed insurrection was underway by employing automatic weapons in Belfast (Lee, 1983: 59–97 passim).

The P.I.R.A. emerged in January of 1970 in a context of renewed violence directed primarily toward the nationalist community. Riots were to increase in number and intensity. The Royal Ulster Constabulary (backed and in some cases restrained by the British army), together with Orange and Green organizations, locked in renewed violent exchange.[4] British troops (ultimately to number some 21,000) fired on unarmed civil rights demonstrators in Derry on "Bloody Sunday" (January 30, 1972), killing fourteen. London suspended the Northern Ireland parliament in March of 1972 and instituted direct rule, with British troops fortifying the nationalist quarter of Belfast and beginning to conduct tens of thousands of house searches (Farrell, 1988: 173–74).[5] On "Bloody Friday" (July 21, 1972), 22 P.I.R.A. bombs exploded in Belfast, killing two soldiers and nine others (Lee, 1983: 182).

In May, 1972, a hunger strike by imprisoned P.I.R.A. members resulted in the conferral of political or special category status by the British. Four years later, the status was suspended but the tactic of the hunger strike was not. In 1981, ten Irish nationalist prisoners died of political starvation in Maze Prison near Belfast as the British insisted on retaining their status as ordinary criminals. The funeral procession for striker Bobby Sands drew 50,000 persons (Farrell, 1988: 181). Between 1970 and 1981, over 10,000 bombings and 28,000 shootings had occurred. By the end of 1984, over 2,000 had died in a decade and a half of violence (*World Almanac*, 1987: 626). A study of the first 2,000 deaths (1968–1980) found that republican forces were responsible for slightly more than 50 percent of the killing, with the loyalists organizations accounting for just under 30 percent and the predominantly Protestant security forces 11 percent of the total (Lee, 1983: 171–73). Others were of undetermined origin.

On the question of republican (nationalist) violence, media accounts have abounded with descriptions of kidnappings, assassinations, bombings, kneecappings,[6] and other acts. It is, however, the question of official terror that escapes center stage. Amnesty International has cited police interrogation procedures including beatings, bending of limbs, choking, cigarette burns, as well as threats of death, imprisonment, and retribution to families (Farrell, 1988: 176–77). In addition, the U.K.'s Prevention of Terrorism Acts (1974 and 1976), intended to ban terrorist organizations, also greatly restricted civil rights. Police powers were expanded allowing the arrest, questioning, and detention of suspects (up to seven days); the search of people and places; and the empowerment of the secretary of state to make an exclusion order removing someone from Great Britain or Northern Ireland (Grant, et al, 1973: 534–35). This led to the detention of over 4,000 Irish people in Great Britain between 1974 and 1979. Security forces in Northern Ireland have also used gas, rubber and plastic bullets and military vehicles as rams (Lee, 1983: 173–78). Since 1971, sixteen persons (including six children) have been killed by rubber and plastic bullets in the North, 15 of them from the nationalist community, with hundreds seriously wounded. Further, forces within the Northern Ireland police have been trained by the covert British intelligence and counterrevolutionary organization, the Special Air Service.[7]

By the mid–1980s, the nationalist leaders in Northern Ireland acknowledged (as had the official I.R.A. two decades before) that decisive guerrilla victory was only a remote possibility, and called for political and legal struggle to supplement the dramatic theater of targeted violence. However, during this period officials sought to step up the uses of "supergrasses" (informers), which led to the long-term imprisonment of nationalists. It was also at this point that some of the more notorious suspected "shoot-to-kill" episodes occurred. In this context, the government of the Irish Republic warned the British that such policies would only radicalize the 500,000 member nationalist minority further and drive them away from the moderate nationalist party (the Social and Democratic and Labour party), and strengthen the hands of the more violent actors in the P.I.R.A.

The Irish Republic secured a consultative role on British policy in Northern Ireland by means of the *Anglo-Irish Agreement* of November, 1985. In return, the republic agreed to cooperation with Britain and the North in opposing the I.R.A. However, the security forces in Northern Ireland, as well as the loyalist organizations, appeared only to step up the violence. In October of 1986, Charles Haughey (the new head of the Irish Republic) declared that the position of the minority in Northern Ireland had actually worsened since the agreement (Farrell, 1988: 179–83). Also in 1985, a distinguished group of international lawyers found

at least 10 prima facie violations of Article 6 (1) of the UN International Covenant on Civil and Political Rights (everyone has the inherent right to life protected by law) and of Article Two of the European Convention for the Protection of Human Rights and Fundamental Freedoms have been committed by the security forces in Northern Ireland in the period in question. (Asmal, quoted in Farrell, 1988: 180).

In summary then, the violence of resistance in Ireland is not to be separated from centuries of imperial British rule. To intervene in the internal affairs of a people, to establish systems of rule and economy, to become active agents in the formation of class and political divisions, and to rely over time on the use of military deadly force to "maintain order" is to play no small historical role in the political theater of terror. It is again the higher terrorism, which helps to explain (if not generally excuse) reactive violence in Northern Ireland today, whether that focused on official targets by more disciplined and popularly supported resistance forces, or the blood lust of vendetta terror that threatens authentic claims to national liberation status. The state in Northern Ireland is not geographically centered in Belfast but in London, a fact that every act of political violence directed at British troops in Northern Ireland, or at leaders or property in Britain symbolically (and tragically) underscores.

On the economic side, the British government courts the investment of external capital in Northern Ireland through touting the pool of cheap labor, and the relative absence of labor unrest. The conflict between better-off loyalist workers and their nationalist competitors is suggestive of caste relations that confound class antagonisms. Similar caste advantages/class disadvantages exist for the Sephardim in Israel (see Chapter 7) and the Afrikaner in South Africa (see Chapter

5). Tax incentives abound, export duties are absent, and the government offers reduced rentals for facilities that are built through public resources as well as grants to build plants and train labor (Lee, 1983: 234–40). In keeping with a political-economy of terrorism, despite its official status in the United Kingdom, Northern Ireland is best understood as a troubled colony of the British crown.

## GLOBAL MARKET DISJUNCTION AND REGIME TERROR

Theoretical attempts in the political economy of terror must address imperial formations. However, the focus on global forces also offers insight into the rise of national regime terror. Particularly important is the competitive disadvantage faced by national economies under various conditions of disjunction between such economies and the forces, demands, and conflictual states of the global market system. The implications of system-wide crisis (such as world depression or global-scale combat) are not the same for all national actors. National economies under conditions of marked decline or isolation are in disjunction and hence vulnerable to the emergence of formal structures of domination through fear. Such conditions only set the historical stage for the emergence of regime terror. More immediate precipitory factors must of course be included in causal analysis.

### The French Revolution and the Jacobin Reign of Terror

> Virtue without terror is fatal. Terror without virtue is impotent. Terror is nothing but justice, prompt, severe and flexible. It is thus an emanation of virtue.
>
> Robespierre

*The Terror*, which produced 10,000 victims, continues to fascinate students of the French Revolution. Yet its roots are to be found in the broader social forces of history.[8] Under Louis XV (1715–74), France had lost most of its colonial empire in wars with the British along with much of its potential for economic expansion. The aristocracy and the church still held most of the land, with the rising French commercialists seeking a return on their growing profits by lending money to the crown. Louis XV was reduced to borrowing more money in order to make interest payments on the royal debt. In a context of bankruptcy, Louis XVI ascended the throne in 1774, facing an alienated and rising new owning class whose members were disenchanted by fiscal crisis, by the British lead in the world economy, and by the tax privileges accorded the aristocracy. In the countryside, the peasantry continued to be burdened by their obligations to the nobility, and a poor crop in 1788 contributed to food riots. Simply conceived, the landed beneficiaries of royalist absolutism still held a relative monopoly on political power, leaving the state poorly prepared to articulate French commercial interests in the world market system (Skocpol, 1979: 51–56).

In the context of crisis, Louis XVI called the *Estates-General* in 1789, an archaic legislature that had not met since 1614, consisting of representatives of the Lords Spiritual (clergy), the Lords Temporal (nobility) and the Commons (bourgeoisie). It was the last that now aspired to be first, and forces of the bourgeoisie (the Third Estate) formed the National Constituent Assembly on June 17. On July 14, 1789, *sans-culottes* stormed the Bastille, igniting a firestorm of repressed resentment throughout the country. Members of the aristocracy were driven out, their property seized, looted, or destroyed.

It was these urban working people who distrusted the representative institutions of the new bourgeois elite, preferring the practice of direct, popular sovereignty. They believed in such checks as the popular initiative, referendum, and recall of deputies, the right to bear arms and the importance of mass education. They were opposed to clerical rule, believing that the priests had historically taught beliefs that legitimated the right of the aristocracy to exploit the labor of ordinary people (Sutherland, 1986: 192–217 passim). Despite the popular revolutionary imagery of the "storming of the Bastille," the *sans-culottes* did not come to control the revolutionary government, and specifically the shadow government of Jacobins led by Robespierre and institutionalized in the infamous *Committee of Public Safety*.

The National Constituent Assembly proclaimed the abolition of aristocratic and other privileges, suffrage for those who paid taxes, the Declaration of the Rights of Man and Citizen, and instituted civil controls on the clergy (who were required to swear loyalty to the new order). The First Republic (1792–95) was declared in September 1792 with the Convention (to be headed by such as Robespierre, Danton, and Marat) in control. However, the pressure to restore royalist rule was by no means at an end. Austria and Prussia (later Britain) sought advantage through military force, and royalist forces (involving local nobles, some priests, and estate stewards and peasants) were staging an ongoing counterrevolution. And in 1793, the major issue for the poor was one of survival in the face of acute shortages. A paranoid obsession with plots became the order of the day, with Robespierre claiming counterrevolutionaries to be behind the food riots, as well as other disturbances. In this setting of external and internal pressures, and in the name of defending the revolution, regime terror took institutional form (1793–94).

The Convention was seeking to defend politically an underlying revolution in property relations and the rise of a new economic order. However, the utopian ideology of change (whether expressed formally in the contractual solution of Rousseau, or simply in the watchwords *liberté, egalité, fraternité* meant different things to different classes. From the view of the rising bourgeiosie, it meant new political forms that would insure the liberal redress of the open market. For the peasants whose agricultural labor accounted for 60 percent of gross national production (Skocpol, 1979: 54), it meant relief from an archaic landed nobility.

For the *sans-culottes*, it meant restrictions on property and an end to the right of any person to control another.

In order to insure the support of urban workers, the peasantry, and the poor, the Convention deputies abolished colonial slavery, instituted measures to help the poor, provided support for public education, and sought to advance the separation of church and state. It was this same Convention that, pressed by military exigencies, fed by rumors of conspiracies and treason in high and low places, and convinced that extremism in the defense of the revolution was a virtue, established the formal structures of regime terror. Their targets were those who defended or symbolized the old order; the forces of reaction that denied open markets and the new bourgeois ideals of rationalism and "merited" (as opposed to hereditary) inequality.

On March 10, 1793, the Revolutionary Tribunal was established to "exercise summary justice in cases involving state security" (Sutherland, 1986: 170). Revolutionary committees were then formed for each district, assuming increasing police powers over time. And on April 6, the Committee on Public Safety was established; a government within a government, impowered to take whatever measures necessary for external and internal defense. Then came the law of March 19, which provided for the trial and execution of armed counterrevolutionaries without a jury and without appeal within 24 hours (Sutherland, 1986: 171). A later law (June 10) denied the accused the right to counsel or call witnesses and gave to the jury the right to convict on the basis of moral certainty. Thus impowered, the Committee on Public Safety moved to guillotine the opposition and sanctioned the "pacification of the countryside" through early versions of a scorched earth policy and free fire zones. In the meantime, the Revolutionary Tribunal and military commissions became killing machines (Sutherland, 1986: 242).

In the wake of the resulting carnage, Robespierre saw the Terror as a method of purification, and in the presence of his zeal, no one felt secure. Forces within the Convention, who had ironically supported terror themselves, were successful in decreeing the arrest of this most infamous member of the Committee of Public Safety. Robespierre's enemies in the Convention declared him and his colleagues "outside the law." Those so designated could be executed within 24 hours without trial. It was Saint-Just, another member of the Committee of Public Safety, who had originally introduced the law as a part of the legal foundation for the regime of terror. Confronted with the National Guard outside his chambers in the Hotel de Ville in Paris, Robespierre tried to kill himself, but the pistol shot only broke his jaw. On the same afternoon, July 28, 1794, the man who called himself *Incorruptible* kept his own rendezvous with the weighted, oblique blade that had become the first symbol of state terror.

This particular form of regime terror had ended, but the paranoia and divisiveness of the era set the stage for the ascendance of a "man on horseback," with his compelling promises of national glory and unity. Between 1795 and 1799, the Directory came to power, with Napoleon Bonaparte as its champion.

In 1799 came the Consulate, with Bonaparte now as First Consul. And in 1804, came the First Empire under Emperor Napoleon I, who led France by the rule of war.

### German Fascism and the Final Solution

> So when I set up the extermination building at Auschwitz, I used Zylon B, which was a crystallized prussic acid which was dropped into the death chamber from a small opening. It took from three to fifteen minutes to kill the people in the death chamber, depending upon climatic conditions.
>
> We knew when the people were dead because their screaming stopped. ... After the bodies were removed our special commandos took off the rings and extracted the gold from the teeth of the corpses.
>
> S.S. Commander Hoess, quoted in Shirer, 1960: 968

A clear expression of state terror was the systematic extermination of millions of the "racially unfit" under the Nazis (Reasons and Perdue, 1981: 575–78, 586–88). Before the invasion of Poland on September 1, 1939, the concentration camps of the Third Reich held no more than twenty or thirty thousand inmates. Initially, the purpose of these camps was to strengthen the regime through programmatic terror directed at its opponents. With the coming of the war years, however, the camps grew in size and number. They provided slave labor for the Reich, and later on subjects for "scientific research." Victims, primarily Jews, but also some Polish and Russian prisoners of war, were exposed to inhuman experimentation. They were given gas gangrene wounds, injected with typhus and jaundice, shot with poison bullets, and forced to quench their thirst with salt water in order to see how long a human being could live. When the decisions were made to implement a "final solution," the death camps of Auschwitz, Buchenwald, Dachau, Mauthausen, Sachsenhausen, and others brought a terrifying, technological efficiency to genocide. In some camps, the disposition of corpses evolved from mass burial to cremation. Once the crematoria (routinely located adjacent to the gas chambers) were done, human remains were at times milled to a fine ash fit for fertilizer.

The organization of genocide depended on the efficiency of population transfer, transportation systems, and deception. Victims were rounded up and many, as in the case of the Warsaw ghetto, concentrated in large urban centers. They were then transported out, frequently by rail, under the pretense of joining work camps. (The gates to the notorious Auschwitz death camp in Poland carried the message *Arbeit Macht Frei*, or Work Makes Freedom.) Once to the camps, under the pretense that they were to receive showers or be deloused, victims were gassed. Gas chambers were routinely disguised, with signs at the entrances reading "baths" and dummy showerheads installed. Musicians from the camp population were recruited, and as they "played for time" ordinary men, women, children, and babes in arms made their contribution to the history of terrorism (Shirer, 1960: 963–79).

The Nazi final solution is a frequently cited example of regime terror, often obscured by narrowly conceived political and psychological inquiries. However, to begin to explain the death camps requires the prior consideration of the rise of a peculiar fascism in Germany. During the 1930s, the Great Depression created for Germany conditions that had already become severe for Italy and Japan during the previous decade. These three nations, which became the "Axis Powers" during the Second World War, were undergoing industrial development but without the control of domestic or international resources (Chirot, 1977: 98–101). In particular, Germany, striving for standing in the core of the modern world-system, had been defeated during World War I and had lost its colonial empire. It was also unsuccessful during the 1920s in finding new industrial markets in the Middle East and South America (Wallerstein, 1979: 31–33). With the loss of the requisite advantages for capital accumulation, depression-era Germany was particularly vulnerable to alterations in the already pronounced asymmetry of its internal class relations. With these external and internal dislocations came the reconstruction of ideological themes of domination that reinforced and redefined state power. Such conditions prepared the historical stage for the rise of the Nazi variety of fascism.

On the one hand, industrial fascism in Germany meant the development of a war economy with the resulting militarization of the culture. The architects of the fascist state gained the support of major industrialists by moving to subsidize the economy through armament credits, amounting to "about 62 percent of total government expenditures, or over 16 percent of total national income by 1938 (Schoenbaum, 1967: 116). However, the Nazi vanguard proved to be the salaried professionals (including many teachers) and technicians, as well as the small landowners and business interests of the "new middle classes" (Cole, 1970). This segment of society had not recovered from the devastating inflation in the wake of World War I that had stripped their savings. It was also this class that feared the coming of a worker's socialism that would take away their claim to higher status and perhaps their dreams of upward mobility. As for those of the strongly organized working class, they proved susceptible to the promise of jobs and something more. Although no German class was immune from the mysticism that came to surround the Fatherland, it remains particularly striking that well-organized, leftist-led workers abandoned the solidarity of labor for one of *supernationalism*. A structuralist analysis of class (which dismisses the role of the ideological factor) fails to account for the cooptation of this stratum.

Fascist movements, notably in Germany, sought to wed national chauvinism with state authoritarianism. This is to say that loyalty to one's country and obedience to the state become sides of the same ideological coin. Fascism thus embraces the supreme authority of the state as a means of settling conflicts among divergent populations (Linz, 1976: 21). But the Nazi form of fascism was something more than belligerent chauvinism and blind authoritarianism. It sought a kind of monolithic synthesis; the emergence of an absolute unity of its people that would subordinate conflicting economic, political, and cultural interests to the welfare of the nation. National unity is often founded in a set of cherished myths held by a population that proclaim the natural superiority of one's nation and values over all others. And once again, patriotism and other ideological or mystical beliefs may become part and parcel of expansionist forces. But in the supernationalism of nazism, a distinctive ideological element was added: the conception of a master race bonded to the fatherland in a mystical union of blood and soil.

Nazi ideology thus integrated two of the more dangerous exclusionary myths of human history into one—the *nation-race*. As always, such symbols acquire legitimacy through the designation of opposites; of "enemy deviants" that define terms and clarify the struggle in dialectical fashion. If there is a master race, there must be inferiors; if there are chosen people, there must be the left-outs; if a superior people find themselves in desperate circumstances, it must be that they have been betrayed. Nazi ideology identified the cast of characters in stark terms. Nazism was opposed to trade unionism, to communism, to the aristocracy, and to the unfair treatment of labor, as well as to the usual assortment of incompetent politicians and military leaders who had "lost" World War I.

It was not necessary to reinvent the full-blown racist ideology of imperial Europe only to redefine the scapegoats. Behind the ideological front and the realignment of class interests came the seizure of property, the blind solidarity, and the legitimation of obedience that foreshadowed the reduction of "surplus population." For the nation-race, bonded in exclusionary purity, there were no ambiguities, no confusion, no uncertainties, and above all no questioning of legitimacy of the state.

### Stalinism: Modernization and Purge

> We spent only a few days at the collective farm and were appalled at the conditions we found there. The farmers were starving to death.... They literally begged us to give them food.
> Soviet Premier Nikita Khrushchev (1958–64) on Stalin's collectivization policies in *Khrushchev Remembers: The Last Testament*

Under three decades of Stalinist rule, the Soviet people became dual victims. Externally, they were attacked by the Nazi Wehrmacht and in the course of "the Great Patriotic War" against international fascism suffered twenty million dead, with many survivors dying prematurely for decades to come.[9] Internally, however, the Soviet people experienced between 1930 and 1953 a reign of regime terror during which open criticism was an offense against the state. But more was lost than freedom of expression. Beneath the silence born of fear, hundreds of thousands were exterminated, and millions died because of state policies (Cohen, 1985:97).

To begin to grasp the Stalinist period is to first address the kind of world that existed when the Bolsheviks under Lenin emerged from the Russian Revolution (1917–21) as the ruling party. First, the country was devastated as a consequence of its ill-fated participation in the First World War. It was the bloody defeat of poorly armed and supplied Russian soldiers on the battlefields of that war that precipitated a mutiny in 1917 (including those in Petrograd). The Bolsheviks ended the war with Germany in March of 1918. Between 1919 and 1921, a "forgotten war" (not forgotten by the Soviets) brought intervention from contingents of U.K., French, Japanese, and U.S. soldiers. The Red Army was ultimately victorious, but the new Soviet state was clearly to enter a hostile world. And the intervention in the Russian Revolution by outside powers was not to be forgotten (Thompson, 1962: 319–80).

Lenin died in 1924, and the leadership of the new society fell to Joseph Stalin. Stalin was heir to Lenin's conception of the state, which began to assume institutional form during the October Revolution and which was consolidated in the context of ongoing internal war. In *The State and Revolution* Lenin argued for the revolutionary transformation of society through state power under the control of a party vanguard. In the name of practical administration, he advocated a hierarchy: "... we want the socialist revolution with people as they are now, with people who cannot dispense with subordination, control and 'foremen and bookkeepers.' But the subordination must be to the armed vanguard of all the exploited and toiling people, i.e., to the Proletariat" (Lenin, 1970: 58, originally published in 1917). Simply put, Lenin advocated a strongly centralized system as a means of consolidating the gains of the revolution, forging unity in a highly fragmented society and seeking to transform its economic base. Unconvinced of the Marxist conception of a more spontaneous and class-wide development of worker revolutionary consciousness, his emphasis on a party elite and organizational efficiency had served the Bolsheviks well in their drive to power. But with his death he passed on a state structure, conceived in the fires of revolution and civil war, with few checks on official authority.

Joseph Stalin was thus first of all a product of the specific conditions of Russian revolutionary history. He found himself at the head of a fragmented society with a poorly developed industrial base in a world whose major powers had signalled their hostility in convincing fashion. In his speech before the First Conference of Russian Managers (Moscow, 1931) he sounded the theme of *state-expansionist development*, where the structures of central management could be used to rapidly eliminate the industrial and technological gap between the fledgling U.S.S.R. and its adversaries.

The history of old Russia is the history of defeats due to backwardness. She was beaten by the Mongol Khans. She was beaten by the Turkish beys. She was beaten by the Swedish feudal barons. She was beaten by the Polish-Lithuanian squires. She was beaten

by the Anglo-French capitalists. She was beaten by the Japanese barons. All beat her for her backwardness—for military backwardness, for cultural backwardness, for governmental backwardness, for industrial backwardness, for agricultural backwardness....
We are fifty to a hundred years behind the advanced countries. We must cover this distance in ten years. Either we do this or they will crush us. (In Horowitz, 1966:14)

Stalinism does not refer to a personality. It is rather a form of nationalism, a fear of backwardness, a conception of state-driven economic development. Stalin presented his fears of capitalist encirclement, founded partly in history, partly in an attempt to build internal solidarity, and partly in an attempt to legitimate the total power of the state. There was a quality of desperation here, an obsession with a people seizing the present and hurling it into the future before they are swallowed up by the past. But though the bureaucratic machinery of the modern state may easily be enlisted in a war of survival, human beings do not so easily yield to demands for total change. In the Stalinist era, efficiency gave way to expediency, the expediency of terror.

During the first five-year plan (1928–32), the party sought to transform the Soviet economy through collectivization and industrialization. Driven by central plans to modernize rapidly, and facing isolation in a crisis-ridden global market, the agricultural surplus was defined as a source of investment for industrial development. Large numbers of peasants were engaged in private farming, and many were reasonably prosperous. An increasing amount of what they produced was requisitioned by the state. The kulaks were wealthy peasants who profited from the labor of poorer peasants, and hence defined as exploiters under the new system. Many fiercely opposed the collectivization of land. Considered a hostile class by the Stalin regime, large numbers were deported to the Ural mountains, Kazakhstan, western Siberia, and elsewhere (Hough and Fainsod, 1979: 152).[10]

The Stalinist employment of terror did not stop in the countryside. Once domination through fear is legitimated in the name of higher purposes and ideals and institutionalized in policies, laws, and programs, it can only spread, feeding upon itself. Once a police force or agency is established on the premise of secrecy, the secrecy is routinely legitimated in the name of state or national security. And the secrecy itself then builds terror as all are left to ponder who will be the next victim. Stalin and his allies came to see in terror a method of political purification, to be directed toward "reactionary elements" within the highest circles of the party and military as well as toward ethnic/national groups, intellectuals, and artists. Perhaps the single most terrifying example is to be found in the *Great Purge* (1936–39). Historian Roy Medvedev (1971: 239) estimated that some four or five hundred thousand people were summarily shot, including high officials. Millions of others were given long prison terms.

So the Soviet national society emerged in tumultuous conflict, ravaged externally by war and internally by contending revolutionary forces. As a declared Marxist state, it was to stand alone in a hostile world shaken in a quarter century by two world wars and a Great Depression. This meant an immediate end to foreign capital, and in the 1930s, a shattering of plans to import vital industrial equipment (Von Laue, 1964: 213). It was not only "behind" in the sense of its industrial and technological base, it was out of step with a global system locked in crises. Stalin also inherited and mystified a conception of power that held that in the hands of a vanguard, the state structure that had emerged historically to maintain and expand the interests of a capitalist class could be put to other instrumental ends. In this orthodox view, the inherent forces of state repression should have been resolved when the state was free from the reproduction of capitalist class relations. That the *problematique* of state power and violence is far more complex is clearly demonstrated by this era.

Some hold that Stalin was at least prescient in his conviction that the unfolding depression would produce war and that the Soviets would be a prime target. However, under Stalinism, the state became something other than the engine of modernization, and a tactical instrument for organizing the national economy and defense. Particularly vulnerable to the systemic crisis of the Great Depression, the Stalinists responded with forced development. In so doing they abandoned Lenin's New Economic Policy (favored by Nikolai Bukharin and in some ways by Leon Trotsky) with its juxtaposition of state controlled heavy industry and a vital, small-scale private sector (Cohen, 1985: 56–62). The state instead became a system for repression and extermination, forcing a recurring debate since the Khrushchev era on the formation of new relations of state power. However, the Soviet dilemma (as with all states) is not merely political. The U.S.S.R. remains linked systemically to the global market system (and its crises), and is still committed to traditional Western conceptions of growth.

## TOWARD REVISIONIST DEFINITIONS OF TERRORISM

In the opening chapter the case was made that the dominant ideology of terrorism masks institutional coercion through fear. In the present argument, the nature of these enduring arrangements have been given theoretical form and brief historical illustration. To this point, the question of terrorism has been clarified by positing the existence of a transnational market system featuring an international and hierarchical division of labor. Within this dynamic order, materially dominant players act to preserve the imperatives of that system, including world market growth; the creation and expansion of developmental organizations; open and secure transnational investment; free trade; technological solutions; reduced labor costs; minimal governmental regulation of the productive process; and the equation of unfettered market forces with public welfare. Taken together, these represent a growth (as opposed to distribution) model of development, the legitimation of which is rooted in the ideology of modernization.

It is within the human consequences of such a system of global reach that the question of terrorism may be joined. Certainly, the disjunction born of world market crisis, or even normative competition, bears a relationship to regime terror, even on the part of Great Powers. It is, however, those societies and peoples without such standing that remain the muted victims. There are probably no more naked indices of living in fear than the stark data on hunger and mortality mentioned earlier. The simply designated "Third World" remains the source of cheap labor and resources, with many of its national economies crippled by debt and unequal exchange. Thus what is "modernized" is a system of global inequality, and what is "developed" are the dependency relations of peripheral underdevelopment. This, simply put, is real terrorism. It is this transnational system that drives the policies of its dominant states, including the use of military force. It is the political/military defense of this international and hierarchical division of labor that is the theoretical nexus for the forms of state terrorism examined in the chapters to come. However, it should be clear that the following definitions have a more general application.

The case has been made that certain of the international and internal practices of the National Security State are designed for the purpose of rule by fear. Whether exemplified in growing arsenals of mass destruction, in purges and assassinations, in death squads and torture, in support for economic violence, or in other methods of terror, it is evident that the state form of terrorism is a brutal reality of immense proportion. Based on our opening chapters, certain specific principles can be formulated that provide some grounds for considering contemporary kinds of state intimidation through fear. Accordingly, state terrorism is evidenced:

1. in police state practices against its own people to dominate through fear by surveillance, disruption of group meetings, control of the news media, beatings, torture, false and mass arrests, false charges and rumors, show trials, killings, summary executions, and capital punishment;
2. in the armed attack by the military forces of a state on targets that put at risk the civilian population residing in another state;
3. in assassination attempts and plots directed by a state toward the officials of other states, whether carried out by military strike, special forces units or covert operations by "intelligence forces" or their third party agents;
4. in the military occupation of a state, whether in the form of direct martial control or in the establishment of a base of operations;
5. in covert operations by the "intelligence" or other forces of a state that are intended to destabilize or subvert another state;
6. in disinformation campaigns by a state, whether intended to destabilize another state, or to build public support for economic, political, or military force or intimidation directed at another state;
7. in military exercises, maneuvers, or "games" conducted by a state outside the territory or territorial waters of that state;
8. in the creation and support of armed mercenary forces by a state for the purpose of subverting the government of another state;

9. in the support, by whatever means, of other states that deny the right of self-determination to nationally conscious populations expressed through popularly supported liberation movements;

10. in arms sales that support the continuation of regional wars and retard the search for political solutions;

11. in the introduction or transportation of nuclear weapons by a state into or through the territory, territorial waters, or air space of other states, or into international waters or airspace;

12. and in the development, testing, and deployment of nuclear and space weapons systems, and all other weapons of mass destruction, by a state that in all circumstances increase the probability of genocide and ecocide, while condemning the poor to continued misery and all humanity to a state of perennial fear.[11]

With such conceptions in mind, we turn to the role of the international media in the "selling of international terrorism."

## NOTES

1. The Department of Energy can more appropriately be called the Department of Nuclear Weapons.

2. Good general references on the contradictions of the warfare economy are found in McFadden and Wake (1983), Fallows (1982), and Barnet (1981).

3. There are widely disparate estimates of the native populations of North and South America. A plausible range for the population north of the Rio Grande in A.D. 1500 is one to ten million (Wax, 1971).

4. These organizations included the Ulster Defence Association and the Ulster Freedom Fighters on the side of the loyalists, opposed by the nationalist I.R.A., P.I.R.A., and the offshoot Irish National Liberation Army.

5. There were some 74,556 searches in 1973 alone (Boyle, et al., 1980: 27–28).

6. Ironically, shootings in the kneecap have spawned a new surgical specialty in Northern Ireland, with new restorative techniques.

7. The S.A.S. was strongly implicated in the resurgence in 1988 of a shoot-to-kill policy, directed at the I.R.A. (*New Statesman*, 1988: 3).

8. General historical references include Skocpol (1979); D. M. G. Sutherland (1986); George Rude (1980); and George Lefebvre (1962–64).

9. The total World War II death toll amounted to some 45 million (*World Almanac*, 1987: 510.).

10. Stalin signed a decree halting mass deportations in May of 1933. However, the world famine of 1932 and 1933 had already begun.

11. Points 2, 3, 5–8, and 10–12 were prepared by the author, and adopted with modifications as part of a conference declaration on the question of terrorism. Others were developed expressly for this volume. (The first point is the work of Ramsey Clark.) The conference was organized by the International Progress Organization of Vienna, a U.N.E.S.C.O. nongovernmental organization.

# 3

# *Mediaspeak: The Selling of International Terrorism*

> The moving finger writes, and having writ, moves on; nor all thy piety nor wit shall lure it back to cancel half a line, nor all thy tears wash out a word of it.
>
> Omar Khayyam

In June of 1985, two hijackers boarded T.W.A. flight 847 in Athens, initiating a voyage of terror for 153 captives, approximately two-thirds of which were citizens of the United States. The crew was forced to fly the plane to Beirut in Lebanon, then over the next two days across the Mediterranean Sea to Algiers, back from that North African capital to Beirut, then to Algiers again, and finally back to Beirut. This odyssey and its aftermath became an ongoing media event, an act of political theater broadcast to an international audience of millions. What began as a shocking ritual in hostage-taking and a cold-blooded execution evolved into a much more complex event with the audience exposed to views, often expressed by the hostages themselves, that ran counter to the "official story" on international terrorism.

## TERROR IN THE SKIES: THE HIJACKING OF T.W.A. FLIGHT 847

The hijacking of T.W.A. flight 847, as the overarching issue of media coverage, cannot be understood in isolation from the higher sociohistorical forces at play. Such forces in turn extend beyond the tragedy of the moment (such as the civil war in Lebanon) to embody the troubled ground of Middle Eastern conflict. For the field of conflict included not only Lebanon, but the so-called Islamic resurgence in Iran (see Chapter 8), the struggle between Palestinian Arabs and Israel (see Chapter 7), and the question of national liberation movements in general. All of this in due course. The point of departure for now shall be the firestorm of criticism encountered by the internationally linked U.S. media, accused by some of losing control of this and other episodes of the story of terrorism.

As events unfolded, the hijackers demanded to contact officials of Amal, a political and militia organization drawn from the long-suffering Shi'ite minority of the Islamic faith. The leaders of Amal at first refused, and the hijackers responded by executing a U.S. Navy diver. The act of vendetta terror was tied by the hijackers to the Bir al Abed massacre. On March 8, 1985, a car bomb exploded in the Bir al Abed suburb of Beirut, intended to assassinate Sheikh Fadlallah, who led Hizbollah in Beirut (see Chapter 8). He escaped, but more than 75 Shi'ite Muslims who happen to be in the neighborhood died (*Time*, June 24, 1985: 22). This bombing was the extension of a C.I.A. program of "preemptive self-defense" by which units of foreign nationals (in this case Lebanese) were to be used in "counterterrorism" operations. The formal finding and the National Security Directive that authorized the C.I.A. to conduct preemptive strikes was signed by Ronald Reagan (Woodward, 1987: 393-94). After the killing of Robert Stetham, an Amal official in Beirut boarded the aircraft, initiating a role for that organization in subsequent proceedings. Through intercession, by Amal in Lebanon and by Algerian officials in Algiers, all but some 39 American male passengers and crew members were released. Those who remained in captivity were ultimately transferred to Amal and finally freed.

In the course of the captivity, T.W.A. hostages and their captors presented not only specific demands but also implicated Israel and its staunch ally, the United States in the tragedy of Lebanon. Israel had invaded Lebanon (for the second time in four years) in June of 1982, with its leaders declaring a national security interest in driving Palestine Liberation Forces from southern Lebanon (see Chapter 7). The Israeli invasion was intended to effectively destroy the P.L.O. in Beirut and to shore up its allies, the Western-oriented Christian Phalange, who sought to extend their political control in the wake of the surging growth of the Islamic Shi'ite population in the region. Thus, a major demand of the T.W.A. hijackers was directed to the Israelis; namely that they were to release some 700 Shi'ite prisoners who had been taken in an Israeli military sweep during its 1985 pullback in southern Lebanon.

The U.S. media were quickly caught up in high political drama. In often live interviews with hostages and captors, Israel was presented as something other than a force for democracy in the Middle East. The taking of American hostages became a symbolic expression of the outrage felt by the adversaries of Israel toward U.S. support for that state. In effect, the captivity of some three dozen Americans was used to point up the similar status of 700 Lebanese. When Dan

Rather (on June 28, 1985) asked hostage Father James McCloughlin of Geneva, Illinois, if he had a message for President Reagan and the other decision-makers in the United States, he reponded that: "I think I'd like to tell the decision-makers . . . that we were taught that our government was of, for and by the people of the country, and not *special interests outside of our nation*, and I would like to see them take that message of Mr. Lincoln very seriously in our regard" (United States Congress, Subcommittee on Europe and the Middle East, July 30, 1985: 145 and 147, italics added). The "special interests" appeared to be a reference to the state of Israel. (Other hostages also questioned the direction of U.S. policy in the region.)[1] McCloughlin later added that he thought the 700 Lebanese jailed by Israel should be released, and he cautioned strongly against military rescue attempts. *Newsweek* (June 24, 1985: 25) reported that many analysts believed that the U.S. Army's Delta Force had been flown to a staging area in the Mediterranean in preparation for a possible raid.

If the question of hostage safety is paramount, then the saga of Flight 847 ended well. All were ultimately released (the Americans in 17 days), including the 700 Lebanese Shi'ites in Israeli jails. However, the issue of the media coverage of this event was not finished. In a letter to the major U.S. networks on the subject of "media coverage of terorrist events and responses thereto," Thomas Luken, a member of the Telecommunications, Consumer Protection, and Finance Subcommittee of the U.S. House of Representatives wrote:

The recent American TWA hostage experience in the Middle East suggests that the American media "have yet to learn how to avoid serving as the 'ransom' that is now paid to terrorists who take hostages." Many of the members of the subcommittee are deeply concerned about the astonishing spectacle of T.V. news shows from the Middle East apparently "co-produced by television and the terrorists." The above-quoted references do not originate with me or other members of Congress, but are statements from respected media spokesmen made since the hostage crisis. I believe they reflect deep seated concerns regarding performances of the networks when they become a major part of making events, rather than simply reporting them. (U.S. Congress, Subcommittee on Europe and the Middle East, 1985: 129)

The question of publicity as ransom is a vital one, but there are larger media-ignored-issues. It was Martin Luther King, Jr. who, in the context of the urban revolts in the United States in the mid–1960s, observed that "riots are the language of the unheard." This was no endorsement of violence, but instead a call to understand its roots. As argued in the previous chapter, conventionally defined terror is not disconnected from institutionalized forms of structural violence. Indeed, the "platform for terrorists" question might well be largely preempted if the media were disposed toward reporting on the higher terrorism. The transcendent issue is not simply whether the broadcast and printed media provide time and ink for perpetrators of outrageous acts.[2] It is rather the relationship between the structural and ideological forces inherent in the "means of influence" on the one side, and the mystification of terrorism on the other.

Argued thus, a critique of the media must address: (1) the definitional or ideological problems associated with terrorism; (2) inadequate coverage of the sources of political violence, with bias favoring coverage of the high drama that gives twisted expression to those grievances; and (3) the role of the media in creating the political climate in which state terrorism is legitimated as "counterterrorism."

The organization of the means of influence, together with the domain assumptions about social reality that are part of media culture, are indeed problematic. But the dilemma goes much deeper than the usually superficial complaints from offended parties who claim the media are too liberal, too conservative, or even a vast (today, a vaster) wasteland. It is only fair to ask whether the media are much more vulnerable to being "used" by agencies of the state, by allies and by other official sources, than by the undisciplined individuals or small groups who indulge in vendetta terror, or by the popularly supported national liberation movements in dominated countries which engage in guerilla warfare. Moreover, it is fair to ask if the media have their own global interests which makes them (whether their personnel are self-conscious or not) part of the ideological problematique of terrorism.

## THE HEADLINE STORY

The U.S. media, both broadcast and printed, demonstrated a recurring interest in the commodification of the terrorism tale in the 1980s. However, there is little evidence that opposing conceptions of terrorism (dominant and utopian) were balanced. (See the literature below.) The debate was instead over the means to be employed (economic boycott, third party force, direct action, etc.) in meeting the self-evident terrorist threat. Thus the official view of terrorism was reproduced by the mainstream U.S. media. On point, the hijacking of T.W.A. flight 847 is an exemplar of vendetta terrorism. However, it is this "kind" of terrorism that became *the* media definition. Throughout the *terrornoia* decade, Western state force and threat of force, whether direct or indirect quite arguably constituted domination through fear. Only a few such cases of the higher terrorism were: support for government by death squad in El Salvador (Chomsky, 1986: 124; Rangel, 1984); surrogate war in Nicaragua (Chapter 9); the 1983 invasion of Grenada (Sono, 1984) and the 1986 bombing of Libya (see below). Nor was the delegitimating and polemical phrase "international terrorism" routinely attached to episodes involving Western allies as we shall see in later chapters.

On the specific question of media conceptions and coverage of terrorism, some sensitizing constructs are in order. To begin, there is the *delayed rejoinder* in which a sensational tale broken with great fanfare is brought into suspicion only later, after the shock value is done and the stereotyping complete. Early charges of international terrorism directed toward the Soviet Union by the Reagan administration, and the conspiratorial confirmation of that theme by Claire Sterling's *The Terror Network* were given enormous play by such as the *Washington Post* and the *New York Times* in March of 1981. The *Post* later ran articles that concluded that "no significant information" could be found that linked the Soviets to "terrorist enterprises" (Parenti, 1986: 149–50). The delayed rejoinder came in January, 1984, almost three years later. Perhaps as with justice, truth delayed is truth denied.

To continue, the media reproduce the double standard of terrorism by *beholding the mote* in the eyes of enemy deviants while "ignoring the beam" in the steely eyes of power. This distinction is evidenced in the focus on "retail" as opposed to "wholesale" terror (the killing of Libyan counterrevolutionaries, numbered at 14 by Amnesty International, compared to the deaths by shadow government terror of 50,000 in El Salvador) (Chomsky, 1986a: 2, 124). *Counterfeit balance* refers to media apologetics for allies; routine assertions that friendly terror must be weighed against violence on the part of opposing forces. The fact that regime terror (usually called something else) far outstrips antiregime guerilla violence or rare vendetta terror is lost, as evidenced in the cases of Honduras, Guatemala, and El Salvador (Herman, 1982: 1970–79). This flaw is often complemented by the *struggling for democracy* myth by which such client states are given media as well as political absolution.

The dominant ideology of terrorism was explored in the opening chapter of this book. Its privatized, psychologized, and "enemy deviant" themes need not be reviewed here, other than to say that the media produce and reproduce these well. The enduring assumptions underlying the nature of terrorism remain familiar. The somewhat promiscuous association of the term with the Soviet Union, Eastern European, and socialist Third World states stand as a variation of the same old Red scare. Other noncommunist national movements and nation-states that are in conflict with the West or that condemn the Western developmental model were also vulnerable. However, the *problematique* of "mediaspeak" and terrorism requires a wider view.

The question of terrorism may not originate and end with the state, or a particular leadership using a defenseless media. It may instead be more persuasive to ask whether the broadcast and printed media are *structurally aligned* with the state in the legitimation of a particular view of terrorism. Claus Offe argues that the state requires the public input of loyalty and confidence to support its output of autocratic administrative decisions (Offe, 1982, first published in 1972). Certainly, among the most crucial of those decisions are those authorizing force or the threat of force. If the media are aligned with the state in the protection and expansion of a given order, then newsmakers are positioned to play a key role in the marshalling of crucial public support. Stated succinctly, the media are structurally predisposed toward the creation and dissemination of a distorted conception of political violence.

People in free-market societies are usually socialized to distrust the state-run media because of such defects. However, in societies in which the media are organizd on a for profit basis, the story of terror, appropriately simplified for mass consumption, may have similar consequences (as well as proving highly marketable.) And, when the media is a part of a transnational corporate economy, still another barrier to accurate reporting and informed analysis may be raised. It is in these and related ways that the media may be thought to be actively involved in the production and sale of a product, of a story part fact, part fiction, but wholly without depth. Hence the media is involved conceptually and commercially in the *selling of international terrorism*. The implications of such disinformation go beyond simple distortion as the following case study bears out.

### Mad Dogs and Presidents[3]

> [A] young man stared at the dusty foot of a child poking out of the rubble. Rescuers dug her out and handed her to a young father, who wrapped the three-year-old body in a blanket, buried his face in it and wept. Later I saw her body at the morgue. Her blue eyes stared upward; her arms reached stiffly out before her. On her wrist she wore a single bangle.
>
> Ruth Marshall in *Newsweek*, April 28, 1986

In April of 1986, 13 F–111 U.S. fighter-bombers flying from Lakenheath Air Base in Britain, joined by 12 A–6 carrier-based aircraft, struck Tripoli and Bengazi, the major population centers of the North African country of Libya.[4] U.S. forces lost one aircraft and its crew of two. But in just 12 minutes over their targets, the planes dropped 100 tons of bombs. Virtually all of the estimated 100 dead on the Libyan side were civilians, including women and children. Spokespersons for the Reagan administration defended the raid as a strike against terrorism. The targets included the personal residence of Libyan leader Muammar Qaddafi, portrayed since the first year of the Reagan administration as the chief instigator and supporter of a campaign of international terrorism directed toward the West. Among the casualties of the raid were Qaddafi's eight children and wife, Safiya, who were hospitalized after the raid suffering from shock and various injuries. Hana, the 15-month-old adopted daughter, died a few hours later. Although denied by the administration, there is more than *prima facie* evidence that the raid was little more than an assassination attempt.

One well-informed Air Force intelligence officer says, "There's no question they were looking for Qaddafi. It was briefed that way. They were going to kill him." An Air Force pilot involved in highly classified special operations acknowledges that "the assassination was the big thing."

"Each of the nine F-111's carried four 2,000-pound bombs. The young pilots and weapons-systems officers . . . were provided with reconnaissance photographs separately depicting . . . where Qaddafi was and where his family was."

The notion of targeting Qaddafi's family, according to an involved N.S.C. aide, originated with several C.I.A. officers, who claimed that in Bedouin culture Qaddafi would be diminished as a leader if he could not protect his home. One aide recalls a C.I.A. briefing in which it was argued that "if you really get at Qaddafi's house—and by extension, his family—you've destroyed an important connection for the people in terms of loyalty. (Hersh, 1987: 20)[5]

The surprising complexities of Libyan-U.S. relations will be explored in Chapter 6. The thrust here is with the media role in the demonology of terrorism. And although few things are certain about disinformation campaigns, there is enough in the way of contervailing evidence to raise grave questions about the veracity of media accounts; accounts that did much to build and spread this lead chapter in the official story of terrorism. To begin, it is arguable that the targeting of Muammar Qaddafi and his family was by April of 1986 a quite predictable extension of "counterterrorism" tactics directed toward this Arab state. Other tactics included naval exercises intended to provoke a Libyan military response (Stork, 1986: 8). Two such exercises, in August of 1981 and March of 1986, resulted in armed conflict in and over the Libyan claimed Gulf of Sirte with all casualties on the Libyan side. Other episodes during the Reagan years included war games conducted in concert with U.S. allies in neighboring states, the ordering of Americans out of Libya, and the introduction of economic sanctions. All were accompanied by accusations of terrorism directed toward Libya by the Reagan administration. Yet the forces of the state have not been alone in constructing this imagery.

In the shadowy and murky world of terrorism, whether state or non-state, it is difficult to separate truth and fiction. Given the stakes involved, especially as a superpower appeared in the early 1980s to be building for a deadly crusade, it would appear that prudence and caution on the part of the media would have been mandatory. But what is now beginning to emerge rather clearly is that some of the major episodes in the saga of Libyan terrorism were manufactured by U.S. intelligence agencies and that others rested on dubious information. However, with only a few late exceptions (such as the *New York Times* piece by Seymour Hersh in 1987), the U.S. corporate media taken as a whole must be judged to have enthusiastically disseminated the official story of Libyan network terrorism. Although some of the more blatant fables drew some long-after-the-fact scrutiny, state and media portrayals of Libya as a major terrorist state strongly resisted negation.[6] More to the point, this particular label is a deadly one because of the kinds of "defensive" violence it sanctions. The dilemma is perhaps best expressed in the words of Omar Khayyam considered earlier in this chapter. Once a judgment of terrorism has been made, and written over and again, it is extremely difficult to recall.

The earliest and perhaps the most sensational account of Libyan terorrism came in the wake of a demonstration of U.S. naval power in the Mediterranean. In August of 1981, U.S. Tomcat fighter aircraft, equipped with sophisticated weapons computers, shot down two Libyan Su–22s over the Gulf of Sirte. The shoot-out occurred over Libyan-claimed territorial water, 60 miles from the Libyan coast. The air battle was a predictable outcome of orders by the Reagan administration that sent the Sixth Fleet into the Gulf of Sirte to conduct war games. The move was decidedly provocative. The Libyan government in a note to the U.S. Department of State eight years earlier had asserted a claim to the gulf, formed by a great indentation in its Mediterranean coastline. Libya's claim, like Canada's claim to Hudson Bay, has not been recognized internationally. But the Reagan administration did not choose Hudson Bay to flex its muscles. Exulting two days after the dog fight, the president declared: "Let friend and foe alike know America has the muscle to back up its words" (*Time*, 1981, Aug. 31: 14–18).

Those who supported the actions of the U.S. military joined with President Reagan in claiming that the United States enjoyed a renewed pride in its armed forces, world respect, and revived confidence as a consequence of the encounter. Columnist George Will contemptuously wrote that "when the tail of a stallion whisks away a fly, the fly has a crisis, the stallion does not" (In Perdue, 1984: 91). Why world respect would follow the swatting of a fly is not immediately clear. There is the danger of counterpolemic here in dwelling too long on chauvinistic chest-thumping in support of provocative demonstrations of imperial power. It may be true that power breeds arrogance; that the ready resort to force reflects a cowboy mentality that endangers world peace. However, such descriptions are reductionist. The issue is not whether one or a number of columnists on the editorial page offer bravado in lieu of analysis. The issue is whether the major broadcast and printed media became an active participant in an historically founded conflict involving real and symbolic global forces.

In the fall of 1981, shortly after the shoot-out over the Mediterranean, security arrangements for the president were tightened. Raymond W. Copson (1982) of the Foreign Affairs and National Defense Division wrote the following in an official government brief:

There was *speculation in the press* that these arrangements *might be related* to the threat of a (possible) Libyan-sponsored assassination attempt in retaliation for the Gulf of Sirte Incident. *The speculation seemed* to be confirmed in early December, when *press reports* indicated that U.S. intelligence officials had received information from an *unnamed* non-American source with first-hand knowledge of Libyan plans indicating that a Libyan assassination team, including Libyan and other Middle Eastern Nationals as well as an East German *might* have entered the United States from Canada over the November 30 weekend. This assassination team (there was later mention of two teams) was said to have plans to kill the President by shooting down Air Force One, the presidential jet; attacking a Presidential motorcade with rocket fire; or shooting at close range with small arms. If the President could not be attacked, the team reportedly was to strike at other U.S. officials or at the President's family. Some U.S. officials *interviewed by the press* were said to be skeptical of the reliability of the source of the conspiracy report, and there was some confusion after the initial report appeared over whether the alleged team was actually in the United States or was preparing to enter the United States from Mexico. Nonetheless, security was tightened for the President and for a number of high officials [emphasis added].

It is clear from a careful reading of this report that the media were being cited to give credibility to the Libyan hit-team caper, a tale that was to become more bizarre (see Perdue, 1984; Sono, 1984; 45–78). Qaddafi denied the existence of a conspiracy or hit teams and challenged the U.S. government to provide evidence. President Reagan responded that "We have the evidence and he knows it." However, no proof of hit teams was forthcoming from the administration. Did the media have the evidence? Ray S. Cline, a former deputy director of intelligence for the C.I.A. and a staunch critic of Libya and Qaddafi stated to journalist John Weisman, "There was no evidence." Jeff Gralnick, executive producer of A.B.C.'s World News Tonight added: "No news organization had any finite proof at all." But still the networks filled the airwaves with sensational accounts, complete with distortion and conflicting details. For example,

1. The number of hit men were reported to be 3, 5, 6, 10, 12, and 13.
2. Two assassins were reported to have entered the U.S. from Canada, from Mexico, then they were not in Mexico, then there were two teams.
3. Their personal habits included wearing cowboy boots, Adidas running shoes, and smoking English cigarettes.
4. N.B.C. reported that the team included three Libyans, three Iranians, one East German, three Syrians, one Palestinian and one Lebanese; A.B.C. reported three Libyans, two Iranians, no Syrians, one Palestinian, one East German, and one Lebanese. C.B.S. reported *no* Libyans, three Iranians, one East German, no Syrians, one Palestinian, and one Lebanese. *Time* reported two Iranians, one Palestinian, one Lebanese, and one German. Columnist Jack Anderson included in the alleged hit team two leaders of Amal (see above), a Shi'ite Muslim political party in Lebanon, opposed to Qaddafi. As noted by Noam Chomsky (1986b: 19), the British press exposed the Amal error, which went largely unreported in the U.S. media. (Anderson later wrote that he had been setup by an unnamed intelligence agency.) The Reagan administration blamed the mix-up on a computer error.
5. On Thanksgiving night (Nov. 26, 1981), A.B.C.'s Frank Reynolds stated that it was known that Libyan agents were "in this country for the purpose of assassinating the highest officials of the U.S. government."
6. On December 4, Dan Rather reported that "a squad of terrorists infiltrated the United States on a mission to kill the President and his top aides."
7. On December 9, C.B.S.'s Phil Jones told viewers that the alleged hit team was sitting in Mexico and that "intelligence reports indicate that the teams have been in contact with the Weather Underground terrorist group." Long after his report, Jones admitted that his story "was sourced by a couple of members for the Senate Intelligence Committee. I have talked with them since and they feel they were had—they used the word "entrapped" by their C.I.A. briefers. He continued, "I've got a great sense of being "had" in this whole thing and the equally disturbing thought is that if the story happened again, we'd be had again." (Weisman, in Perdue, 1984: 92)

Those who doubted the veracity of the tale appear to have been correct. Over five years later, Seymour Hersh reported the following quote from a Reagan administration insider involved in the task force authorized by then Secretary of State Alexander Haig to study the Qaddafi "problem":[7] "This item stuck in my craw. We came out with this big terrorist threat to the U.S. Government. The whole thing was a complete fabrication (Hersh, 1987: 24)." By August of 1986, the *New York Times* confirmed what had been slowly dawning on many in the media in the following aside:

On the basis of information provided by an official that was later shown to be unreliable, American agencies were put on alert in December 1981 to defend against a team of Libyans who had purportedly entered the United States to attack President Reagan. The information was reported by news organizations causing a furor that officials now view as unfounded. (In the *Spokane Spokesman-Review*, August 6, 1987: A10).

The "hit-team" tale, because of the emphasis on the targeting of the president, appears to have been the opening salvo intended to target Qaddafi. It was later recanted with far less fanfare than it was originally reported. One book, published later in the Reagan administration's second term, documented a C.I.A./N.S.C. obsesssion with Libya that apparently came to be shared by the president. Although exploring the dubious intelligence on which covert actions were planned (including one bizarre attempt to convince Egypt to invade Libya) (Woodward, 181–86, 419–20), this journalistic account also personalizes and fragments the issue. The "revelations" centered on former C.I.A. Director William Casey and the inner workings of the agency. (The real story is found in the nature of the Libyan Revolution and will be explored in Chapter 6.)

It is arguable that the most dramatic story on terrorism was that agencies of the U.S. government were building a set of escalating tactics designed to eliminate a political opponent defined within the Reagan administration as a threat to U.S. and Western interests (Woodward, 1987: 409–10). To wit, in February of 1983, Libya was accused of planning an invasion to overthrow the government of Sudan. The facts were that such an invasion would require the advance of columns 600 miles across the desert to Khartoum (while U.S., Egyptian, and other pro-Western forces were sleeping, apparently), and that Egyptian and Sudanese intelligence knew nothing about it. "The U.S. responded to the fabricated plot with an elaborate show of force, enabling Secretary of State Shultz, who had been denounced as too faint-hearted, to strike heroic poses on television while announcing that Qaddafi 'is back in his box where he belongs' because Reagan acted 'quickly and decisively' against this threat to world order" (Chomsky, 1986b: 19).

After the hijacking of T.W.A. flight 847 (see above), White House planning on terrorism intensified. On December 27, 1985, unattached Palestinian suicide squads struck the Rome and Vienna airports, killing 21 people, among them five Americans. On this occasion, the media reported strong administration assertions of Libyan sponsorship of this act of vendetta terror.[8] However, a State Department report issued in January of 1986 was only able to speak of *alleged*

*Libyan involvement*, with the only "evidence" being the possession of Tunisian passports by three of the gunmen; passports supposedly traced by the C.I.A. to Tunisians who had worked inside Libya, one eight years earlier.

On the other hand, there is evidence of the presence from time to time in Tripoli of the Palestinian renegade Abu Nidal (Sabri Al Banni),[9] linked in Western accounts to the Rome-Vienna killings. Libya then, driven perhaps by a sympathy to the Palestinian cause, has left itself open to the administration's tendency to measure guilt by association. However, Abu Nidal has traveled widely throughout the Middle East, not simply in Libya. If the occasional sanctuary provided Nidal makes Libya (and other states) responsible for his acts, it should be remembered that the ties between the Reagan administration and the Nicaraguan Contras (no strangers to atrocities) have been much stronger than those between Nidal and Libya (see Chapter 9).

However, there is a more important point to be made. Given the suffering and rage of the young Palestinians who carried out these attacks, there is little need to legitimate conspiratorial theories by pointing to a "mastermind." It requires little organization, little funding, and little military skill to smuggle weapons inside public buildings and to open fire. All it takes is fury, guns, and a willingness to die. Still, the charges of Libyan responsibility for the Rome-Vienna episodes were not sustained by either the Italian or the Austrian governments. And by the summer of 1986, Western intelligence (including the United States) had changed their tale, coming to embrace the Israeli official story that Syria (Israel's most formidable adversary) was responsible for the slaughter in Rome and Vienna. However, this change came too late. By March of 1986, the U.S. Navy had again conducted exercises in the disputed Gulf of Sirte. Code-named "Operation Prairie Fire," the games were designed to provoke a Libyan attack (Stork, 1986; Chomsky, 1986b). This time, the Libyans fired SAM missiles at intruding aircraft.

Echoing the Reagan administration's claim to be preserving the right of "innocent passage" according to the "law of the sea," the media again provided legitimation for "Operation Prairie Fire." However, what is at issue as Chomsky notes (1986b: 20) is not the law of the sea but the "law of the air." For its part, the United States claims a *200-mile* "Air Defense Indentification Zone" within which its air forces will exercise the right of self-defense. The media as a whole essentially missed this contradiction; as it missed the point that a superpower naval flotilla (probably nuclear-armed) was in the Gulf of Sirte to intimidate by threat of force. Also missed was the point that Qaddafi did not live in Libya by himself. That 3.5 million Libyans would be terrorized by the presence of a superpower armada is clear. And there is more. A British engineer in Tripoli testified that before the missiles were fired by Libya, American aircraft had not only penetrated the 12-mile limit (claimed by the United States to represent the extent of Libyan territorial waters), they had also flown over Libyan land. "American warplanes made their approach using a normal civil airline traffic route and followed in the wake of a Libyan airliner, so its radar blip would make them on the Libyan radar screen'' (in Chomsky, 1986b: 20). Bluntly put, U.S. aircraft were apparently used as bait.

The SAMs fired by Libya missiles missed their targets, and over the next week, U.S. naval forces followed the policy articulated by the Pentagon, which was "to shoot at any Libyan boat that enters international waters in the Gulf of Sidra for as long as the U.S. naval exercise in that region continues—no matter how far away the boat might be from U.S. ships" (in Chomsky, 1986b: 20).[10] In pursuance of this policy of a free fire zone in the gulf, U.S. naval forces sank several small Libyan boats with a loss on the Libyan side of over 50 sailors. There were no American casualties and the Libyans did not respond further. However, the stage was set for the high drama to come.

Just as the mainstream U.S. media appear to have largely missed the real story of "Operational Prairie Fire," it may have also missed (until Seymour Hersh's delayed and diminished rejoinder) the next chapter. On April 5, 1986, a bomb exploded in a West German discothèque frequented by U.S. Army personnel. One soldier and a Turkish woman were killed. Turkey did not feel compelled to order a military response. However, the American reaction was predictable. Soon after, the Reagan White House claimed to have intercepted Libyan messages that provided the standard "irrefutable" evidence that Libya ordered the bombing. Once again, the nation on whose soil the violence occurred (in this case, West Germany), challenged the U.S. version of events.[11]

Inside the U.S. National Security Agency, the standard channels for translating the messages were suspiciously bypassed, a move that dismayed the N.S.A.'s own North African experts. And those who purport to understand Libyan politics should have known that Libya considers black Americans an oppressed group. It is plausible to argue then that the La Belle disco, known to be frequented by black soldiers, would be an unlikely target (Hersh, 1987). However, the die was cast. On April 8, Ronald Reagan authorized a military strike on Tripoli and Bengazi. On April 9, he went on television to describe Muammar Qaddafi as the "mad dog of the Middle East" (Stork, 1986: 8). With Israeli intelligence pinpointing Qaddafi's home, the raid on Libya, code-named "Operation Eldorado Canyon" struck on April 14. On that evening, the great communicator echoed a now familiar theme, that "our evidence is direct, it is precise, it is irrefutable" (in Chomsky, 1986b: 21).

How did the media respond to the raid? When Libya was attacked, *Time* (April 28, 1986) headlined the story *Hitting the Source: U.S. Bombers Strike at Libya's Author of Terrorism*. No headline said: *U.S. Bombers Strike Qaddafi's Family: Kill 15-Month-Old Daughter, Wound Young Sons* or *U.S. Bombers Kill Libyan Civilians*. After describing some of the carnage of the raid, *Newsweek* correspondent Ruth Marshall (or her editor) rationalized "No one gave any sign of second thoughts, of wondering whether Libya had brought this sorrow on itself by dealing in terrorism" (*Newsweek*, April 28, 1986: 30). In the same issue (p. 21), *Newsweek* writers demurring on the targeting of the Qaddafi family offered the curious argument that "a free society will tolerate killing civilians in bombing raids but not government sanctioned murder."

The *Washington Post* and the *New York Times* editorialized in support of the raid, while a Yankelovich poll commissioned by *Time* rushed to show that 71 percent of the American people were in support. And when the United Nations General Assembly condemned the raid as a violation of international law in November of 1986, holding that Libya was entitled to compensation, that story paled alongside continuing pronouncements of Libyan terrorism. Of course, the U.S. government did not wait to make its case in international law, and present its evidence before the United Nations International Court of Justice. The Reagan administration had already denied the jurisdiction of the court on the question of C.I.A. covert action in Nicaragua (see Chapter 9). Again, the U.S. media failed to raise serious questions at the moment of currency, but the official story was to have a postscript.

On October 2, 1986, Bob Woodward of the *Washington Post* broke a story of Reagan administration disinformation on Libya. In August, John Poindexter of the National Security Council, later to be a key figure in the Irangate episode (see Chapter 8), had authored a memorandum. In it he called for a campaign to be waged through the media, designed to make Muammar Qaddafi "think that there is a high degree of internal opposition to him within Libya, that his key trusted aides are disloyal, that the U.S. is about to move against him militarily." State Department spokesperson, Bernard Kalb, used to release the false story to the press, resigned in protest. Columnists and pundits editorialized for days, lamenting the breakdown of trust. But once again, the mainstream media isolated the disinformation issue from the larger history of U.S.-Libyan relations.[12]

## THE MEDIA PRISM

There are two aforementioned frameworks by which the role of the media in Libyan-U.S. relations can be analyzed. First, there is the question of the dissemination of "disinformation." In the language of Chapter 1, this is an issue of particular ideology by which falsehoods are invented by self-conscious agents to advance political ends. Thus at the level of particular ideology, the media become a "mark," deceived by political actors into distorting the truth. However, at the level of total ideology, the much more serious issue of a media structural predisposition to actively enter the "war on terrorism" is joined. So conceived, the information order, in response to external and internal systemic forces, plays a proactive role in the political theater of terrorism, and in so doing defends a wider world.

### The Other Anti-Semitism: Stereotyping the Arab World

Ideological analysis may begin by exploring the role of stereotypes in domination. The ease with which Libya was made a dominant player in the mediaspeak on terrorism rests in part with powerful imagery, both negative and unchallenged. There is substantial evidence that the Western media prism refracts the official story of terrorism through stereotypes of the Middle Eastern, Arab, and Islamic world in general, and the Palestinian movement in particular (see Said, 1978 and 1981; and Michalak, 1984). To this point, a national poll conducted by the Washington, D.C.-based *Middle East Journal* found such descriptions as "barbaric and cruel," "treacherous," "warlike," "rich," and "mistreaters of women" used to typify Arabs. Of course, stereotyping and ignorance of a people go hand in hand. During the Iranian hostage episode in the United States, some 70 percent of Americans surveyed identified Iran as Arab, while another 8 percent indicated they did not know whether Iran was Arab or not (Lamb, in Sheehan, 1985: 162–63). OPEC is also perceived as an organization of Arab states, when 6 of its 13 members are not Arab (Shaheen, 1985: 162).

One communications analyst finds that these "myths are incorporated in the instant Arab kit, which includes belly dancers' outfits, headdresses, veils, dark sunglasses, flowing gowns and robes, oil wells, evil mysticism, limousines, and camels. We see Arabs as billionaires, bombers, or belly dancers—villains of choice. . . . They are described as terrorists, their society as violent, and their religion, Islam, as radical" (Shaheen, 1985: 163, 162). The power of such stereotypes, to support dominant conceptions of terrorism, is clear. Yet, despite the absence of substantial quantitative data, it is valid on face that crimes against the person in the Arab world are far rarer than in the United States.

It is perception, not reason that prevails when the question of terrorism is joined. Thus in the summer of 1986, in the wake of the raid on Libya, the growing fear of "terrorist reprisal" against Americans abroad produced predictable consequences. When *Newsweek* (April 28, 1986) commissioned a Gallup poll, one question was "If you had the opportunity to travel overseas this summer, would you take the trip or refuse it because of the threat of terrorism?" Seventy-nine percent of the respondents said they would refuse the trip. It is clear that such fears reveal a lack of proportion. (One would statistically be in greater danger driving to the airport.) While the British complained about "chicken Americans," tourists sought a safe haven at home, this despite the fact that European rates of crimes against the person are miniscule in comparison to those of the U.S.[13]

Arabs are also Semites and are clearly victimized by this "other" anti-Semitism. From where do such stereotypic perceptions come? Few American people have direct, first-person knowledge of the Arab world, of Islam, of the Middle East, and the question of Palestine. Far fewer still have been victims of conventionally defined terrorism. To some extent, it must be acknowledged that the fear of Arab terrorism among the American population has been cultivated, and that this cultivation clearly implicates the American media. This does not mean that other of the "institutional means of influence" are without fault. For example, fundamentalist Christianity inside the United States (whose churches and televangelists frequently view Israeli dominance as the fulfillment of biblical prophecy) clearly contributes to the real anti-Semitism in the United States. Nor does it mean that the U.S. educational system has been successful in promoting rational analysis of the critical issues in the Middle East. However, compared to the other ideological institutions, media influence is virtually universal and potentially life-long for the population. In a context of alienation, the media becomes both a tranquilizer and a source of the *sharpening of images* for dramatic effect. And the process is not confined to television.

The motion picture industry has historically traded in the imagery of terror and violence. However, in the more recent past, the Arabs may be emerging as the new Hollywood Indians. Only a few examples from the 1980s would include: the portrayal of an Arab renegade state holding the father of the teen hero hostage in *Iron Eagle*; the "humorous" stereotypes of Arab violence in *Jewel of the Nile* and *Ishtar*; the kidnapping of a beautiful, successful stockbroker by an OPEC oil minister in *Harem*, the deceitful Palestinian who betrays Sigourney Weaver in *Half-Moon Street*, and the cold terrorism of Palestinians that shatters the "naïve" sympathy of Diane Keaton for the Palestinian cause in *The Little Drummer Girl*.

Perhaps a prime case study is *Delta Force* released in 1986. It is a fictionalized account of the hijacking of T.W.A. flight 847, but with a "Rambo" ending. The real T.W.A. hijacking was ended through international negotiation, with only one hostage lost to vendetta terrorism. In the movie, the Delta Force commandoes rescue everybody, suffer one casualty, and slaughter dozens of Arab terrorists. Many such films, along with their television counterparts, are designed for an adolescent audience (at least for an adolescent mentality). They stand as a form of political socialization rooted in stereotypes of the Arab world.

On a related point, the Arab world is predominantly of the Islamic faith. (Although it should be remembered that approximately fifteen million Christians are numbered among the 140 million Arabs.) It is not necessary to ignore conflicts in the Islamic world, but like the "Christian" war in Ireland, these can be shown to have economic, political, and social roots. However, religious terms such as "Christian" and "Jewish" are not used generally by the media to describe acts such as the bombing of Libya by the Christian United States, or the bombing of Palestinian camps by the Jewish Israel. Nor should they be. Such adjectives obscure the nature of the conflict and malign all Christians and all Jews.

Unfortunately, terms such as *Muslim* and *Islamic* are used to describe the Middle Eastern forms of nonstate terrorism. For example, *Time* (June 24, 1985) titled its report on the T.W.A. hijacking analyzed earlier in this chapter: *Terror Aboard Flight 847: Muslim Hijackers Hold Americans Hostage on a Murderous Journey*. *Newsweek*'s (June 24, 1985) lead was: *An Odyssey of Terror: Once Again a Band of Islamic Fanatics Puts Ronald Reagan on the Spot and Underscores the Vulnerability of Americans Around the World*. According to the Islamic Center of Washington, D.C., there are over one billion Muslims, only a handful of which executed this hijacking. The services of other Islamic Arabs in Algiers and Lebanon were indispensable in ending it.

### The Western *Weltanschauung*

Sensitivity to the role of stereotypes in terrorism is only a point of departure. In Chapter 1, the dominant ideology of terrorism was explored. Narrowly, it is the official state view of what terrorism is, who the terrorists are, how terrorists behave, and which targets terrorists mark for violence. At the higher level of Western *Weltanschauung*, its properties include: (1) hedonistic definitions of rationalism (which hold that choice is based on a "cost-benefit" analysis of pleasure versus pain); (2) a preference for privatized explanations (that center in the analysis of personalities and motivations); and (3) the tendency to view the existing institutional order of Western societies as a global solution, and fundamental changes in that order as a problem. Dependent on official state sources,[14] and bearers of the Western worldview, the media are culturally predisposed to produce and reproduce the dominant ideology of terrorism. Yet the questions of source validity and the higher biases of First World interpretations of reality are insufficient to explain the ideological *problematique* of terrorism. And although media stereotypes of enemy deviants harden the official story, there is more to domination than conventional ignorance. The terrorism story bears the marks of an international information and communication order, and it is to the structural properties of that order that we now turn.

### THE INTERNATIONAL INFORMATION AND COMMUNICATION ORDER

To a large degree, the issue of structurally founded media biases on the question of terrorism turns on the larger issue of a Western-dominated international information and communication order. The Western media are often likened to a democratic forum in which all ideas and all points of view receive a fair and impartial hearing. It is clear, however, that the construction and dissemination of information favors the wealthier, more powerful states where the technological revolution in communication has taken root. In the mid–1980s, the Associated Press (AP) and the United Press International (UPI) of the United States, Reuters of Great Britain, and AFP (Agence France Presse) operated in some 110 countries and dominated the selection of the "newsworthy" for much of the globe (Misra, 1985: 23). On the bottom of the international information order are the one-third of developing nations that are without a national news agency of their own (Hammoudi, 1985: 32). The top-down flow means that poorer nations (and some not so poor, such as Canada, certain South American, and other semiperipheral states) must consume the cultural and ideological content that comes with globally relevant information (Dorfman, 1985). If this world communication order is fully integrated into the transnational market system, a structural predisposition to defend that order can only follow. Such real conditions cannot fail but color how the media reports on movements for change that threaten to introduce disequilibrium into the very order that sustains their existence. Similar predispositions may obscure "friendly" state force or threat of force designed to dominate through fear when such are employed to maintain that system.

To this point, the Mustapha Masmoudi paradigm of media imbalances may be reformulated to critically assess the world information order. The *cross quantitative disparity between North and South* refers to the sheer gap in news volume between core and periphery; a disparity that assumes great significance when placed in the context of the aforementioned *inequality in information services*. To these may be added the *hegemonic* factor, which holds that imperialism has a cultural component. Stated simply, developing nations are judged by foreign standards, not merely cultural but especially by their openness to a Western model of development. The lack of *authentic information* on the developing world means that conflict, poverty, and societal problems are interpreted not by victims but by the representatives of privileged states. The imbalance in this order is also seen as a *survivor of the colonial era*, by which direct control is replaced by more subtle ideological forms that ignore the role of exploitation in the process of underdevelopment. And finally, the programming content of the existing international information and communication order contributes not only to cross-cultural pollution, its escapist, materialist, and privatized themes reproduce the powerlessness of *alienation* (in Sono, 1985: 48–49).

## Commodification and Terrorism

With such a global view entrenched, we turn to pertinent cases on the nature of the U.S. mass media. In the United States, the broadcast and publishing industries take the form of privately owned, diversified corporations, with worldwide holdings. They are driven by the same imperatives that mark the financial, petroleum, automotive, or other industries within the corporate economy.

The predominance of private ownership in the broadcast industry does not mean that radio and television are either socially or politically independent of the corporate capitalism that dominates the American economy. . . . In fact, as in other industries, the ownership-pattern of television stations is one of local monopolies, regional concentrations, multiple ownerships, multi-media ownerships and conglomerates. Similarly, one might expect to find shared social and political values. (This does not mean that all stations are either Republican or Democratic. Rather, they share elements of corporate philosophies, particularly the drive toward profit.) (Tuchman, 1974: 3)

It is clear that the media in the United States are privately held, notwithstanding some public broadcasting. (U.S. public broadcasting is increasingly dependent on corporate sponsorship and telethons that solicit money from the viewing or listening audience). It is also clear that the profit imperative, expressed materially in ratings and advertising revenue, drives not only entertainment programming but also news programming. Thus what is offered as hard and unbiased information is subject to the market rules affecting any commodity. For the U.S.

television networks in particular, news divisions now face increasing pressure to win the race for ratings. A larger audience share means higher advertising revenues. Viewed in this context, stories with dramatic overtones can only be defind as saleable commodities. By this standard, the terrorism story is clearly a "high impact piece," frequently picked to lead the evening news. When defined as mindless attacks on innocent American citizens, the question of terrorism is merged with powerful currents of nationalism. Portrayed starkly, in terms of good versus evil or civilization versus barbarism, stories on terrorism represent a simple morality play. As such they require little investment of intellectual energy, either on the part of the networks or their audience. Here then, are the mundane elements of the soap opera with villains and innocents sharply etched, with sacred values clearly symbolized, with stories produced for dramatic effect.

### The Means of Influence: The Networks

There is more involved in the structural understanding of the ideology of terrorism than its commodification. As important as the ratings game may be, the place of the U.S. media in the world corporate order should not be overlooked. For if the media represent a dominant ideological institution within a broader global system, it follows that a central role for the media will be the legitimation of that system. Turning specifically to television, the organizational nature of N.B.C., C.B.S., and A.B.C. is instructive. Despite some slippage in ratings, not only do these networks remain dominant in the broadcasting industry but their size, patterns of ownership, global holdings, and the diversified nature of their business reveal their integration into a world corporate order. It is these elements that form the structural prism through which the events of the modern world are refracted.[15]

The National Broadcasting Company, Inc., was organized in 1926 by R.C.A. Corporation to develop radio broadcasting as a vehicle for the sale of radios by its parent corporation.[16] N.B.C. (with 200 TV and 600 radio affiliates) led the entertainment division of R.C.A. Corporation, but broadcasting sales of 2.4 billion dollars in 1984 amounted to less than 25 percent of R.C.A.'s total sales. As of 1986, the business of R.C.A. also included electronics; leasing automobiles and trucks (through its subsidiary, the Hertz Corporation); and the provision of domestic satellite communications services (through R.C.A. "Americom"); and global communications services (through R.C.A. "Globcom"). R.C.A.'s business also included insurance (North American Life), the manufacture and sale of carpets (Coronet Industries), and the distribution of prerecorded videocassettes.

The integration of R.C.A. Corporation into an international division of labor is reflected in its manufacturing holdings in Mexico, Taiwan, and Canada. Divisions of R.C.A. International Development Corporation were found in these three countries, as well as Italy, England, Bermuda, Brazil, West Germany, France, and Malaysia. Further, as a U.S. government contractor, R.C.A. designs, engineers, and manufactures military and space electronics equipment and systems. These products include, but are not limited to, satellite systems, early warning ballistic missile defense systems, and lasers. Military and space equipment and systems are also sold to other governments. And finally, R.C.A. offers services consisting of the operation, maintenance, and technical support for Department of Defense, NASA and other U.S. and foreign government programs. At the beginning of the 1980s, these were known to include the Missile Tracking System for the Air Force's Eastern Test Range; the Navy's Atlantic Underseas Test and Evaluation Center; the Atlantic Fleet Weapons Training Facility and telecommunications operations in Puerto Rico; the Army's White Sands Missile Range and others. An R.C.A. subsidiary was also known to operate and maintain the Ballistic Missile Early Warning System in Great Britain (Reasons and Perdue, 1981: 56–57).

However, the story of N.B.C. cannot be simply reduced to the story of R.C.A. Corporation. The structural law of concentration in the corporate order has been reflected in a growing pattern of takeovers in the United States during the 1980s. Given impetus by the Reagan administration's ideal of an unregulated marketplace, "mergermania" saw the acquisition of R.C.A. by General Electric on June 9, 1986.[17] The General Electric Company is a highly diversified, transnational corporation, with revenues in 1986 of almost 37 billion dollars. At the beginning of 1987, G.E. controlled the following international affiliates: Canadian General Electric of Canada, Sadelmi-Cogepi of Italy, General Electric Plastics B.V. of the Netherlands, General Electric de Brazil, General Electric de Venezuela, and General Electric de Mexico. In addition to its 217 domestic manufacturing plants, G.E. (as of early 1985) owned 116 manufacturing plants in 24 other countries.

The General Electric Company does substantial export business, and has majority or minority interests in manufacturing and distributing products and providing services (including financial) outside the United States. As of the mid– 1980s, it was heavily involved in communications and electronics, electrical construction equipment, transportation systems, motors, and robotics. As a primary military contractor, G.E. sells a variety of engines to the armed forces of the United States. These range from steam-turbines for ships to the F110 engine that powers some of the U.S. Air Force and Navy's F–16 and F–14 fighter aircraft. G.E. engines power a variety of bombers, helicopters, and transports. Most of the company's aerospace business (including products for space sciences, electronics and microelectronics, ordnance systems, avionics, computer software, and simulation and control systems) is done with the U.S. government. Thus G.E. ranks as a world-class corporate player, a prime military contractor, and the real owner of N.B.C.[18]

The Columbia Broadcasting System, Inc. is the second of the "big three" U.S. broadcasting networks, and, like N.B.C. and A.B.C., underwent massive changes in the 1980s. The C.B.S. story is somewhat unique in that the corporation embarked in 1986 upon a restructuring effort, at least in part in response to the perception that it was a likely takeover target.[19] C.B.S. business through the mid–1980s was conducted through four operating groups: C.B.S./Broadcast, C.B.S./Records, C.B.S./Publishing (including Holt, Rinehart and Winston, Praeger, W. B. Saunders, and a magazines division), and an "others" group that dealt in toys, software, and technology. Of the 4.9 billion dollars in revenues earned by C.B.S. in 1984, some 2.7 billion (55 percent of total) was from its broadcasting divisions. Hence, over 45 percent of its revenues came from its other diversified holdings; a pattern not to be maintained.

The subsidiaries controlled by C.B.S. in the mid–1980s included companies in Sweden, Belgium, Australia, England, France, the Federal Republic of Germany, Italy, Japan, South Africa, Venezuela, Holland, Denmark, Norway, Switzerland, Spain, Costa Rica, El Salvador, Panama, Guatemala, Mexico, Peru, Canada, India, Portugal, Chile, Kenya, Malaysia, Cyprus, Finland, Austria, Argentina, Columbia, Brazil, Greece, Hong Kong, and Israel. Its 1986 total revenues were 4.75 billion. A subsequent restructuring saw C.B.S. moving back into its broadcasting roots where it began doing business in the late 1920s. In 1986 and 1987 it moved to sell its magazine, book, and music publishing operations. The final step was an agreement to sell its records holdings to Sony Corporation in November of 1987. The cash holdings of C.B.S. as reported by the Associated Press on November 20, 1987, amounted to 2.5 to 3 billion dollars.

The American Broadcasting Co., Inc., as of the mid–1980s remained a highly diversified information, entertainment, and communications company.[20] Its further integration into the corporate economy was underscored in 1986 when A.B.C. merged with Capital Cities Communication, which acquired the broadcasting giant for 3.375 billion. Capital Cities/A.B.C. owns and operates television and radio stations in a number of major U.S. markets, selling 53 cable television systems to the Washington Post Co. in 1986. As of the mid–1980s, Capital Cities published ten daily and 27 weekly newspapers, as well as a large number of specialized publications (many through its Fairchild subsidiary) intended for a business and professional audience. In 1986, the newly merged corporation had net revenues of 4.12 billion.

The pattern of media integration and concentration is not unique to the broadcasting business. Ownership of the printed media has reached the point where (by the early 1980s) only 20 newspaper "groups" controlled more than half of daily newspaper sales in the United States. Groups have not been interested in acquiring newspapers in cities where there exists real competition for the circulation and advertising markets. Thus some 98 percent of all newpapers are the sole newspaper in their cities. Correspondingly, early in the 1980s, 11 U.S. corporations received over 50 percent of the revenues from book sales, 20 giants took in over half of the magazine sales, and 10 firms claimed the majority of the audience for commercial radio (Reasons and Perdue, 1981: 63–69; Bagdikian, 1983: Chapter 1, and Shaheen, 1985: 169).

The question of who owns the mass media may be rephrased as who owns the news.

Ten business and financial corporations control the three major television and radio networks (NBC, CBS, ABC), 34 subsidiary television stations, 201 cable TV systems, 62 radio stations, 30 record companies, 59 magazines including Time and Newsweek, 58 newspapers including the New York Times, the Washington Post, the Wall Street Journal and the Los Angeles Times, 41 book publishers, and various motion picture companies like Columbia Pictures and Twentieth Century Fox. Three-quarters of the major stockholders of ABC, CBS, and NBC are banks, such as Chase Manhattan, Morgan Guaranty Trust, Citibank, and Bank of America. (Parenti, 1986: 27)

So then, taken as a whole, what can be logically inferred from the structural organization of the U.S. media? First, despite blinding changes in the specifics of ownership, there remains a pattern of full integration into the U.S. corporate economy, which in turn is the lead player in the global market system. Quite aside from what might be preferred by professional journalists, knowledge and information is a product, like any other, where market share, return on investment, and potential for expansion constitute the bottom line. Moreover, in addition to the intrinsic biases of the dominant Western *Weltanschauung* are the market forces that press for the commodification of international and other news events. Commodification in turn means to choose stories for dramatic impact, and to then shape their telling along simple lines without regard for historical context. And commodification also means the decline of journalistic revelance, as witnessed in the virtual disappearance of the unprofitable hour-long documentary from the major U.S. television networks. Against these considerable forces, broadcast and print journalists have little to offer except a professional code that calls for fairness, balance, and accuracy. However, in a world where television newspeople survive on the basis of being telegenic; where the audience is asked to judge media personalities rather than quality of information, where the "national newspaper," *U.S.A. Today*, gives virtually equal space to sports, business, personal living, and "hard news," the real question of a story is not "does it fairly inform?" but "does it sell?"

Also relevant is the symbiotic relationship between agencies of government and the press. Contrary to the enduring imagery of independent journalists who supposedly gather objective information on which to base their stories, reporters are heavily dependent on "official" sources who typically insist on anonymity (Gans, 1979). This suggests, especially for stories based on murky sourcing and ambiguous information (such as terrorism), that U.S. media accounts bear the imprint of such as the C.I.A., National Security Council, the State Department, the Oval Office, friendly government official sources, and others. None of these have an obligation to tell the truth, indeed there is often a duty to lie or selectively recall events in the "interest of national security." Examples at the highest level include Lyndon Johnson's 1964 claim of an attack on U.S. forces in the Gulf of Tonkin; Richard Nixon's assertion that U.S. forces had observed the neutrality of Cambodia before he ordered the invasion of that country in May of 1970;

and Ronald Reagan's 1986 emergence as an "international arms dealer" for Iran.

## CONCLUSION

The U.N.E.S.C.O. initiatives of the 1970s and 1980s on a new international communication order (as well as a new international economic order) predictably drew fire from the Western media and Western states. Such events symbolized the growing Third World resistance to monopolism, whether expressed in the concentration of global wealth or in the power to define events. An equally predictable reaction came when the Reagan administration led the United States to withdraw from U.N.E.S.C.O. (followed forthwith by the loyal Thatcher government in Britain), and to withhold dues from (and threaten bankruptcy to) the United Nations. All this aside, it is not only the peoples of the Third World who are faced with the abuses of mediaspeak. A citation from *Reshaping the International Order: A Report to the Club of Rome (1977)* is perhaps more pertinent over a decade after its original publication:

Public opinion in the industrialized countries will not have real access to full information until communication patterns are liberated from the market-oriented sensationalism and news presentation which characterize them at present and until they are consciously stripped of ethnocentric prejudices. The widening of the capacity to inform must be viewed as an essential component of attempts to create a new international order, and, as such, the monopolistic and discriminatory practices inherent in current international information dissemination must be deemed as one of the worst, though subtle, characteristics of the present system. (In Sono, 1985b: 47)

It is within this larger context that the official story of terrorism must be judged.

## NOTES

1. The view that an Israeli lobby directs U.S. Middle Eastern policy represents a far too instrumentalist view of state relations as will be argued in Chapter 7. Nevertheless, hostage remarks that appeared sympathetic to the "other side" embarrassed both Washington and Tel Aviv.

2. In the case of the T.W.A. hijacking, it was actually the disconcerting commentary from some American hostages that undermined the official story.

3. "Mad Dogs and Presidents" is Joe Stork's term. Ronald Reagan used "mad dog of the Middle East" in reference to Muammar Qaddafi of Libya. The rhetorical dehumanization of an enemy is a routine step in the legitimation of deadly force.

4. Useful general references include Chomsky, 1986a and 1986b, Stork, 1986, and Hersh, 1987.

5. This legitimation is unfounded. In the Arab world in general, and in bedouin culture in particular, the family is a sacred institution and an attack of this sort could only be defined as barbarism. That Libyans would respond differently to a bombing raid

than would other victims is another Western, stereotypical view of Orientalism—specifically, that a high-tech raid on a family will produce a "loss of face" for the Arab.

6. In September of 1988, George Bush reminded the electorate that he had supported the bombing of Libya and challenged his rival to do the same.

7. In the bipolar world of Secretary Haig, Libya and Muammar Qaddafi were the Middle Eastern counterparts to Cuba and Fidel Castro. Both were on the "other" (Soviet) side (Stork, 1986). This rather curious view of Libya runs counter to what is known about that society and its institutions (see Chapter 6).

8. In his news conference of January 7, 1986, President Reagan said "The Rome and Vienna murders are only the latest in a series of brutal terrorist acts committed with Qaddafi's backing" (Reagan, 1986).

9. Abu Nidal is a *nom de guerre* meaning "father of struggle."

10. The U.S. calls the gulf "Sidra" and Libya calls it "Sirte." As there is a bay of Sidra in the southernmost waters of the gulf near the town of Sidra, and as Sirte is located closer to the mouth of the gulf, it appears more reasonable to follow the local custom.

11. The AP later reported on January 11 of 1988 that West German police identified Christina Endrigkeit, linked to two imprisoned Palestinians, as the prime suspect in the La Belle bombing, and offered a reward of $93,000 for her capture. Mention of Libyan complicity was conspicuous in its absence.

12. A more recent milepost in Libyan-U.S. conflict began to unfold in the winter of 1988–89 with U.S. claims that Libya was building a chemical weapons plant. Libya responded that the facility was a pharmaceutical plant and invited international inspection. Then came the shoot-down of two Libyan jets by U.S. fighters. Although the U.S. charges at this writing are unproven, there is no controversy on the matter of the enormous U.S. C.B.W. capability.

13. In 1983–84, the U.S. homicide rate was 1,114 percent higher than that of the United Kingdom, 844 percent, that of Greece and the Netherlands, 750 percent, that of Spain and Denmark, 672 percent, that of Sweden and Norway, 608 percent, that of West Germany, and 554 percent, that of France (author's calculations based on World Health Organization data, 1986).

14. Joe Stork (1986) argues that many of today's antiterrorism experts are yesterday's anticommunism experts. Others are former or current members of state intelligence services. Yet these state experts are also the media experts, routinely interviewed on the terrorism issue.

15. The specifics of network business changes rapidly of course. But the rapidity of that change only confirms the obvious point: that the information industry is subject to the imperatives of growth, profitability, restructuring, diversification, protection of market share, merger, and so forth.

16. The profile of R.C.A./N.B.C. that follows is drawn from *Moody's Industrial Manual*, 1986:4326–4333, 1988:349.

17. The following profile of General Electric Co. is drawn from *Moody's Industrial Manual*, 1986:351–63, 1988:348–57.

18. Since its acquisition of R.C.A., General Electric sold R.C.A. Global Communications to M.C.I. Communications for 160 million. G.E. also sold other R.C.A. holdings.

19. The following corporate profile is constructed in part from information in *Moody's Industrial Manual*, 1986:1133–36, 1988:1084–87.

20. See *Moody's Industrial Manual*, 1986:2539–41, 1988:2654–55.

# 4

# *The Real Nuclear Terrorism*

> Many other were around them, a pathetic tide ebbing away from the burning city. There were children with their clothes burned off, their eyelids and lips swollen, some of them unable even to open their eyes. Most people were naked, their clothes ripped off by the force of the blast. They moved like ghosts, their skins, burnt by the flash, peeling and hanging off them in shreds—Close by, in the shallows of the river, a young woman was holding a baby very tightly, sobbing... "he's dead... dead, My baby, my baby." The woman waded deeper into the river until she was no longer to be seen.
> 
> Toshi Maruki, *The Hiroshima Story*

> In the United States, the logical place to explode (a nuclear) device would be the governmental nerve center of the country, Washington, D.C. The device could easily be placed on a boat on the Potomac River. Controlled by a timeclock set days or weeks ahead of time. It could explode when the President was in the White House, and the Congress and the Supreme Court in session. Washington would be demolished.... What would happen next? Would a panicky silo commander or a submarine captain assume it was an act of war and unleash a salvo at the Soviet Union? Who knows?
> 
> Bernard J. O'Keefe, Chairman of E.G.&G., Inc.,
> in congressional testimony, Nov. 9, 1983.

Very different images of nuclear terrorism emerge when the Hiroshima experience is juxtaposed with the official view. From the official perspective, a hypothetical situation is imagined wherein hostile states or shadowy and ill-defined terrorist organizations acquire a nuclear device and actually detonate the weapon or use it as an instrument of blackmail. As evidenced in the statement by Bernard O'Keefe, past chair of the National Association of Manufacturers in the United States, such acts of renegade terror are seen to pose a clear and present danger. In response, the U.S. House of Representatives in 1983 passed a resolution (#233). It called upon the president to enter into negotiations with the Soviet Union on the question of reducing the threat of accidental thermonuclear war triggered by acts of terrorism (United States Congress, Committee on Foreign Affairs, House of Representatives, 1983).

## NUCLEAR RENEGADES: THE OFFICIAL STORY

The assumptions that underlie the official story on nuclear terrorism are familiar. Predictably, the dramatic imagery focuses on outsiders, driven by fanaticism, perpetrating a sneak attack on the United States or its allies. O'Keefe, author of *Nuclear Hostages*, contributed to the dominant ideology of nuclear terrorism by noting that "tens of thousands of Middle Easterners have been technically trained in the United States, and it would require only a small fraction of 1 percent of these to accomplish the task (of producing a thermonuclear device)" (United States Congress, Committee on Foreign Affairs, House of Representatives, 1983: 12). He specifically named Fidel Castro and Muammar Qaddafi as logical sponsors of such acts. This official construction of terrorism again plays on the Arab and socialist worlds, as well as two revolutionary leaders who oppose the West. The terrorists once again are the outlaws engaged in outrageous behavior. In the words of one consultant, "small numbers of unsophisticated angry people can travel the globe in the span of 1 day, can communicate with each other almost instantaneously, can carry high technology weapons . . . and can drive the superpowers into a conflagration from which humankind cannot escape" (U.S. Congress, 1983:11).

With the threat so defined, the issues become those of crisis management designed to improve the communication links between the superpowers so that terrorists cannot begin the doomsday process. At a slightly different level, this conception of nuclear terrorism focuses attention on the safeguarding of U.S. government buildings, airports, and military installations. Defined in this way, nuclear facilities must be made failsafe, so that fissionable material does not strangely disappear, or that fanatics do not do damage to a reactor, with the resulting horror of the China Syndrome. The cast of characters is thus familiar, as is the conception of the problem itself. According to the official view, the enemy deviants are hostile, mobile, and sinister representatives of the Third World who will stop at nothing. They symbolize dark forces, conspiracies, and pathological personalities. Through the possible triggering of World War II, they represent a threat to humanity.

It is not necessary to dismiss the official view as a conscious effort to deceive. To the contrary, desperate people might indeed come to acquire a nuclear device, or to sabotage by other means nuclear power plants or weapons facilities. Nor should one dismiss the importance of crisis management, by means of improved data-sharing (including intelligence), enhanced communication networks, and crisis-control centers. The success of such efforts is, of course, a function of mutual trust between the U.S.S.R. and the United States. Indeed, a century ago it might have taken months to deliver a declaration of war. This must be compared with the specter of superpower nuclear armed submarines routinely prowling the depths of the oceans, prepared to launch missiles that would reach their targets within minutes. Further confirming the importance of crisis management is the fact that in times past, armies have been capable of inflicting bloody losses, but their weapons were not those of human extinction.

Still, when all is said and done, the official view of nuclear terrorism substitutes imaginary scenarios about what shadowy enemy deviants might do, for the far more certain analysis of the spiraling arms race involving today's nuclear weapons states. Crisis management notwithstanding, it is within the cold and calculated rituals of the modern state that we find the familiar specter of institutional domination through fear. It is at this higher level that the full resources of modern science are applied to the questions of mass destruction. It is within this sphere that the five billion people on this island earth are transformed into captives. It is here that the "best and the brightest" consider the means of ecocide, and give new meaning to the word *holocaust*.

Perhaps the greatest challenge for critical theory is to reframe the terrorism debate. This is true for the nuclear issue as for others. In the pages to come, dominant ideological systems and symbols are again the focus of the analysis. Conventional conceptions of nuclear terrorism reduce the level of the debate, ignoring the arsenals of the state and routinely dealing with the renegade scenario (Laqueur, 1987: 314–20). (Laqueur retains a chapter on the "Philosophy of the Bomb." The meaning of philosophy, from *philos* and *sophos* meaning "love of wisdom," may be stretched here. But what is at issue in this chapter is the higher terror embodied in the "Philosophy of the Nuclear Bomb.")

## TERRORISM UNLIMITED

At an international conference on the "Question of Terrorism" held in Geneva in 1987, Nobel Peace Laureate Sean McBride of Dublin referred to the global fear unleashed by the nuclear weapons states. "The terrorist who holds a hostage for ransom is not very different from the head of a government who threatens to use nuclear weapons to force another State to yield to its demands. They are both ignoring not only the Rule of Law but the elementary principles of morality" (McBride, 1988: 35). Quite aside from the conventional view of nuclear terrorism as something that may be used to coerce or threaten powerful states, is the realization that those states hold within their arsenals the ultimate fate of the earth. It is clear that the use of nuclear threat to intimidate, subjugate, or control comes neither from so-called radical or revolutionary states, nor from groups that oppose more powerful states. It can be quite logically argued that, for whatever the historical reasons, the nuclear arsenals of nuclear weapons states constitute terrorism without boundaries. However, in keeping with the language of domination, official practices are commonly legitimated as matters of national security and always as sane and rationally considered.

It was Thomas Merton who noted that "It is the sane ones, the well-adapted ones, who can without qualms and without nausea aim the missiles and press the buttons that will initiate the great festival of destruction that they, the sane ones have prepared.... No one suspects the sane, and the sane ones will have perfectly good reasons, logical, well-adjusted reasons for firing the shot. They will be obeying sane orders that have come sanely down the chain of command. And because of their sanity they will have no qualms at all" (quoted in Pfohl, 1985: 1). Perhaps, in this terrifying world of a nuclear death race, there is a need for alternative defintions of sanity and new conceptions of security.

The real nuclear terrorism is already here, and its human effects are evident if only poorly understood. It shall be argued that these effects are not simply economic and political but social, cultural, and psychological. The people living in nation states who wield nuclear force are assured that such weaponry is in the national interest. And because the research, development, testing, and deployment of such weapons are done by rational and patriotic experts, people are told that they need not fear. In essence, the official view is that the only way to avoid human extinction is to be constantly prepared to unleash the forces of human extinction. In the United States, this balance of nuclear terror is expressed in the acronymn *M.A.D.*, for Mutually Assured Destruction. But as surreal as this doctrine of war may be, it stands to be surpassed by the new statespeak of martial capitalism known as *discriminate deterrence* (see below).

It is clear that the relationship between terrorism and the nuclear arsenals of the state cannot be ignored, and the complex institutional and ideological supports for that relationship must be analyzed. It is also clear that such an analysis cannot be unduly limited to a consideration of what happens if and when the warheads strike. Also to be explored are the real consequences of permanent threat; what happens if the missiles never fly, and the bombs never fall. There are three dimensions to this expanded thesis: (1) the martial issue of the extinction of life; (2) the economic issue of waste and world inequality; and (3) the social issue of the negation of human nature. The first of these raises the question of ecocide. "Eco" is from the Greek *oikas*, which means "house." Ecocide thus means the finishing, not merely of life, but of that which shelters and sustains all living forms.

### The Heat, the Cold, and the Dark

> The immediate consequences of a single thermonuclear weapon explosion are well known and well documented—fireball radiation, prompt neutron and gamma rays, blast, and fires. The Hiroshima bomb that killed between 100,000 and 200,000 people was a fission device of about 12 kilotons yield

> (the explosive equivalent of 12,000 tons of TNT). A modern thermonuclear warhead uses a device something like the Hiroshima bomb as the trigger—the "match" to light the fusion reaction. A typical thermonuclear weapon now has a yield of about 500 kilotons (or 0.5 megatons, a megaton being the explosive equivalent of a million tons of TNT). There are many weapons in the 9 to 20 megaton range in the strategic arsenals of the United States and the Soviet Union today. The highest-yield weapon ever exploded is 58 megatons.
>
> Sagan, 1983: 257

A 58-megaton weapon has a yield that equals almost 5,000 Hiroshima-size bombs. In fact, in today's nuclear arensals, Hiroshima-size bombs can be delivered by artillery, depth charges, torpedoes, and surface-to-air or air-to-air missiles. By mid-1983, the United States had produced 30,000 deliverable nuclear warheads, 12,000 of which could be directed toward the Soviet Union. The Reagan administration sought to spend another 222 billion dollars between 1983 and 1989 to add another 17,000 nuclear weapons to the U.S. arsenal by 1993 (Fulbright, 1983). The United States *in 1977* already possessed enough nuclear weaponry to annihilate the 218 cities in the Soviet Union with a population of 100,000 or more over 200 times (Sivard, 1977: 1).

In the event of a major exchange, estimates of quick death range from several hundred million to the World Health Organization's figure of 1.1 billion people (the latter estimate assuming that other than N.A.T.O. and Warsaw pact nations would be involved.) The number of critically injured who would require unavailable health care would perhaps approach another 1 billion persons. Given such an event, the basic services and organizations of society would collapse. Medical care, water, electricity, fuel, transportation, communication, food supplies, sanitation, and civil services would all be devastated. Although it is routinely stated that only military objects are targeted, many of these are near major population centers. And planning for thermonuclear war requires striking war-supporting industrial plants, transportation systems, and energy facilities (Sagan, 1983).

Even the technical language used to describe the magnitude of nuclear explosions contributes to the desensitizing that socializes a people to live with the unthinkable. Such are measured in "tons" of T.N.T., but a nuclear blast is both qualitatively and quantitatively different from one involving high explosives. A nuclear explosion releases energy in three forms: blast and wind, heat and nuclear radiation (Sartori, 1983). With regard to the first of these forms, shock waves travel from the point of explosion at more than the speed of sound. The waves create *overpressure*, crushing pressures that peak at high levels beyond those exerted by the normal atmosphere. The shock waves are accompanied by winds traveling at the rate of hundreds of miles per hour. A one-megaton burst at 6,000 feet could be expected to crush multistory reinforced concrete buildings, and generate 500 MPH winds up to 1.8 miles from the point of explosion.

The first effect of the explosion on the target is the heat that moves at the speed of light. While chemical explosives can produce temperatures of only a few thousand degrees, peak temperatures from a nuclear explosion may reach "tens of millions of degrees, comparable to the interior of the sun" (Sartori, 1983: 41). Those looking at the fireball directly would most probably suffer permanent blindness, while firestorms such as those occurring in Hiroshima would threaten to boil or asphyxiate blast survivors who reached shelters. Heat at ground zero at Hiroshima matched the surface of the sun, and burn victims who survived became charred zombies who walked with arms outstretched so as not to touch their burned skin. It might be remembered that in the whole of the United States there are hospital facilities for only 1,300 burn victims and perhaps 65,000 intensive care patients (Allen, 1985: 928, 931). Given a nuclear strike, many of these facilities would be incapacitated.

Of course, death need not come quickly. The gamma rays and neutrons produced by a nuclear explosion would be absorbed by the cells of the body, producing radiation sickness and death. Of the Hiroshima population of 340,000, 130,000 died within three months of the bombing, and 70,000 more by 1950. The dying continues, with leukemia the major killer of survivors, occurring at a rate five times higher than normal as late as 1971. Also among the Hiroshima victims were increases in various cancers, bone marrow disease, genetic defects, cataracts (Allen, 1985: 928), and among atomic bomb survivors exposed *in utero*, excesses of severe mental retardation and small head size (Neel, et al, 1985). It is this extension of death and dying far into the future of a people that is often missing from the official predictions concerning the loss of life due to nuclear detonation (Tsipis, in Sartori, 1983: 40).

Another dimension of nuclear terrorism seems to have escaped many planners who (as we shall see) have talked glibly in terms of "survivability" in the wake of a nuclear exchange. When a shoddily constructed dam in West Virginia collapsed flooding the community along Buffalo Creek, Kai Erikson (1978) provided a distinctly sociological focus to the phrase *Everything in Its Path*. For when the flood waters hit, more than lives and property were destroyed. In addition, the complexity of social relations, the support, the nurturance, and the reliability and trust that together constitute a human community were lost.

When this argument is considered in relation to the question of nuclear terrorism, the implications are clear. Those who survived would experience not simply the collapse of buildings, but the destruction of normative systems. They would know not simply the dread of pain, but the loss of trust, of cherishing, and of social order. At a concrete level, this means a short-circuiting of the international economy, the worthlessness of currency, and the development of black markets based on bartering. Work and the rituals of everyday life would become meaningless. Hoarding, looting, scavaging, and total suspicion would become the new norms of survival. In the case of the United States, this ultimate anarchy could emerge where in 1988 over 120 million rifles and shotguns, and 60 million handguns were in the hands of private citizens (National Rifle Association, 1988: 7). At a more philosophical level it may be argued that the collective life in which human beings are embedded, the larger whole which offers *social* identity, would be shattered. In the process, the entire meaning of being human would be transformed.

At the social-psychological level, the responses would be both immediate and long-term. Assuming some period of warning (no more than 30 minutes given a confirmed ICBM launch, much less with submarines and planes), massive attempts at urban exodus could assume no other form than chaos and panic, leaving many caught in the open. Accordingly, leaders might choose not to provide warning at all. Struck without warning, survivors would find that in a fraction of a second, the known had been transformed into the unknown. And beyond the instant shock of mangled corpses in the place of friends and families, and moonscape emptiness where once there were parks and trees and other living things, would be the enduring terror of psychic trauma.

Survivors would know the guilt of being spared, or as with some of the victims at Hiroshima, the endless guilt that would follow the fleeing for one's life in blind terror while leaving loved ones behind.

One-third of those within 2 kilometers of the hypocenter left someone behind... Tazu Shibama, an English teacher, lost a cousin that way. Her cousin's mother promised to stay with her daughter, who was pinned beneath a beam the mother couldn't lift. The mother came to Shibama's house the next day in tears, carrying a teacup filled with her daughter's ashes. "I promised Tomoko-*chan* to die with her but when the fire almost burned me up I left her," she told Shibama. "She did not know why she left," says Shibama. "But I think that's human nature. She's dead now but she never smiled again after her child died." (Silberner, 1981: 297)

Survivors would also know a world in which those physicians who lived were forced to make Dantesque triage decisions to determine who would receive whatever medical treatment remained. They would know a world in which suicide would escalate, euthanasia was no longer a debate, where the disposal of corpses would become a major industry, and where each of the living would watch in dread for the symptoms of radiation disease (Allen, 1985). Of course, there are many in a society at any time who face a certain death, but they usually rely upon social supports that would certainly suffer degrees of breakdown in the nuclear nightmare. And finally, what of those who in all societies are most dependent on the nurturance provided by others? How would the cold, dark world of "the day after" look through the eyes of a child, the emotionally disturbed, the developmentally disabled, the dependent aged, and the already seriously ill?

There is a uniqueness to these prospects of survival terror. For it is not simply the loss of life and the physical destruction that are at issue. Among the *hibakusha* (explosion-affected persons) of Japan, the fear, the depression, the anger remained. They lived imprisoned with their memories, often unable to trust the future, to hold jobs or to leave their homes. The firebombing of Tokyo was as destructive in loss of life and property, but the psychological profile for survivors is not the same as with the *hibakusha*.

The problems, say researchers, occurred because the destruction occurred all at once, in such an unexpected and incomprehensible manner and wiped out all social structures—the family, the workplace, schools, governments, hospitals, homes.... In Hiroshima 96 percent of those within 500 meters of the hypocenter—including entire school populations—died by November. One-third of Japan's total war dead perished in Hiroshima and Nagasaki (Silberner, 1981: 297)

There is a nuclear variation of the optimism that appears to undergird the dominant ideological system in the United States. By this view, even the mushroom cloud has a silver lining. Surely, happy nuclear warriors have argued, some life would remain. Or in the words of one Reagan administration official, 'eventually the ants build another anthill'' (see below). However, a discussion of the ecocidal prospects of nuclear exchange requires a wider view, one that considers the assault upon the sustaining earth. In a U.S. conference held in Cambridge, Massachusetts, in the fall of 1983, another anticipated consequence of nuclear exchange was considered. That consequence is commonly known as *nuclear winter*, and its importance transcends the astronomy on which it is based because of its potential to reframe the terrorism debate.

Narrowly conceived, the conception of nuclear winter is based on a series of scientific assumptions about what could be expected to happen to the earth's climate when subjected to the after-effects of nuclear explosions. Such blasts can be projected to propel massive amounts of dust and radioactive products into the air. They can further be predicted to produce huge firestorms with their resulting smoke and soot. Yet there is more than radioactive fallout to consider here. Nuclear fireballs can be expected to ignite nitrogen, which in turn would produce nitrogen oxides. These oxides would subsequently attack the ozone layer in the atmosphere that protects human and other life from the sun's ultraviolet rays. So after the soot and dust comes ultraviolet radiation. But before that comes the nuclear winterkill.

Should massive nuclear pollution (dust, soot, smoke, particles) saturate the atmosphere, it will absorb the sun's light and in turn cool the surface of the earth.[1] What remains are the scientific projections of climatic devastation. Assuming the explosion of only some 500 to 2,000 of the total 50,000 nuclear warheads in the arsenals of the superpowers alone, the survivors of the initial exchange would face cold, darkness, and the death of vegetation. With the settling out of particle pollution from the atmosphere, would come the bombardment of the earth with ultraviolent rays (Editors, Bulletin of the Atomic Scientists, 1985; Sagan, 1983). Nuclear pollution would not conveniently remain in the atmosphere above the original targets of war. It would be moved by weather systems to affect the whole of the earth. So beyond the terror of the strikes and counterstrikes, beyond the immediate death and dying, beyond the psychosis that would effect the survivors, is the specter of total ecological war.

## Nuclear Legitimation: Bomber, Missile, and Other Sanity Gaps

The political economy of nuclear terrorism calls for the exploration of the dialectical relationships that constitute the nuclearized warfare state. It follows that special historical consideration must be given to nuclear warhead production, and the consequences of that production for the range of social relations. In the sections to come, that range will not be limited to a narrowly conceived "relations to the means of production" but will be expanded through considering the role of nuclear imperial force in global order. Nuclear domination through fear thus emerges as something other than a confirmation of Proudhon's natural corruption of the nation state. Nor is it a simple product of Ogburn's "lag" between technological advance and trailing cultural constraints; or the Adlerian pathological expression of a "will to power." Instead, nuclear weapons misproduction embodies and symbolizes hierarchical relations on a global scale. In its processes, wealth is transferred, labor is corrupted, and the means of coercion built and concentrated. Perhaps in a more limited scope, no higher form of alienation can be imagined than that of commissioners, designers, and makers of the nuclear warfare state, busily deploying the means for negating human history.

Given the crudeness of the production technology and the relative scarcity of materials, the U.S. nuclear stockpile grew to only some seven hundred warheads by 1950. However, with the growth of vast production facilities (at Los Alamos, New Mexico; Oak Ridge Tennessee; Livermore, California; Aiken, California) and the growth of test sites, gaseous diffusion and feed-processing plants, and other sites for the manufacture and assembly of specialized warhead components, the stockpile reached a level of almost 32,000 total warheads in 1967. Since that point, the actual upper limit of the stockpile has actually declined. This should not be interpreted as an authentic slowdown, as the nuclear weapons industry is an exemplar of planned obsolescence. As older, less sophisticated, and less deadly weapons are retired, new ones are developed and deployed.

To illustrate the principle of more nuclear bang for the stockpile, during the 1970s both the U.S. ICBM and SLBM missiles were the beneficiaries of improved guidance systems that provided greater accuracy and allowed for the *MIRVing* of strategic weapons.[2] MIRV is an acronym for *multiple independently targeted reentry vehicle*. This means that a single missile can carry several reentry vehicles, each of which can be directed at a separate target. During the 1970s, total megatonnage for U.S. ICBM and SLBM missiles appeared to decline, while the missile force as a whole became more deadly (Norris, et al., 1985: 107).

Three milestones in the history of the U.S. nuclear stockpile revolve around allegations made in the 1950s of a "bomber gap," succeeded in the 1960s by a "missile gap," and finally in the 1980s by the designation of a "window of vulnerability." During the Eisenhower administration, the United States responded to its own inflated estimates of a U.S.S.R. bomber threat in two ways. First, it stepped up the production of its own B–52s, and second, it unleashed a crash program in the construction of 7,000 nuclear air-defense missiles. By the early 1960s, a vast "response capability" had been created including 274 Nike Hercules batteries, 439 Bomarc missiles, 2612 interceptor aircraft, and hundreds of radars with crew members exceeding 200,000 (Norris, et al., 1985). What was the size of the Soviet force that legitimated this escalation? On the other side of the "bomber gap" were 125 propeller powered TU95 Bear and 45 jet-engine Mya-4 Bison aircraft. Was the U.S. nuclear escalation a *response*? The 170 Soviet bombers were deployed in 1956. In *1955*, the U.S. had deployed 264 B-52 G/II bombers with twice the Soviet range (drawn from data in Arkin and Fieldhouse, 1985: 45, 46).

With the end of the "bomber gap" (and the obsolescence and dismantling of the missiles it created) came the new threat raised by Senator John F. Kennedy in the 1960 presidential campaign against Eisenhower's vice president, Richard M. Nixon. Kennedy's charge of a "missile gap" represented a startling distortion of U.S. nuclear superiority. The year 1987 marked the 25th anniversary of the confrontation between the U.S. and the U.S.S.R. over Soviet missiles in Cuba. According to then Secretary of Defense Robert McNamara, in October of 1962, the United States warhead advantage stood at 5,000 to 300 (in Lukas, 1987: 27). More specifically, according to official U.S. government sources, in 1961 U.S. strategic forces contained 1,530 weapons subject to launch on tactical warning and 3,267 others requiring 14 hours of preparation. Soviet strategic forces "were estimated to contain 10 to 25 ICBMs, 200 bombers, and 'about 78' submarine-launched ballistic and cruise missiles, none of which were kept routinely on alert in peacetime" (Gottfried and Blair, 1988: 128).

The Cuban missile crisis is instructive as a means of demystifying the legitimations of expertise intended to assure a people of the ultimately rational nature of the state. Billed in history and the media as the Kennedy administration's "finest hour," JKF's national security adviser McGeorge Bundy (free of the shackles of state service) described the event as a "battle of blunders" featuring brinksmanship, miscalculation, and political facesaving. At its zenith, the Strategic Air Command had 700 nuclear-armed B-52s airborne ready to strike on command; nuclear tipped ICBMs and missile armed submarines stood at Defcon (Defense Condition) Three; 100,000 troops and a thousand warplanes were poised to invade Cuba; and a U.S. naval armada blockaded the island. In return for U.S. agreements not to invade Cuba and to remove the missiles it had installed in Turkey (which borders the U.S.S.R.), the Soviets "blinked" and dismantled their missiles in Cuba. And the world stepped back from the nuclear abyss (Whited, 1987: 5).

Unfortunately, it is easier to revise history than to change institutional reality. Also duing the anniversary year of the Cuban missile crisis, Reagan appointee Kenneth Adelman (of the curiously named U.S. Arms Control and Disarmament Agency) argued in Bonn, West Germany (Feb. 2, 1987) that since 1972, the Soviet inventory of strategic nuclear weapons[3] had quadrupled, while the U.S. arsenal had only doubled (Pasti, 1987: 1). Adelman thus expresses the "window of vulnerability" legitimation (an ideological permutation of the Kennedy and

Eisenhower "gaps" of decades ago) to intimate that U.S. security is threatened. On the productive side, fear continued in the 1980s to serve as an impetus to military spending in general, and the development of more technologically sophisticated systems of nuclear destruction in specific. But was the vulnerability thesis credible?

It is clear that the Soviets did not sit on their hands while the Eisenhower and Kennedy administration used the new Red scare to cloud the story that the U.S. was running an arms race with itself. Yet focusing on U.S.-Soviet strategic nuclear forces (designed to deliver a nuclear strike to each other or to a third nation), it is clear that at no time during the period 1950–86 did the Soviet Union possess either a qualitative or quantitative advantage in nuclear warheads, when all delivery systems are taken into consideration. It is true, that in 1986, the U.S.S.R. held a 6,420 to 2,175 advantage in ICBM warheads. However, U.S. nuclear strategy has always emphasized the nuclear "triad" consisting of ICBMs, SLBMs, and bomber aircraft.

In 1986, the United States held a 5,632 to 3,175 SLBM warhead advantage, and a 4,104 to 430 advantage in warheads to be delivered by bombers (bombs and cruise missiles).[4] Thus, the number of total strategic warheads favored the United States by 11,911 to 10,025. But more important, over 80 percent of the U.S. strategic warheads are aboard aircraft and submarines. Those few submarines not already at sea, as well as the nuclear armed planes, would be launched at the first confirmed warning of an attack (Nuclear Weapons Databook, 1987). Of course, the existence of the nuclear triad also bears testimony to the power of intraservice rivalry, as each branch wants its share of the nuclear weapons pie.

The nuclear weapons race is legitimated in part by dehumanization. "Each side confirms the other's official propaganda that it really is led by the very sort of morally reprehensible beings that only an equally reprehensible policy can protect against" (Perkins, 1985: 34). During the 1980s the polemic on the United States side accelerated in the context of an unprecedent arms buildup, with the U.S.S.R. portrayed as an "evil empire." More to the point, the Reagan administration held that it would not be bound by the (unratified) SALT II (Strategic Arms Limitation Treaty) of 1979 as the U.S.S.R. was violating its limits. However, Wolfgang Panofsky, chair of the National Academy of Sciences Committee on International Security and Arms Control, argued in 1986 that the Soviets were in compliance.

Specifically, since SALT II (1979), the U.S.S.R. had never exceeded the SALT I limit on ballistic missile launchers or violated its commitment not to undercut the SALT II limits on total strategic warheads or MIRV style ballistic missiles; had not constructed a single new fixed ICBM silo; had not tested a new "heavy" ICBM; had not increased the number of warheads on existing ICBMs; had provided advance notification of tests of multiple missile launches and extraterritorial test flights; had produced 30 or fewer Backfire bombers per year; had not deployed the Backfire with long-range cruise missiles; and under

SALT I and II, had removed 1,007 ICBMs, 233 SLBMs and 13 Yankee class nuclear missile-carrying submarines (1986: 38). Of course, even the treaty-making process becomes a stimulus to the arms race under the assumption that only weapons superiority brings the opponent to the bargaining table, and only weapons strength can be used as "bargaining chips." The *reductio ad absurdum* of this argument is that the cause of the nuclear weapons race is the arms control process itself.

### The Ideology of Nuclear Deterrence

The growth of nuclear stockpiles is legitimated by powerful ideological currents. Again, it is patriotic reverence for the nation-state, comprised of equal parts of grandeur and fear, that inhibits critical thought. In a world seeking to establish a new unity, a new internationalism, what is now celebrated as patriotism may be redefined in future history. There must come a time when national chauvinism is regarded in the same ways that ideas of racial, sexual, ethnic, and class superiority are being redefined today. Given the power of the forces that sustain it, however, it may be that nationalism will prove to be the final bigotry.

But on the nuclear issue, other more specific legitimations are at play. One of these is "expertise," which holds that the defense of national interests are matters for scientists, technicians, managers, specialists, and a leadership class. The idea of expertise is a logical extension of Western hierarchy and rationalism. Accordingly, the guardians of reason and knowledge carefully weigh the options before embarking on a carefully charted course. It is interesting to contrast this view with the uncertainties among the community of early nuclear physicists gathered near Alamagordo, New Mexico, in preparation for firing the first nuclear shot on July 16, 1945. Physicist Robert Krohn speculated that the atmosphere might be ignited, "in which case the world disappears." Another referred to the build-up among the physicists of an "almost hysterical anxiety." Various members of the braintrust formed a betting pool on the magnitude of the blast. Edward Teller bet on 45,000 tons of T.N.T., while Robert Oppenheimer bet on 3,000. Enrico Fermi took side bets on the "possibility of incinerating the State of New Mexico (Allen, 1985: 927)." In the 1950s, U.S. "atomic soldiers" (Rosenburg, 1980) dug in within a mile of "ground zero," convinced that they had nothing to fear, while school children were shown films advising them to "duck and cover" in the case of atomic attack.

When scientific rationalism is put to the ends of power, a moral numbing can be expected. Within the technical community, a compartmentalization of life sustains the irrational processes of the nuclear warfare state. For Sartre, the pretense that voluntary acts are compelled relieves the role-player from the agony of choice. There is doubtlessly some existential degree of "bad faith" here, but Western science has long offered its practitioners ideological deliverance. In the name of value neutrality, the technicians' role is fragmented so that the larger ends of labor need not be debated. These ends, ultimately irrational and immoral, are defined as the responsibility of others. And a critique that addresses the social costs of science stands to be labeled polemical. Perhaps the intellectual point may be made by considering only a single weapons system in the arsenals of the superpowers.

As of 1986, the United States had deployed eight Trident submarines. While submerged, a single boat has the capability of launching 24 missiles simultaneously. Each of these MIRV-type missiles carries eight to ten independently targeted nuclear warheads. Each of these 100 kiloton warheads has a yield 8.5 times greater than that of the bomb dropped on Hiroshima (from data in U.S. Congress, Congressional Budget Office, 1986: 2, 10). Each of these warheads carried by each of these 24 missiles can travel a distance up to 7,000 nautical miles and strike within 300 feet of its target (Clark, 1984: 427). Thus some 240 cities can be devastated by one boat. As presently planned, the United States will deploy 20 Trident submarines by the year 2,000 to replace its Poseidon class submarines. In 1986, each of the 28 Poseidon boats was armed with 16 MIRV missiles, each with 10 to 14 warheads. One dated Poseidon carried more explosive capability than contained in the total firepower used by all combatants during World War II (Kurtz, 1988: 9).

Of course, the submarine missile marathon, as others, continues with each new weapon only a stimulus to its successor. Citing a "gap" in the "hard-target capability" of Trident I missiles, the Reagan administration announced in 1986 its intention to employ the Trident II. Its warheads, with greater explosive power and accuracy, would be able to attack targets such as Soviet ICBM silos hardened against nuclear blasts. "By the year 2,000, approximately 4,800 hard-target warheads would be deployed on Trident II missiles on 20 Trident submarines, resulting in more than a fourfold increase in the number of U.S. hard-target warheads deployed on ballistic missiles" (U.S. Congress, Congressional Budget Office, 1986: xi). Weighing this bottomless pit of nuclear terror, one may question the "rationalism" and "expertise" that conceived, researched, designed, and deployed the Trident and its counterparts.

What happens when this icy style of the technological weapons fix enters the minds of human actors? In the early 1980s, Robert Scheer revealed that the Reagan administration had developed a National Security Decision Document based on the assumption that nuclear war can be won (1982: 3). Certain of the quotations he gathered provide further grounds for a critique of state rationalism.

1. Louis O. Guiffrida, head of the Federal Emergency Management Agency: "It would be a terrible mess, but it wouldn't be unmanageable" (1982: 3).

2. William Chipman, F.E.M.A., responding to a question on whether U.S. institutions would survive an all-out nuclear exchange with the U.S.S.R.: "I think they would eventually, yeah. As I say, the ants eventually build another anthill" (1982: 4).

3. James B. Edwards, former Secretary of the Department of Energy: "I want to come out of it number one, not number two" (1982: 4).

4. Charles Kupperman, a Reagan appointee to the Arms Control and Disarmament Agency: "It is possible for any society to survive ... nuclear war is a destructive thing, but still in large part a physics problem" (1982: 6).
5. T. K. Jones, Deputy Undersecretary of Defense for Strategic and Theater Nuclear Forces, offering a tip on how to survive thermonuclear war: "Dig a hole, cover it with a couple of doors and then throw three feet of dirt on top ... it's the dirt that does it ... if there are enough shovels to go around everybody's going to make it" (1982: 18). (It appears that Jones's solution is for each to dig a shallow grave.)

**The Nuclear Warfare State**

The inherent structural and ideological forces that sustain the warfare complex were considered in an earlier chapter. The cost of the nuclear component of the national security state is, however, deserving of special treatment.

The United States since 1945 has manufactured some 60,000 nuclear warheads in 71 types configured for 116 weapons systems costing some $750 billion. This amounts to an average production rate of about four warheads per day for 40 years. With the current rate of spending on warhead production exceeding that of the Manhattan Project, the present stockpile of some 25,500 warheads is once again on the rise. (Norris et al., 1985: 106)

While 750 billion is no small sum, it comes from adding up all dollars spent as if each had the same purchasing power. Another approach is to control for inflation by using 1986 dollars for the 1945 to 1986 period. In fiscal 1986 dollars, the Department of Defense had spent 1.7 trillion dollars on nuclear delivery systems (planes, missiles, etc.) and other support costs. During that period, the Department of Energy (and its predecessors) had spent $209 billion in fiscal 1986 dollars. By the late 1980s, the nuclear weapons component of the warfare state had thus cost the American people approximately two trillion 1986 dollars. (Norris, et al., 1985: 108). This enormous investment not only nurtures the imperial power of the modern state, it builds bureaucratic empires, provides state capital for nuclear war contractors, missile sites, and air and naval bases. It means budgets, profits, jobs, and economic impact in the local communities of wealthy nation-states. But, viewed from the bottom, these expenditures constitute a form of theft, not merely in the philosophical sense of human regard for those in need, but in the structural sense of the transfer of wealth from periphery to core. Those whose driven underdevelopment has fueled the development of others, now face the twisted development of nuclear domination.

The nuclearization of the warfare state cannot be minimized by drawing a line of demarcation between nuclear and conventional forces. Of course it is true that nonnuclear weapons and forces exist. However, given the centrality of nuclear weapons in military planning and readiness, and given that the superpower military infrastructure must be prepared above all to fight a nuclear war, it follows that the calculus of warfare terror must be considered with the nuclear factor first in mind. If a carrier such as the Nimitz carries nuclear "city-busters," it matters not that this vessel can be used in conventional war. It embodies the threat of nuclear force, and the very *perception* of that capability adds exponentially to its standing as an instrument of state terror. The U.S. naval policy of refusing to specify which of its warships entering the ports of other countries are carrying nuclear weapons, also serves to maximize the means of intimidation.

The nuclear warfare state is misnamed if one assumes its nature is national. The infrastructure required to support its arsenals, as well as the battlefields and targets that are paramount in its planning, simulations, and exercises, are global. It includes:

hundreds of laboratories, testing sites, and electronic support facilities. It encompasses the factories, military bases, transportation networks, command centers, computers, and satellites that feed the system. It is the lifeblood of the war plans. The infrastructure knows no boundaries and observes no borders: the battlefields are virtually everywhere. Scores of nations are linked, wittingly and unwittingly; all of them are on the front lines. Just as the distinction between war and peace is blurred, so is the distinction between military and civilian. The nuclear infrastructure has a priority claim on all resources. . . . About 70% of U.S. tactical nuclear weapons are stored in foreign countries and are on ships at sea. (Arkin and Fieldhouse, 1985: 2, 4)

## Weapons Immortality: Star Wars

It is ironic that public fears associated with nuclear weaponry appear to have been used during the Reagan years to justify a new escalation in weapons technology. The high-sounding Strategic Defense Initiative (S.D.I.) included proposals for space-based laser weapons that would burn through enemy ICBMs in flight, "high frontier" vehicles fired by hundreds of killer satellites, orbiting mirrors, particle beams (charged protons and electrons), and the nuclear-pumped X-ray laser weapon termed Excalibur (Bowman, 1984: 362–65). Estimates of the cost of a fully deployed system of space-based weapons ranged upwards of one trillion dollars. But, given the history of the nuclear stockpile, the capacity of such a system to absorb resources appeared indefinite.

However, new legitimations took root in the United States during the mid– 80s about the officially labeled S.D.I. In the context of surging U.S. and European public opposition in the United States and Europe to early Reagan administration intimations on winning a nuclear war (see above), the president in his March 23, 1983 National Security Address to the Nation (in Kurtz, 1988: 158) cloaked the futuristic weapons system in new clothing. The official story emerged that S.D.I. would rid the world of nuclear weapons, while serving as a purely defensive weapon to be used against long-range Soviet nuclear missiles. In a telling demonstration of statespeak, the goal of a verifiable nuclear freeze was coopted from a grassroots movement, and its high moral ground transformed into a stimulus for further weapons production. All too predictably, the "tough defense" legitimations were followed by strong public support.

It is logically contradictory (if not politically surprising) that the deployment of space weapons at any point in time would constitute a clear threat to an authentic defensive system: the satellites intended to provide early warning of surprise attack (Bowman, 1984: 360–61). And official legitimations notwithstanding, the space weapons envisioned for the S.D.I. system were not inherently "defensive" despite the ideological assumptions. ("Our" weapons systems are defensive, "theirs" are offensive.) Nothing remains to prevent such weapons from being directed offensively toward ground targets. Indeed, the Soviet "fear" of S.D.I. from its announcement appeared to be precisely this.

It was clear that its futuristic weapons would lose effectiveness when the ICBM warheads they were supposed to destroy separated from their launch rockets. This would introduce an incentive to strike silos early, perhaps before launch in a period of international crisis (Bowman, 1987: 15). The offensive targeting of other ground targets would clearly be within the capabilities of the laser systems, which form an integral part of S.D.I. technology (Kurtz, 1988: 175–76). And contrary to official assurances, the proposed Star Wars X-ray laser weapon Excalibur was to be powered by a nuclear explosion in space (Broad, 1983: 17). Thus a hydrogen explosion was to power the laser beams, and in the process destroy the Excalibur weapon.

The testing of a project that requires nuclear explosions only strengthens nuclear doctrines of war, adding another barrier to deescalation. The Reagan administration's refusal to join the 18-month unilateral moratorium on nuclear testing declared by the U.S.S.R. in the mid–1980s did advance star wars experimentation. However, the popular view that the administration's S.D.I. program was the root of its failure to denuclearize remains an unconvincing variation of technological determinism. The deployment of this and other advanced weapons system is an expression of the relations of intimidation.

By the late 1980s only technological religionists considered it possible to make this highly imaginative system fail-safe (with even the Office of Technology Assessment reporting in June of 1988 that computer software of unprecedented and untestable complexity would be required to fire its weapons). S.D.I. (if deployed) could thus be used only to supplement nuclear weapons systems, not to replace them (Kurtz, 1988: 168–70). Stripped of exaggerated claims, it was a system for protecting missiles, not population centers. As such, its deployment would represent a clear violation of the ABM (Anti-Ballistic Missile) treaty between the Soviet Union and the United States (approved by the U.S. Senate, Aug. 3, 1972). In effect, the system could offer only a shield with offensive capabilities to the sword of offensive weapons (Kurtz, 1988: 175).

## The Doctrine of Discriminate Deterrence

The critique of star wars must transcend its technological faults. This technology, as all others, is context-bound; it is the instrumental purposes of scientific applications that are at issue. And these purposes are defined by doctrines of war and driven by imperial forces. The objective of the "control of space in wartime" is only one component of the doctrine of *Discriminate Deterrence* (Commission on Integrated Long-Term Strategy, 1988: 2) prepared for the U.S. Secretary of Defense and the Assistant to the President for National Security Affairs.

Discriminate deterrence calls for the funding of a continuum of deadly force contingencies. The rationale is that "to help defend our allies and to defend our interests, we cannot rely on threats expected to provoke our own annihilation if carried out" (1988: 2). Stated simply, new threats are needed including "emerging technologies of precision, control and intelligence"; a "mix" of nuclear and conventional weapons including "strategic defense"; "versatile mobile forces"; "assistance to anti-Communist insurgents"; and "discriminate nuclear strikes" among others, all funded by budgetary growth "at a steady rate commensurate with our growing economy (1988: 2–3)." Ideologically, the "new" doctrine stands as both dialectic expression and facillitator of the same old martial captialism projected on a world scale. As such, it reflects and drives the forces of the Global Security Economy, including those of accelerating arms production and diversification, while legitimating the deployment of the military means of domination through fear.

**Social Negation**

There now remains the issue of social negation. Given a mixed history of cooperation and competition, harmony and strife, peace and war, the authentic nature of human being and the potential for change may be obscured. If human beings are bent on Hobbesian self-destruction, and are constrained only by fears of self-preservation, then nuclear terrorism is a logical extension of the darkness of the human spirit. But there are other more optimistic assumptions, rooted first in a conception of the social being, who seeks to survive and flourish through forming social alliances with others of his or her own kind. Perhaps a consciousness of that social nature is essential to harness the human power of science, technology, reason, and contemplation to wage authentic peace.

To argue the elimination of nuclear arms presupposes that humankind can rise above destructive myths and practices to form a new international order. Perhaps above all, this vision of peace first asks those who hold it to believe that human nature as human society is perfectable. This does not mean that human beings are somehow independent of the historical basis of society. However, if rule through terror is defined as natural then the material, political, and ideological forces that drive the arms race will be dismissed out of hand.

The point is that the nuclear death race has the gravest consequences for the human species, even if these weapons of destruction are never used. To this point, one variation of the peace through weaponry position is commonly termed nuclear deterrence. In the hope of pushing the debate off of a myopic point and counterpoint, a *consequentialist argument* may be used to assess the deterrence strategy, and its underlying doctrines of war. Such strategies have moved from a simple conception of massive retaliation in the event of a nuclear strike. Today, the doctrine of discriminate deterrence includes the strategy of "counterforce." Such assumes that a rival will be better deterred if nuclear force is used in *gradations*, and that nuclear forces as well as cities should be targeted. As long as deterrence is rooted purely in the concept of massive retaliation, nuclear war is clearly understood to be a form of suicide. But with the counterforce strategies founded in rapid development of nuclear weapons of varying yields, in improved missile guidance systems, and in multiple targeting, new "consequences" now follow. To be specific, contemporary counterforce assumptions encourage the belief that nuclear war can be limited, and that it can be won. This in turn contributes to the growing suspicion that one side is preparing for a first strike (Perkins, 1985: 32).

What further permutations await the ideology of nuclear deterrence? Driven by the imperatives of expansion, but legitimated by national grandeur, anti-Soviet terrorist demonology, and the ubiquitous communist threat, the doctrine of deterrence would be expected to escalate: from massive retaliation to counterforce, and ultimately toward a new form of "prevention," a first-strike capability. That agents of the state believe they have a first-strike capability is not likely to be announced. But the feverish quest for that capacity stands to be legitimated by the elite and those who serve as only another exercise in deterrence. Given the history of arms escalation, and corresponding escalations in the ideology of deterrence, the enemy nation would be thought to be even more credibly "deterred" by the belief that its retaliatory capability could not survive a first strike.

Yet it is not a single person, nor the players responsible for this tragedy, who are alone imperiled. Stripped of its calculations, its contingencies, and its gamesmanship, nuclear deterrence rests on the premise that the nuclear warfare states, in the name of their own security, have the right to back up their interests with a versatile program of discriminate and indiscriminate destruction. The firing of the shot, or the theft and conversion of resources from the have-nots, are not all that matters. The escalating growth of these arsenals can but destroy the future prospects for an authentic international harmony. To find security in nuclear or other weapons is to depend on state terror to intimidate or dominate adversaries, routinely on a world stage, but always in the name of keeping the peace. This is, in a variation of Rousseau, the peace of the nuclear dungeon.

The species has survived in that tiny speck of time called the nuclear era. But the continued reliance on the threat of human extinction to preserve life on this planet is not only irrational, it tears at the fabric of trust and community that is essential to the flourishing of human life. This then is the ultimate meaning of social negation: it is the creation of the forces of domination that set the human being against his or her own nature. The real nuclear terrorism strikes fear in the hearts of real people. In both the United States and the Soviet Union, research on children shows that they have inherited a world that is qualitatively different from that of previous generations (Reifel, 1984). It is the young whose knowledge of nuclear war brings the fear of powerlessness and loss of support, and who resent (especially in adolescence) those adults who appear indifferent and impotent. In earlier times, the question of the future was how to improve it. Now, the question is whether there will be a future at all.

## SUMMARY: THE WORLD'S BUSINESS

There are many who choose to view the nuclear weapons issue from inside the ideological prism of the national security state. These include government lawyers, trained in international law, who cite *raison d'état* in defense of the changing and escalating doctrines of nuclear deterrence (Meyrowitz, 1985). By this interpretation, the nation-state must retain independence and supremacy that cannot be limited by international law, otherwise the state is no longer sovereign. A quite different interpretation of the relationship between the states and global order is that, whether one likes it or not, states will press national interests to maximum advantage on the world stage. Both of these ideas lead to the same conclusion—specifically that international law and multilateral organizations lack the right and/or the power to limit sovereign states.

That there can be no rightful international norms that limit state interests has its analogy in the argument that there can be no group norms that limit individual members. In both cases, the only law is that of force, whether practiced by the strongest of nations or the strongest of persons. It is abundantly clear that the rise of the nuclear warfare state is not purely a matter of national sovereignty. Just as individual rights end where others suffer, so do national rights end where the whole of humankind is threatened. The nuclear death race has transformed the whole of humanity into nuclear hostages. It appears irrational and arrogant to argue that those who live outside the nuclear weapons states have no "standing" in this debate, yet this is precisely what the argument of *raison d'état* assumes.

The second point, which deals with the impotence of international organizations, is more difficult to critique. Certainly, it is true that effective international law still awaits the coming of well-developed global systems for making, judging, and enforcing rules concerning those relations among states that impact the fate of the earth. However, it is one thing for those who speak for the state to note the difficulty in erecting workable systems of international law, and quite another for powerful states to ignore or actively subvert that process.

Ultimately, then it is necessary to develop a transcendent principle, a *raison du monde*. The concept of national sovereignty, and the chauvinism that too easily coexists therewith, will not yield ground easily. Nor will the argument that states have the right to legitimate self-defense (even though "self-defense" and state terrorism often appear joined at the head). Still, it should be clear that national sovereignty, whatever its other problems in definition, does not extend to ecocidal weapons systems. Otherwise, it is as if the nuclear weapons states reserve unto themselves the right to commit national suicide, and to take everybody else with them. Given then the fact that nuclear (and perhaps later high tech weapons) are qualitatively different from all others, their control and elimination are clearly the world's business. And it is at this point that the building of a new conception of international security can begin.

If this argument is sound, it follows that all human beings have the right to insist upon the creation of nuclear free zones for their countries and territorial waters. All human beings have the right to insist that all nuclear weapons states declare the no-first-use of nuclear weapons, that a comprehensive test ban treaty be negotiated, that the arms race not be extended into outer space, and that the systematic and verifiable destruction of nuclear stockpiles begin. If the squandering of resources on the means of domination embodies a global class war on the wretched, then denuclearization is by definition a step toward international transformation.

So argued, a resolution by the foreign ministers of over 100 Third World nations meeting in Havana is instructive. As reported by *Prensa Latini* and the Associated Press on May 5, 1988, the resolution called for the staged, total elimination of nuclear arms, and encouraged multilateral negotiations, in the framework of the United Nations. Some, of course, dismiss resolutions and their assumptions as empty, and indeed words are insufficient. But the premise of the work at hand is that ideas and ideology matter, not as detached abstractions, but as powerful forces when they seize the minds of real players caught up in the relations of global power and change.

## NOTES

1. Although recent modifications of the 1983 projections have been advanced in some quarters, these do not question the feasibility of climatic catastrophe, but its degree.

2. An intercontinental ballistic missile (ICBM) is powered by a rocket engine and travels outside the atmosphere for part of its flight. SLBMs are submarine-launched ballistic missiles.

3. *Strategic weapons* refers to nuclear weapons with intercontinental ranges of more than 3,400 miles. Tactical weapons are short-range systems to be used on the battlefield.

4. A cruise missile is an unmanned, self-propelled, guided missile that flies at low altitudes to avoid radar detection. It can be launched from air, ground, or sea.

# 5

# *Racial Terrorism: Apartheid in South Africa*

Among blacks, the death of Black Consciousness leader Steve Biko is one of the better known. He was detained on August 18, 1977, in good health. Twenty-six days later he was dead. These grim facts are not disputed by the South African Government: (1) Biko was held naked in solitary confinement from the 19th of August to the 6th of September. (2) He was taken to the interrogation room on the 6th of September. That night he was handcuffed and shackled by leg irons, locked to the walls, and left to sleep that way. (3) He was not removed from the irons for two days, by which time he was mentally confused; his hands, feet, and ankles were swollen and cut; his clothes and blankets were soaked in urine. (4) He was taken naked in the back of a Land-Rover 750 miles to a prison hospital. He was given a mat and died on the stone floor of his cell.

American Friends Service Commitee, 1987

Each trade agreement, each bank loan, each new investment is another brick in the wall of our continued existence.
J. B. Vorster, former Prime Minister of South Africa

And what if the Church and the State is the mob that howls at the door?
W. B. Yeats

In the context of the ongoing political violence in South Africa, the nature of the struggle is transformed to fit one of two varieties of the dominant ideology. In the view of the state and those who support it internationally, the violence of resisters is labeled terrorism. In the view of reformers, the regime (as well as the violence of resistance) is condemned. Neither of these addresses the global foundations of *apartheid*. As with other forms of settler terrorism, the roots of S.A. racial separatism are to be found in the historical relations of colonialism; relations that have changed more in form than in substance since the Dutch established a European outpost in the mid-seventeenth century. The point of departure for this inquiry will be U.S. relations with South Africa in the 1980s. But as always, the forces at play transcend the policies of a particular administration. In this sense, the modern exemplars who speak are locked in the transcendental and dialectical relations of conflict.

## THE RED SCARE IN BLACK AFRICA

U.S. policy on southern Africa has been driven materially by the forces of capital accumulation (that have taken specific form in South Africa as shall be demonstrated) and ideologically by fervent anticommunism. Alexander Haig, a former officer with general rank, who had served in the Nixon administration before becoming the president and chief executive officer of the United Technologies Corporation, testified before the House of Representatives early in the decade.[1] Citing the importance of South African minerals and the escalation of "Soviet proxy activity in the third world," he argued that "the era of the resource war has arrived" (United States Congress, Subcommittee on Security and Terrorism, 1982: 2). Assistant Secretary of State (for African Affairs) Chester Crocker, in an address to the American Legion in Honolulu on August 29, 1981, had already offered an elaboration of this thesis. He began by noting that U.S. economic interests in that portion of the African continent below the Sahara are heavily concentrated in the south.

This concentration of our interests reflects southern Africa's tremendous mineral wealth and the relative sophistication of the area's economies—especially those of South Africa and Zimbabwe. Southern Africa accounts for over 40 percent of sub-Saharan Africa's GNP, 70 percent of its industrial and 60 percent of its mining output, 80 percent of its steel and 85 percent of electricity consumed. The area contains immense deposits of many strategic minerals which are vital to industrial economies like ours. . . . (Crocker, 1981: 1)

The specifics of the "economic and national security interests" argument will be addressed in due course. However, from an African perspective, such positions embody the legitimations of imperialism. The concept of a "resource war" between superpowers and their partners bypasses the question of just who it is that resources belong to. When a dominant state enters the global arena on the grounds of what's good for its own economic investment or its own strategic interests, the legitimate rights of indigenous people become secondary. The selective view is that what's good for the interests of dominant states is good for the world. The structural position of less powerful resource states insures an opposing conception.

Crocker also reiterated Haig's insistence on viewing southern Africa as a "contested area" with the U.S.S.R. and its allies seen as major threats in the region. This is a restatement of a longstanding view in the United States (a view that became perhaps more pronounced under the Reagan administration) that the black oposition to white supremacist rule in the Republic of South Africa and Namibia (the colonial name of which is South-West Africa) could be attributed to external Communist intervention.

Faced with large-scale foreign intervention, the pressure of African guerrilla groups, and strains in its relations with its traditional Western partners, South Africa has significantly expanded its defense potential in recent years. The republic, through a sustained self-sufficiency drive, is now an important regional military power. It has clearly signalled its determination to resist guerilla encroachments and strike at countries giving sanctuary (Crocker, 1981: 1).

Once again, a consideration of political language is instructive. Here, the South African military escalation is described in terms of "defense potential" and its political system becomes a "republic." (The country is officially the Republic of South Africa.) If one conventionally defines republic as a state in which the electorate rules directly or indirectly through elected representatives, the problem with the South African republic is that it denies full electoral standing to nonwhites. It is by definition a racist republic. Nevertheless, the term republic is a legitimating one that gives credibility to the South African government every time it is used.

Further, Crocker described South African border-crossings into neighboring states as strikes at "sanctuaries" for guerrillas. The guerrillas were in turn defined as allies of the Warsaw pact. This tendency to view the forces of change as the problem, and the forces of the existing order as defensive has the unsettling effect of placing the United States, its allies, and the international order they represent, on the side of white supremacist rule. In its zeal to identify and oppose the ubiquitous Communist threat, U.S. policy in southern Africa has historically contradicted its own stated purposes and participated dialectically in the ongoing negation, not only of apartheid, but the larger forces that sustain it. For if the system of white supremacist economic and political rule in South Africa is "anti-Communist" and the lead antiapartheid forces are Soviet proxies, what conclusion is to be drawn by the people of southern Africa, the continent, and the Third World? Once again, it is anticommunism in its material and ideological forms, that helps to build the anticapitalist formations of African socialism as alternatives to modern settler rule.

The U.S. obsession with terrorism in the 1980s was easily transposed to the South African revolutionary context. On this point, in a series of hearings before the Senate Subcommittee on Security and Terrorism, the thesis was developed that the Soviet Union, East Germany, and Cuba were responsible for the "fomenting of terrorism in southern Africa." In the words of that subcommittee's chair, these states "actively and often successfully seek, under the overall control of the Politburo in Moscow, to utilize, infiltrate, and manipulate so-called 'national liberation movements' around the world " (U.S. Congress, 1982: 2). From this viewpoint, the Senate subcommittee conceived of terrorism as a political instrument used to reach the alleged goal of "Communist world domination." Specifically, the African National Congress and the South-West African People's Organization, who have resorted to armed struggle, were (and continue to be) portrayed as exponents of Soviet interests.

Such allegations require an inquiry into the history of the resistance movement in southern Africa, and this will follow in due course. However, it is noteworthy that the Senate Subcommittee on Security and Terrorism did not entertain evidence and testimony on the political, economic and social structures of racial domination in southern Africa.[2] This tends to again build the ideological monopoly on terrorism in the United States, marked by a selective perception of only those violent acts that threaten Western states or their allies. Consequently, the role of the West (from its colonial empires to its modern corporations and system of world-market trade) in erecting and supporting the continuing structures of white supremacist rule in South Africa can only be ignored.

## THE SOUTH AFRICAN NATIONAL EMERGENCY STATE

In the late 1980s, the state security system of the R.S.A. remained in the hands of the military and a nationalized police force under the Department of National Security (Tatum, 1987: 25). More specifically, its structure resembled "a military dominated system of secret committees responsible for coordinating the activities of the South African Defence Force (SADF), police intelligence, secret security agencies and other governmental departments. . . . " (Sono, 1987: 6). More formally, this network was known as the National Security Management System (NSMS), established in 1979 to develop a "total strategy" to control and negate the antiapartheid movement. At the pinnacle of the NSMS stood the State Security Council where the harsh 1985 and 1986 states of emergency appear to have been ordered. Headed by a former head of Military Intelligence, the State Security Council came to effectively supplant the South African cabinet. Under the direct control of the prime minister, the SSC provided the means to take expedient action in the name of national preservation. At a lower, but still national level, it presided over 13 interdepartmental committees.

At the regional level in the late 1980s, the structure of the National Security Management System featured at least ten Joint Management Centres that corresponded with the military command districts into which South African territory is divided. At the grassroots level some 500 local committees were charged to gather intelligence and forward it up the chain of command. Whatever the level, the "total strategy" was to maintain the social, economic, and political institutions of apartheid by breaking the opposition. In August 1986, the Joint Management Centre in Johannesburg sought to end the nonviolent resistance of a rent boycott in the townships of the Vaal Triangle. Tactics included the formation of collection action groups, the eviction of tenants, the use of computers to store intelligence information, and the recruitment of the young to reeducation camps where they would be taught to convince their parents to pay rent. The legions of young "detainees" held under the increasingly permanent state of emergency[3] were offered early release contingent upon their agreeing to attend two-week crash courses in political indoctrination.

In the recent history of South Africa, recent emergency restrictions have legitimated the often unrestrained employment of the police power of the state. The South African Police (SAP), the municipal police, the South African Defence Forces, and the homeland (Bantustan) police, aided by part-time Citizen Force army units, have constituted the official enforcement apparatus. The dominant strategy, in a country where whites constitute only one-seventh of the population, is to induce the victims of apartheid to cooperate with the white regime. Thus much of the less savory work of political repression has been carried out by police-recruited vigilantes whose tactics include arson and assassination. Black police have been recruited in increasing numbers, often from the desperately impoverished rural areas, to keep order in the townships. In November of 1986, the *Johannesburg Citizen* reported an announcement from the South African minister of law and order that the police forces would increase from a level of 56,316 to 96,300. The rationale for the building of a modern police state, which survives in part through nurturing black on black violence, is familiar. The minister of law and order cited the need for maximizing the "ability to control terrorism" (Sono, 1987: 9).

It is clear that the organization of the South African national emergency state raises the question of institutional domination through fear. It is important to remember that the assault is more than the denial of abstract rights; it is more than a case of violation of international law. Certainly laws and rights are involved, but the real terrorism of apartheid has broken bodies as well as statutes and crushes the spirit as well as the ballot box. Under the national security state, police powers are unrestrained resulting in wholesale detention of those suspected of sympathies toward the antiapartheid movement. In too many instances, detention has meant the brutality of torture.

Over 90 percent of 40 released detainees who were examined by physicians reported details of being hit with a rifle butt, beaten with a whip or heavy stick, or being punched, kicked or slapped. A quarter complained of being stripped and suffering assault to their sexual organs. Eight of the forty former detainees said they were given electric shocks and three that they had a canvas bag or hood pulled over their heads during interrogation. (Sono, 1987: 13)

Apartheid adds literal meaning to the phrase "suffer the children." According to estimates by the opposition Progressive Federal Party of South Africa, the state of emergency that commenced in June of 1986, had resulted by early winter of 1987 in the detention of some 25,000 persons (Asmal, 1988: 128–29). According to the Detainees' Parents Support Committee that mounted a "free the children campaign," some 10,000 of these detaines were under the age of 18.

Most were in their teens, but a number of ten-year-olds were included. As most of these children were not formally charged, it can be concluded that the random detention of children was designed to provide a lesson in terror. They were held in cells, often overcrowded, cold, and filthy. The allegations of physical torture were commonplace, and the experience of being caged apart from familial and community support represents a clear form of psychological coercion.

## REGIONAL DOMINATION

But the terrorism of apartheid is not confined to the internal level. In southern Africa, a wave of national liberation intensifying in the 1970s saw the coming of African rule in Zimbabwe (formally Rhodesia), Mozambique, and Angola, ending the vestiges of settler colonialism in the region. Although the new states represented no direct military threat to the South African regime, they declared early on their solidarity with (while providing some support and sanctuary for) the national liberation forces who have restored to armed struggle against the apartheid regime. Under enormous pressure from the South African military and RSA-supported counterrevolutionary forces,[4] these states were forced to enter into agreements with the RSA that have limited their support of the African National Congress (ANC) and the Namibia-based South-West Africa People's Organization (SWAPO) (Mazrui, 1986: 308–9).

Perhaps of greater long-term significance, nine states of southern Africa formed the Southern African Development Coordination Conference in an attempt to challenge South African economic domination in the region. In response to the growing threat, South African military spending reached the level of 4 billion rand in the mid–1980s (from 44 million in 1960) (Asmal, 1988: 142). According to the United Nations Centre Against Apartheid, South Africa's fight to maintain white supremacy has featured "direct military invasion and incursions, the use of mercenaries and groups of nationals hostile to the governments of independent states, economic sabotage and pressure, the assassination of individuals, virulent propaganda and, in general, attempts at political and economic destabilisation. These methods have been used in different combinations and to differing degrees against all the African countries that border on South Africa or South African-occupied Namibia'' (cited in Asmal, 1988: 18). For example, South Africa conducted a massive invasion of Angola in 1981, ostensibly to strike at SWAPO. According to the United Nations Security Council and the U.N.'s International Court of Justice, the South African occupation of Namibia is itself illegal, thus an act of aggression against Angola in the name of the defense of Namibia was, clearly without merit.[5]

South Africa legitimates its war against the ANC as a war against terrorism. This version of history, which renders the apartheid system a victim instead of a perpetrator, found support in the policy of the United States during the 1980s. (As demonstrated earlier, the Reagan administration waged both an ideological and a shooting war against international terrorism, making this the cornerstone of its foreign policy.) Candidate Reagan, prior to his first election, described not only the ANC, but SWAPO of Namibia, and Z.A.N.U. and Z.A.P.U. of Zimbabwe as terrorist organizations (U.S. Senate, Executive Report no. 97–98, 1981). These are mentioned because they are from southern Africa, but the U.S.-constructed list of terrorists has been a lengthy one.

It is now true that the ANC in South Africa and SWAPO in Namibia carry on armed struggle. Yet the African National Congress, formed in 1912, is the most senior liberation movement in Africa. And prior to the 1960 massacres at Sharpeville and Langa, it had adopted a position first of negotiating with the white South African government, and then a strategy of nonviolent civil disobedience. Since its founding in 1960, the Southwest African People's Organization has opposed the occupation and domination of Namibia by South Africa. It is recognized by the United Nations as the sole, legitimate representative of the Namibian people. And of course, it was the armed struggle of the Zimbabwe African National Union (Z.A.N.U.) and the Zimbabwe African People's Union (Z.A.P.U.) that brought an end to white rule in what the colonizers called Rhodesia. The Z.A.N.U. Patriotic Front became the ruling party in Zimbabwe with its independence in 1980 (Danaher, 1984: 65–72; 109).

The international community (with the notable exception of some Western states such as the United States and Great Britain) has chosen to focus on the illegitimacy of the apartheid regime, instead of the allegations of terrorism directed toward the African National Conference. It should be understood that South African apartheid, and the institutional structure it symbolizes, stands against the flow of African history. With the coming of continental decolonization, the late twentieth-century white supremacist state stood as an historical anachronism. Given the sounding of the political voices of newly independent states in the international arena, apartheid came to be conceived of as a crime against humanity. This is evidenced in the International Convention on the Suppression and Punishment of the Crime of Apartheid of 1973, and in the declaration by the U.N. General Assembly that the "racist regime of South Africa is illegitimate and has no right to represent the people of South Africa." The General Assembly did more than condemn apartheid. It also declared the "legitimacy of the struggle of the oppressed people of South Africa and their liberation movements" to be considered the "authentic representative of the overwhelming majority of the South African people" (Asmal, 1988: 133).

The point is that these movements were and are considered legitimate forces of resistance, certainly by the natives of sub-Saharan Africa. However, they did not conform to the political vision advanced by the U.S. administration in the 1980s. This policy, pleasantly termed "constructive engagement' by its architects, called for the United States to maintain friendly (diplomatic and commercial) relations with the R.S.A. Thus, with the heavy pattern of total investment maintained, it would be possible to influence the peaceful transition from apartheid. In the process, Western-style institutions could be retained, and the role of South Africa in the global market system preserved. This is the crux of a beguilingly palatable conception of social reform in South Africa. It is not merely the resort to armed struggle that is found objectionable, though the hope to improve nonviolent methods of conflict resolution is a laudable one. It is the fear that armed struggle may produce new institutions that prove to be independent of undue influence from the Western world.

In assessing the stated objectives of constructive engagement, it is clear that the commitment to "peaceful change" in South Africa was not extended to other regions. (See Chapter 9 on Nicaragua for example.) Such a critique should not be confined to current events involving the United States.[6] This nation-state was founded in a war of colonial secession. Its expansion came primarily at the expense of the indigenous peoples of North America. Since 1776, the United States has fought eight wars (some undeclared) against foreign powers; a civil war; a century of intermittent conflicts with its natives; and it has intervened repeatedly in Central America, the Caribbean, the Mediterranean, the Western Pacific, and the Persion Gulf. The size of the U.S. nuclear arsenal and its version of the modern warfare state were discussed earlier, as was the militarization of space. One may question whether these are the historical and political credentials of nonviolence. This history of armed intervention notwithstanding, the Congress of the United States chose to include language associating the African National Congress with terrorism in its Comprehensive Anti-Apartheid Act passed in October of 1986.

## R.S.A. INSTITUTIONAL TERROR

The recurring argument then, is the continued predominance of a double standard of terrorism, better fitted for ideological warfare than analysis. The official story denies, ignores, or falsifies the global nature of that form of institutional terrorism embodied in South African internal and international relations. To wit, as of the mid–1980s, South Africa's infant mortality rate was 12 per thousand for the white population, compared with 69 per thousand for urban Africans, and 282 per thousand for rural Africans. The black South African death rate due to malnutrition was estimated at 96 per day, and its rate of illiteracy was 50 percent (Danaher, 1984: 111–12). The economic terror of apartheid continues to be evidenced in a record of virtually no gains for the African majority after a century of Western-style industrial development (Greenberg, 1981).

R.S.A. regime terror is reflected in the industrial world's highest rates of prison population and state execution. It is evidenced in mass detentions, numbering 35,000 in 1984 alone (Sono, 1986: 2). It is poignantly and personally recorded in the death in 1977 of Black Consciousness leader Steve Biko, who became the forty-fifth known black activist to die in police custody (Danaher, 1984: 126), and in the 1964 Rivonia trial where Nelson Mandela and seven other leaders of the ANC were sentenced to life imprisonment. It is etched in the 1960 massacres at Sharpeville and Langa where police fired on unarmed demonstrators killing 67, wounding 186, including many women and children and many shot in the back (Danaher, 1984: 68). It is founded in the Soweto rebellion of 1976, which took 575 lives, and resulted in the wounding of almost 4,000 persons and the arrest of 6,000 more.[7] (The Soweto rising was sparked by police firing on Soweto schoolchildren protesting an education bent on the maintenance of structural inequality.) The historical reliance by this state on deadly force and massive structures of "internal security" to control its own population continue to falsify its claim to legitimacy.

## INTERNAL COLONIALISM

Descriptive accounts of state terrorism, however graphic, only serve to raise the level of abstraction. The emergence, institutionalization, and maintenance of white rule in South Africa is a chapter in the larger history of European conquest. This particular story began in 1652 with the establishment of a colony in Cape Town by the Dutch East India Company.[8] These early colonists brought in slaves from the Dutch East Indies and other parts of Africa, in order to augment the indigenous labor force made up of the San (Bushmen) and Khoikhoi (Hottentot) tribes. Early in the eighteenth century, many of the Dutch, German, and French Huguenot colonists began the "trekking" movement into the north and east. The colonists were known as Boers (Dutch for farmers) and as they sought land they clashed with African Bantu-speaking tribes, which were well-organized and difficult to subdue.

### Settler Isolation and the Ideology of the "Chosen"

As the settlers moved inland, they became geographically estranged from the Cape Town colony, and in that context of economic conflict and isolation, began to develop the specific institutional and cultural structures of separatism. On the productive side, the trekkers developed a subsistence-based agricultural economy. Culturally, they took the name *Afrikaner*, which literally means "African," thus asuming a symbolic identity. This identity signalled both a break with Europe, as well as a claim to authentic native standing. However, through adopting the name Afrikaner, the trekkers symbolically transformed the original inhabitants into aliens in their own land. Further marking their geographical and growing cultural isolation, the Boers developed a language called Afrikaans, which became increasingly removed from the original Dutch. But it was on the ideological side that the Afrikaners developed the clearest manifestation of their separatism, thus establishing support for the more sophisticated institutions of racial domination that emerged later.

The trekkers found in the dogma of sixteenth-century Calvinism the legitimation of a chosen people called by God to transform and dominate a wilderness. Calvinism was a harsh protestantism, integrating predestination and total depravity. But it also offered the promise of irresistible grace and the certain preservation of the saints. For the early Boers, this faith represented more than a link to tradition. Calvinism was a set of core principles of faith, to which were added the more specific legitimations of racial supremacy. Correctly understood, Calvinism was filtered through the prism of settler life and refitted for the task of ideological domination. Thus, while Calvinism withered elsewhere, it flourished in South Africa. But as with other idea-systems of control, its religious content took political form.

Merged with racism, Calvinist predestination was to be transformed. Not confined to the matter of the elect and damned in the afterlife, it became instead a mandate to establish Afrikaner control of the native population and ultimately Afrikaner nationhood. Depravity became more than a general condition of wretched humanity. It was instead reinterpreted along racial and cultural lines to describe the subject population. And of course, *irresistible grace and the certain perseverance of the saints* conferred upon the Afrikaner a divine mission, well expressed in Psalm 105: "He brought forth his people with joy, and his chosen with gladness, and gave them the lands of the heathen, and they inherited the labor of the people." As with the conquering Israelites, so with the Afrikaner.

But we need not rely on biblical passages or remain in earlier centuries to understand the imperial transformation of theology. D. F. Malan was a minister in the Dutch Reformed Church who became prime minister in 1948 when the Afrikaner Nationalist Party took power. These were his words:

It is through the will of God that the Afrikaner People exist at all. In his wisdom He determined that on the southern point of Africa, the dark continent, a People should be born who would be the bearer of Christian culture and civilization. In his wisdom, He surrounded this People by great dangers. He sent the People down upon unfruitful soil so that they had to toil and sweat to exist upon the soil. From time to time he visited them with droughts and other plagues. But this was only one of the problems. God also willed that the Afrikaans People should be continually threatened by other Peoples. There was the ferocious barbarian who resisted the intruding Christian civilization and caused the Afrikaner's blood to flow in streams. There were times when as a result of this the Afrikaner was deeply despairing, but God at the same time prevented the swamping of young Afrikaner People in the sea of barbarism. (Quoted in Moleah, 1984: 71)

Viewed through this particular permutation of settler dogma, the struggle for land, resources, rule, and cultural superiority became a holy war.

## Ideological Permutations and Neo-Apartheid

The imploding contradictions of social relations in South Africa in the post-Sharpville era brought a state legitimation crisis. The institutions and ideology of racial domination were not only meeting better organized and mass-oriented internal resistance, the naked use of force increasingly branded the R.S.A. as an international pariah. Western claims that capitalism and authentic democracy were inextricably tied were being falsified beyond denial. U.N. resolutions of condemnation and the 1963 voluntary arms embargo were perhaps symbolic.

More substantive was the flight of foreign capital, and the archaic nature of the South African labor market. Apartheid was poised to assume a new political and ideological dress. Between 1960 and 1970, the ruling Afrikaner Nationalist Party put in place a policy of *separate development*, creating a homeland (bantustan) system for its "African Nations" (Lipton, 1985: 29–37).

The historical consequences of this structure of divide and rule will be examined in due course. For now, it should be noted that the ideology of apartheid in the 1960s was transformed on two levels. First, its legitimation base was to replace God-ordained genetic superiority with new claims of cultural dissimilarity. It was not that God intended domination, but the differences in the customs and lifestyles of peoples that mandated separation. Second, the demand for democratization would be answered through fragmented "citizenship" in the new *tribal-states*. However, the retribalization policy was no more effective in addressing the archaic nature of the R.S.A. labor market than in meeting growing demands for self-determination. It remained rigid and fractured with the state attempting to regulate the flow of workers to mines, towns, and farms (Lipton, 1985: 47). The opposing interests of the Afrikaner and British divisions of the R.S.A. white caste, embodied in state bureaucratic controls and patronage on the one side and major private sector domination on the other, will be explored in due course. But the need for skilled black labor, together with the unification of black resistance expressed in both nonviolent and violent forms, led to further permutations in the 1970s. Ideologically, these were expressed in the familiar language of reform, and politically in the form of more cosmetic alterations in petit apartheid (see below). But this reformulation was to resemble more the modernization of apartheid than its negation.

**Caste Capitalism**

The conflict between Afrikaner and African is only one element of the complex history of South Africa (Tatum, 1987: 35–36). Perhaps 40 percent of the white population is descended not from the trekkers but from the British. In 1795, the British occupied the Cape as a means of strengthening their colonial possessions elsewhere in the continent. The occupation became permanent in 1806, and sovereignty followed in 1814. Dissatisfied with British rule (and especially afraid that British law would not sanction the slave labor on which the Boers depended), the settlers organized a mass exodus in 1836.[9] The "Great Trek" saw the movement of some 10,000 persons 500 miles inland, where they were to encounter the Zulu nation. There, in December of 1838, they defeated these indigenous tribespeople at the battle of Blood River. The trekkers then created independent republics known as the Transvaal and the Orange Free State but were driven out of Natal by the British in 1844. It was the discovery of diamonds and gold in the final three decades of the nineteenth century that signalled the beginning of the end for the independent Boer states (Karis, 1963: 471–83).

Cecil Rhodes was at the forefront of the British move north, personifying a pattern of imperialism that, in concrete terms, brought miners, roads, railroads, and military force to southern Africa. Although the British had failed in an earlier attempt at intervention in the Transvaal, the second Anglo-Boer War (1899–1902) proved to be an all-out struggle for domination between the Afrikaners and their more powerful adversaries. The British responded to the Boer guerrilla tactics by torching farms and establishing a system of concentration camps in which 26,000 men, women, and children died. Such tactics brought an end to the war but the cause of Afrikaner nationalism now had its martyrs.

With British rule then assured, a typical pattern of advanced colonialism emerged. The British moved into urban centers, forming the economic apparatus necessary to exploit the land and resource wealth. Despite their position of economic advantage, the British settlers found their position a tenuous one. They were outnumbered by the embittered Afrikaners, and both divisions of the dominant white caste were aware of the threat to white rule represented by native Africans. Driven by a sense of the greater danger, the old European adversaries formed an antagonistic alliance, and the British government responded by recognizing the Union of South Africa in 1910. Comprised of the Transvaal, the Orange Free State, Natal, and the Cape, its all-white parliament was intended to insure that the means of state domination would remain in white hands. Thus there emerged a political alliance between the warring masters of South Africa.

In the first quarter of the twentieth century, the economic centrality of the British in the Union of South Africa was to insure that the Afrikaners lost more ground. With the development of industry, the poorly educated Boers were forced off the land and, without mastery of the English language, thrown into competition with blacks for jobs. They were the beneficiaries of government-sanctioned discrimination, but the once proud trekkers found themselves looking up at the British owners, and living in the growing urban slums. In the meantime, those remaining on their farms were losing much of their black labor to the mines. In response to this growing marginality, there emerged the political arm of the Afrikaner—the National Party. Founded by the Boer general J. B. M. Hertzog in 1914, the party came to power first in 1924. But its intensive nationalism had yet to mature (Robertson and Whitten, 1978; Thompson, 1964).

By the 1930s, the Afrikaner Broederbond ("band of brothers") was becoming a powerful political force. Working underground, it began to recruit not only the disgruntled farmers but the teachers and ministers who would be in a position to promote the new ideology called apartheid. That ideology had been formally developed at the seminary at Stellenbosh, near the Cape of Good Hope, by Boers who had not joined the Great Trek of a century before. Now, aided by the Dutch Reformed Church (which was determined to keep alive the theology and dogma of "chosenness"), apartheid became a purified nationalism founded in religious zeal. However, the new ideal of separation was to become more than an article of faith. In 1938, the Broederbond led a reenactment of the Great Trek of 1836. On a hill outside Pretoria, 100,000 people gathered to demand a monument.

The Voertrekker Monument stands today, a ring of wagons carved in stone (Temko, 1986).

Yet the ideology of apartheid, drawn curiously from the wellsprings of a people both despised and despising, dominated and dominating, was to be etched in something other than a monument of stone. When institutionalized, this idea-system came to mean both the state preservation of white supremacy and the repudiation of British imperialism. These dreams of grandeur were only temporarily interrupted by the Second World War. South Africa entered the conflict on the side of the Allies, but that move was bitterly opposed by the Afrikaner nationalists. In the words of Kevin Danaher:

Opposed to humanist notions of the state as a device created by humans for their own use, Afrikaner Calvinism viewed the state's monopoly of force and authority over the individual as a divine gift. The emphasis was on discipline and obedience to this higher authority. The parallels to Nazism in Germany and fascism in Italy were direct and explicit. (Danaher, 1984: 66)

It is unnecessary to rely on ideological similarities in the credos of the nation-race that emerged in Nazi Germany and in South Africa. The extremist New Order and Ossewabrandwag factions sought to block South Africa's joining of the allied cause by dynamiting railroads, communications facilities, and some civilian targets. They also engaged in armed assault on the police and military (Bunting, 1964). A commandant of the Ossewabrandwag was B. J. Vorster who declared in 1942 that the National party stood for "Christian Nationalism," which was "an ally of Nazism" (Laurence, 1979: 149, quoted in Danaher). Dr. H. F. Verwoerd, a graduate of Stellenbosch, as a wartime editor supported nazism. Both Verwoerd and Vorster, ideological allies of fascism during the war, were later to serve as prime ministers of South Africa under the reign of the National party. But it was to be Hendrik Verwoerd who, as minister of native affairs under the government of D. F. Malan, became responsible for translating the ideology of apartheid into law.

When the National party unified the Afrikaners to win the elections of 1948, the Malan regime moved quickly to use the power of the state to compensate for the economic disadvantage of the lower white caste. This meant that Afrikaners were to be supported in the labor market, with preferential treatment accorded them in both the public and private sectors of the economy. This included, but went beyond, the establishment of state corporations that provided management and employment opportunities for the Afrikaner. Before 1948, some 30 percent of the South African white-collar workforce were Afrikaner. By 1970, that percentage had doubled (Temko, 1986).

The position of advantage in the labor market did not come at the expense of the British South Africans who were entrenched at the top of industry and commerce. It was paid for instead by the nonwhite majority, whose position of subordination was further insured by a set of laws establishing the practices of "petit apartheid." Such laws mandated registration by race to insure "apartness" in the future, and a reconstruction of institutions and living patterns to end the minimal sorts of racial integration that had occurred. Schools, families, unions, political parties, hospitals, neighborhoods—all came to embody in material form the ideology of apartheid.

Reference was made earlier to the establishment of a "homelands" policy in the 1960s, the cornerstone of the N.P.'s system of "grand apartheid." Only the R.S.A. recognized some of these "mini-reserves" as independent states. The Bantustans held only 13 percent of the land and were strangely lacking in the lush topsoil and rich mineral reserves South Africa is noted for. In the period between 1960 and 1980, some 3.5 million Africans were forcibly resettled to the reserves (International Defence and Aid Fund, 1982). This massive population transfer is best understood as a grand design of labor control, founded in the premise of divide and rule. It makes manifest in stark geographical terms the formation of a cheap labor reserve, while continuing to offer white dominated capitalism the advantage of black disadvantage.

The internal colonialism of these bantustans is best illustrated by the organisation of their economies. In the case of Kwazulu, Ciskei, Bophuthatswana and Lebowa, they are areas which provide cheap and available labour for white industries and domestic service "bussed" to and from their houses by excessively long bus and train journeys up to 140 km each day. For the mines, the immoral system of migrant labour continues, whereby men working on contracts of up to three years are housed in all male compounds. Notwithstanding the abolition of the notorious Pass Laws in 1986 under which up to a quarter of a million Africans were arrested each year, influx control under more sophisticated arrangements ensures that the families of these migrant labourers cannot legally join these male workers. (Asmal, 1988: 130)

It is the economic centrality of black labor and the emergence of apartheid as a system of labor discrimination that is at issue in South Africa. This conception includes, but is not restricted to, the point that Afrikaners have compensated through the power of the state for much of their historical economic disadvantage. Nor is it sufficient to argue that the power of the state has denied the black worker "equal opportunity" in the labor market. The Western tendency to see apartheid as only a political problem ignores the broader societal and global forces at play. This is to say that much of the opposition to apartheid in the West is a narrow and selective opposition to the naked racism expressed in both ideology and law. The critique is narrowly focused on the contractual unfairness of this system, marked by the absence of legal entitlements, including the vote. In effect, the Western complaint detaches polity from the base of class relations. However, as the Afrikaners have used their majority to compensate in part for their economic disadvantage vis à vis the British, they are well aware of the power of the state, including the potential to nationalize industries.

It was perhaps with a view toward centralizing power, while offering token representation to potential junior partners in privilege, that a constitutional reform plan was approved by the South African electorate in 1983. This established separate parlimentary chambers for "coloured" and "Indian" segments of the population. However, in the main these chambers legislate separately on the group affairs and have little support from those they are supposed to represent. More important, the new governmental structure served to consolidate the power of the chief executive, now termed the president (Danaher, 1984: 24–25). This centralization appears to fit well the needs of the S.A. National Emergency State.

Most of the South African symbolic reforms in the 1980s, pushed by the regime headed by Pieter W. Botha, came on the fringes of apartheid in response to fierce black resistance and mounting international pressure. The focus of political change was at the level of petit apartheid under which black trade unions acquired legal standing and the bans on interracial marriage, sporting events, parks and beaches, and other forms of de jure social segregation were lifted or modified. Given the need or skilled black labor, a relative few workers received more training (Lipton, 1985: 59–60). Such symbolic moves alienated the most reactionary elements of the National Party, and crystalized the opposition on the far right. However, more contemporary reforms must be understood structurally as attempts to make the systems of control more efficient, and as safety valve mechanisms intended to spare the real apartheid. The contradiction in South Africa is that political rights that confer the power of the state will not be peacefully surrendered unless and until new class formations of privilege coopt members of the lesser castes. Otherwise, the power of the state could too easily become a force for nationalization and distribution.

Apartheid is more than a system of racial domination and cultural imperialism; its preeminent function has been the control of the labor market. Indeed, the dependence of the white caste on native labor has been a constant in South African economic history.[10] Continued growth and prosperity for labor-dependent sectors thus remains a consequence of relative share of the surplus value of nonwhite labor. Apartheid may then be shown to differ from earlier colonial patterns of domination, rooted in economic exploitation but expressed in race, in its embodiment in the power of the modern state. Certain of its more outrageous *social and cultural* elements (embodied in petit apartheid) are at least somewhat expendable. However, viewed holistically, the real apartheid is a caste/class system of internal colonialism fully integrated into a global market system. And as apartheid in South Africa both reflects and reproduces that global system, it may not be expected to yield to purely political and social reforms.

## GLOBAL APARTHEID

A more formal expression of the "official story" on the reform of apartheid is that South Africa's homelands (held on the basis of communal tenure) and the control on labor movement represent precapitalist formations. So argued, these are in a state of dysjunction with more contemporary, "rationally-developed" formations, to be spurred on by U.S. and Western assistance. Thus it can be held that to improve the human capital of the working masses is essential to an industrial society, and that improvements in the education, and training of that workforce, as well as growth in unions, and the concomitant growth of political consciousness all mean that irrational apartheid must give way; that a free market produces free people. While such factors may indeed precipitate new class formations, it is unlikely that S.A. caste capitalism can create new privileges and allegiances rapidly enough to negate their revolutionary (as opposed to accommodating) potential. As shown, South Africa's evolving formations of internal colonialism have functioned historically to reconcile the conflicting interests of the class divisions in the white caste. Further, to extend (or surrender) political emancipation to exploited non-whites is to invite the transformation of S.A. capitalism (see Sizwe, 1979). With such in mind, it is time to raise the theoretical level.

An earlier reference was made to the Reagan administration's policy in southern Africa, formally termed "constructive engagement" by Chester Crocker. Crocker stated its premise succinctly in 1981 arguing that "with the right mix of aid, policy reform, and a strongly reinvigorated role for the private sector, African peoples will opt for the growth and freedom . . . inherent in the free world's international economic system" (Crocker, 1981). The thesis is not a novel one. It is the ideological expression of global market imperatives that has historically legitimated (and in some ways driven) U.S. foreign policy in South Africa and elsewhere (see especially Chapters 8 and 9). Reduced to its essential premise, through multinational business as usual, growth and prosperity will ease the transition from apartheid and all South Africans will benefit. Viewed through an African prism, this may be the logical equivalent of the argument that what benefits the plantation benefits the slaves. However, the claim can be examined more specifically in history.

The base development of the South African economy has followed a distinctive pattern: a minority group of colonizers, both Afrikaner and British, expanded industrially through the domination of a cheap black labor force. This development has historically been facilitated and maintained through the active support of what Chester Crocker referred to as "the free world's international economic system." In point of fact, the Western world's economic system has been in South Africa for a long time, beginning with the ventures of the Dutch in 1652. This may appear to be a sufficient period in which to test the thesis that what's good for the free world's international economy is good for all South Africans. However, if one chooses to ignore most of the history of European conquest, this particular version of trickle down ideology still appears wanting. In the first three decades after World War II, while the R.S.A. gross domestic product increased by over 2,000 percent, little of this reached the black majority (Schmidt, 1985: 6).

Based on often sketchy R.S.A. sources (which have often excluded routinely impoverished residents of the Bantustans from official statistics), some portrayal of wage differentials can be attempted. In private manufacturing and construction, the ratio of white to African wages between 1915 and 1982 reached its lowest point in 1944/45 (4.2–1) and its high point in 1970 (6.0–1), before retreating to 4.4 in 1982 (Lipton, 1985: 387). The pay of African miners, consigned to this most dangerous of occupations and continuing to live for the most part away from their families, improved in the wake of improving gold prices in the 1970s. However, S.A. sources projected the white to African wage ratio at 5.5:1 for 1982 (Lipton, 1985: 388). Statistics are notoriously unreliable for agriculture, but some 25 percent of the African workforce were employed in this poorly paying sector in the early 1980s, receiving much of their compensation from payment in kind (Lipton, 1985: 382, 388). Of course, wage analysis alone only obscures the real face of caste capitalism in the R.S.A. where African *ownership* is insignificant. Indeed, the control of African labor presupposed their movement (sanctioned in law by the Land Act of 1913) from their own small farms (Tatum, 1987:7–12).

The claim of international trickle down can be juxtaposed with the counter argument of global apartheid. The thrust of this argument is with the role of the leading states of the world market system in the emergence, institutionalization, and maintenance of apartheid. The point of departure for modern S.A. Western-style development in the late nineteenth century was its mining industry. It was in fact engineers and managers from the United States who played major roles in the development of that industry. By the end of the century Americans ran approximately 50 percent of South Africa's mines, while American companies became the major source of mining equipment. And it was those who managed the mines, not the National party of the Afrikaners, who established the South African system of labor control (Danager, 1984: 47). (As one critic was to observe later, "Apartheid has meant an extension to the manufacturing economy of the structure of the goldmining industry" (Leggasick, 1974: 47).)

By the end of the nineteenth century, U.S. firms such as Singer Sewing Machine, Kidder, Peabody Co., Mobil, and General Electric were in South Africa. They were followed after the turn of the century by Ford and Kodak. U.S. companies played critical developmental roles in metals, the motor industry, agricultural equipment, and petrochemicals. Although interrupted from time to time, U.S. corporations have provided computers and other advanced technology which the S.A. police and military have employed in the automating of apartheid. Firms such as General Electric, Honeywell, and Allis-Chalmers assisted in the building of the nuclear industry in this nation, which is widely acknowledged to possess nuclear weapons (Danaher, 1984: 48). A national analysis is insufficient, of course. In 1985, West Germany and Japan along with the United States were S.A.'s leading trading partners (*World Almanac*, 1987: 612). Another major player continues to be Great Britain, which under the Thatcher government steadfastly opposed and minimized economic sanctions against South Africa on the part of the Commonwealth (where on this issue the 48 former British colonies truly remain under the Union Jack). Western transnational corporations are responsible for about 90 percent of the trade in petroleum and petroleum products (Othman and Kiss, 1986: 13), a fact of vital importance for South Africa, which has no independent oil supply.

In the past decade, U.S. corporate ties to South Africa came to be the subject of a divestment movement in the United States. As the movement peaked in the mid–1980s, some universities, religious bodies, and branches of local and state government sold or were developing strategies to sell their stock in U.S. corporations dealing with Pretoria. By 1986, some 50 universities and colleges had divested completely and public employee funds had traded stock valued at 3.4 billion. Between January 1, 1986, and October of 1987, 96 U.S. firms severed their direct investment links to South Africa leaving a total of 167 companies so tied. Yet many of the firms who "quit" the country did so in name only. Some firms, like G.M. and I.B.M., sold their subsidiaries to South African groups, which continued to market and service their products. On October 22, 1987, the Investor Responsibility Research Center announced that the curtailment of U.S. investment in South Africa was of little consequence, because many U.S. corporations established licensing and other agreements with former subsidiaries. Thus the economy of South Africa continued to have virtually unrestricted access to U.S. products and technology (*Spokane Spokesman-Review*, 1987: B6).

Despite the false front, antiapartheid forces (including the African National Congress) continued to support the divestment movement in the United Sates. This contributed to the symbolic isolation of South Africa, to the provision of moral support for those risking their very lives, and to the raising of consciousness among non-South Africans about the global nature of apartheid. Perhaps it can be argued that the United States and other member states of the "free world international economy" were already isolated, at least in a moral sense because of the commercial support for apartheid. In late 1981, the U.N. General Assembly adopted by large majorities 16 resolutions in condemnation of apartheid, seeking help for its victims and calling for international pressure. The United States voted yes on 2 of the 16, no on 12 and abstained on 2. (For a critique of the U.S. voting record in the U.N., see Beaubien, 1982.)

There is evidence that Israel has also collaborated in the South African government's policy of regional destabilization (Beit-Hallahmi, 1987). Faced with isolation, South Africa has sought to develop ARMSCOR, its government-owned company that produces and exports weapons. Israel worked openly with South Africa before the U.N. embargo of 1977, and since that time some South African arms look suspiciously like Israeli hardware. For example, the display unit of a computerized firing control system that controls the firing of as many as eight artillery pieces bears a startling resemblance to the Israeli David system. And the Skorpion antiship missile is identical to Israel's Gabriel missile. (Not only Israel, but South Korea and Taiwan appear to be collaborating with South African arms development.) Finally, the S.A. Cheetah fighter aircraft is an upgrade of the French Mirage 3E supplied in the mid–1960s.

The ties between Israel and South Africa are structural and historical. Both reflect the properties of garrison states marked by a blurring of the lines between civilian and military identity and rule, and the ready resort to armed force to control native populations. Former S.A. Prime Minister General J. C. Smuts was a fervent supporter of a separate Jewish state and had an Israeli kibbutz named after him. The name of D. F. Malan is inscribed in Israel's Golden Book of the Jews, and former chief of the Israeli Air Force General Weitzman declared that South African pilots virtually "laid the foundation" of the Israeli Air Force. In the early 1960s, the relationship chilled in the context of Israeli attempts to strengthen relations with African states. However, in the wake of the Arab-Israeli wars of 1967 and 1973, the continuing crisis of the Palestinian Arabs, and in response to initiatives led by Libya and the Organization of African Unity, Israel lost standing in Africa. Tel Aviv then moved to restore the relationship with the R.S.A. Diplomatic relations were elevated to the ambassadorial level in 1974 and Cape Town and Haifa were declared sister cities in 1975 (Metrowich, 1977: 134–37). (For more on the structural formation of Siege States, see Chapter 7.)

## SUMMARY: THE SOUTH AFRICA OF TOMORROW

The first strategy of colonialism, external or internal, is divide and rule. South Africa's strategy of retribalization extends a patronage system to African petit officials who await the withering of apartheid. Some have denounced the design. After five years of independence, Prime Minister George Matanzima of Transkei declared that South Africa viewed the bantustan as a "labor reservoir" (Tatum, 1987: 10). Of enduring significance for the factionalization of the resistance movement has been the role of the Zulu tribe, and its political arm, Inkatha. Led by Chief Gatsha Buthelezi of the Kwazulu bantustan, Inkatha has historically sought coexistence with Pretoria and trumpeted the cause of change through greater foreign investment (Danaher, 1984: 43, 70). Through 1987 and much of 1988, Inkatha and anti-apartheid forces led by the Congress of South African Trade Unions were locked in violent combat.

Official S.A. African surrogates have historically extended Pretoria's regime terror whether as members of the S.A. or the homeland police. Unofficial surrogates, clearly tied to the South African police, include the violent "vigilantes" used in one notorious instance to massively remove people from Crossroads, a black township. Under conditions of omnipresent fear and loathing in the 1980s, youthful resistance assumed a violent turn. Groups calling themselves simply "comrades" turned on collaborators and resorted from time to time to the trademark "necklace" execution by which a gasoline soaked tire was tied around the neck and ignited (Tatum, 1987: 82–84). Any authentic contribution of the comrades will be judged in their ability to retreat from a single-minded punishment of collaborators to form alternative structures of governance in the townships, and to inspire participation on the part of older Africans.

The unitary appeal of the African National Congress (banned since 1960) can be juxtaposed with the continuing fragmentation in some quarters of the resistance movement. Its original Freedom Charter (Brownlie, 1971: 437–47) was adopted in 1955 by 3,000 delegates from all walks of life who met at Kliptown, Johannesburg. In addition to the ANC, the South African Indian Congress, the Coloured People's Organization, the South African Congress of Trade Unions, and the Congress of Democrats participated. The charter and its later amplifications form an ideological link between liberation and a distinctive African socialism intent on economic justice. It is grounded in a condemnation of European colonialism, and the inclusion in the struggle of other ethnic minorities. The ANC charter establishes the premise of nonracial democracy; holding that South Africa belongs to all who live in it with black and white as equals. ANC ideology calls for an Assembly of the People to replace the S.A. parliament, local self-government, and the preservation of the authentic multiethnic culture of its diverse national groups.

On the productive side, the ANC has stood for the transfer of mineral wealth, banks, and monopoly industry to the ownership of the people as a whole. In addition to public ownership of the major means of production, ANC ideology has historically favored land reform, equality before the law, human rights (free speech, the right to assemble, to publish, to worship, and to educate) and employment rights (including equal pay for equal work for men and women of all races, unemployment compensation, and the right to form unions, to sick leave, and to maternity leave on full pay). Also embraced have been freedom of movement, decent housing, rent and price controls, and free medical care and hospitalization. On the international side, ANC ideology calls for negotiation to end disputes, and declares that "Democratic South Africa shall take its place as a member of the OAU and work to strengthen Pan-African unity in all fields. Our country will actively support national liberation movements of the peoples of the world against imperialism, colonialism and neo-colonialism" (Brownlie, 1971: 447).

It is clear that the ANC offers a clear repudiation, not merely of S.A. racial separation and domination but the global design of the apartheid system. Breaking free of the economic domination of the capitalist world market will be extraordinarily difficult and can advance only in stages. However, the authentic development of the devastated African continent is dependent on the establishment of new horizontal relations among its states, in concert with the progressive minimization of the vertical ties between periphery and core that strengthen dependency. A democratic South Africa, with its immense wealth and industrial base can become in the twenty-first century, an engine for new regional and (in concert with progressive sub-Saharan and North African states) a more encompassing continental development. And it is within this higher drama that S.A. state terrorism continues to be played out.

## NOTES

1. Haig held positions in each dimension of the elite triad identified by C. Wright Mills. After resigning from United Technologies he briefly served as secretary of state

under the Reagan administration and later mounted an unsuccessful bid for the Republican nomination for the presidency in 1987.

2. Certainly, the U.S. Congress is not of a single mind on the apartheid question, though few appear to explore the global nature of this system. However, the subcommittee in question offers an exemplar of the dominant ideology of terrorism in R.S.A., with the framing of international issues in terms of the "Soviet menace."

3. On December 3, 1988, the Associated Press reported that South Africa was well into its third year of emergency rule, by which antiapartheid activists would continue to be jailed without charge, press controls would be tightened further, it would be illegal to quote members of any of the banned resistance groups, and it would be unlawful to promote the boycott of elections that retain the structure of white rule. In 1988, a total of 32 organizations were banned including the largest antiapartheid organization, the United Democratic Front.

4. UNITA (National Union for the Total Independence of Angola) in Angola and RENAMO (Mozambique National Resistance) in Mozambique are strongly tied to the R.S.A.

5. On December 22, 1988, the Associated Press reported that South Africa signed an agreement to end its 73 years of control of Namibia and to make the continent's last colony a politically independent nation in 1990. SWAPO was not a party to the accords. Whether Namibia will experience a social transformation and an end to settler domination and whether South Africa will remain neutral will be the questions of the 1990s.

6. For an exploration of the theoretical link between U.S. militarism and imperialism, see Magdoff (1970).

7. For an excellent analysis of the society-wide scope of the Soweto rising, see Hirson (1979).

8. Important general references for this section include Fredrickson, 1981; Robertson and Whittier, 1978; Wilson and Thompson, 1969; Moleah, 1984.

9. It was not that British colonists looked upon the blacks in Africa as equals. The British conception of empire was rooted in a paternalism by which colonial subjects of the crown were cast as the beneficiaries of enlightened rule. This view of enlightened imperialism clearly would have been contradicted by the enslavement of the subject population. However, there is a material side to this argument that is perhaps more telling. Owing to their central industrial position in a system of world-market trade, the British were not dependent on archaic forms of slave labor. Hence, slavery was abolished throughout the British empire in 1834.

10. Whites constituted 15.7 percent of the total population of S.A. in 1980; Asians 2.8 percent; "coloureds" 9.0 percent; and Africans 72.5 percent, with the last two categories expected to grow proportionately in the future (Marger, 1985: 203).

# 6

# "Terrornoia" and Zonal Revolution: The Case of Libya

> Libya's wealth and Qaddafi's ideology may pose threats to other governments in Africa. Nigeria, the second leading U.S. supplier of imported petroleum, has a vast Islamic population—thus there is some fear that an ideology emphasizing a return to traditional practice and the sharing of national wealth along socialist lines could have much appeal.
>
> U.S. government analyst Raymond W. Copson, Foreign Affairs and National Defense Division

> The Americans fear that his [Qaddafi's] charisma and egalitarian philosophy ... may attract many in Africa even beyond the 250 million Moslems who appear to be his prime target. The Reagan Administration and some conservative African regimes fear that he may influence the socio-economic and political order on the continent to the detriment of their economic and political interests.
>
> *Africa Now*, February 1983

For the United States in the 1980s, the "war on terrorism" has been conducted on a variety of fronts, including the ideological, with the media enlisted to construct the dominant imagery for the politics of fear. Yet the question of terror does not remain at the level of ideas alone. Whatever the level of analysis, from the organized behavior of the modern state to the random acts of vendetta, the question of terrorism takes human form. Both victims and victimizers are real; they are men, women, and children caught up in cycles of violence and pain. On the larger ground of history, terrorism is ultimately about relationships; both the logical connections that must be made if one is to define, analyze and explain, as well as the social associations that bind people in more or less enduring patterns of cooperation and conflict, order and change, repression and struggle.

To define terrorism is to first identify the common properties of what appear to be drastically different forms of dread and fear. This means to tie the more dramatic images of violent death, with the private pain of the "other victims." When an 11-year-old citizen of the United States named Natasha Simpson was killed in a raid of rage carried out in the Vienna airport in December of 1985, she was rightfully mourned in much of the world as a victim of terrorism. But when terrorism assumes its more subtle face, when it appears as hunger and malnutrition and disease, or when its victims are crushed by the military and police power of the state, something is lost in translation.

The massive scope of the greater tragedy is somehow beyond the personal images that drive the "human interest" story so captivating to the Western media. In a privatized society, it is as if the social or collective nature is lost, and only individual tragedy can be recognized, named, and responded to. The "One" retains a face, and the suffering of the One constitutes a crime against the person. But the "many" somehow lose that uniqueness required in a privatized society to confer existence. Their terror is dehumanized by the cold formality of statistics; the broad sweep of their tragedy only insures anonymity. Thus, to those for whom the individual is the only reality, a crime against humanity is somehow unreal, it is unfathomable, it is an abstraction. In this quintessentially Western obsession with the person, people disappear.

The relationships in question go beyond the connections that help us define the greater terror. Real people, as they play out the drama of everyday life, are caught up in objective relations of differing form and scope. At a higher level, the explanation of terrorism commands us to examine the conflict of differing social worlds representing differing forms of economic organization and political rule. In its global context, the question of terrorism is bound up in the point and counterpoint of rival nation-states; in forms of colonialism old and new, and in the struggle between those who perceive themselves the guardians of civilization and their blood-foes seeking liberation through all available means.

But what happens when a state astride the modern world economy confronts another that has only recently asserted its independence from colonial forces? What if the first state is consigned by its status in history to protect, defend, and expand that international market system? And what if the second state, relatively small and weak, is also playing out an historical role? What if it seeks alignment with other movements and states and offers ideological and material support to those committed to the transformation of whole societies? And what if ultimately this small state on the periphery offers a grandiose utopian vision calling for an end to existing hierarchical relations among rich and poor nations on a world scale? In such a confrontation, the conditions are ripe not only for political violence, but for the polemic of terrorism.

## LIBYAN TERRORISM: THE OFFICIAL STORY

An understanding of Libya must be gained through historical inquiry, but the official story on Libyan terrorism is of recent vintage. Despite the clash between Libya and the West since the Al Fatah revolution began (September 1, 1969), it was not until the 1980s that the question of the Libyan revolution was transposed into the now familiar language of international terrorism. As noted by Reagan administration Assistant Secretary of State for African Affairs Chester A. Crocker, both Ronald Reagan and his first secretary of state, Alexander Haig, expressed early in the first year of the Reagan presidency their serious opposition to "Libyan misconduct, including support for international terrorism and interference in the internal affairs of other countries" (United States Senate, Commitee on Foreign Relations, 1981: 2).

Summarizing broadly, the Reagan administrations's early view can be reduced to a few broad contentions detailing the Libyan menace. On May 29, 1981, Alexander Haig charged that Libya's oil revenues "are almost exclusively diverted to the purchase of armaments, the training of international terrorists and the conduct of direct interventionism in the neighboring states of Northern Africa" (quoted in Perdue, 1985: 41). On July 8, U.S. Assistant Secretary of State Crocker continued this line, accusing Libya of developing a diplomacy of subversion in both Africa and the Arab world. But, more to the point, according to Crocker: "It is a diplomacy of unprecedented obstruction to our own interests and objectives" (U.S. Senate, 1981: 2). Further, under Muammar Qaddafi, Libyan goals were defined by Crocker as dangerously far-reaching, involving the possible unification of an Arab and Islamic bloc. These forms of unification, including such constellations as Pan-Islamism or Pan-Arabism (and Pan-Africanism), were seen to threaten the existing order of territorial boundaries. Again, in the official view, the purpose of such a vision was expansionary: the absorption of "Arab and Muslim leaders into a Libyan-dominated state" (U.S. Senate, 1981: 2). And finally, Libya was linked with the Soviet Union as states that "share many common goals in Africa" (U.S. Senate, 1981: 4).

The objectives of Libya, as expressed by Assistant Secretary Crocker in 1981, were further seen as a threat to the state of Israel. In what was to be a recurring theme of the Reagan administration, Libya was accused of supporting "Palestinian terrorist organizations" (U.S. Senate, 1981: 3). In like manner, the claim was made, supported by some African leaders with strong ties to the United States, that Libya was actively involved in internal efforts and movements committed to the subversion of their governments. In service of these aims, Libya's Qaddafi was held to employ a variety of methods. He was accused of drawing neighboring nationals into Libyan military units, of funding African political parties, of providing financial assistance to opposition newspapers, of providing budgetary support for certain African goverments, of using diplomatic facilities to support clandestine operations, of military aggression (in the case of neighboring Chad), and of assassinating Libyan opponents abroad.

With the die of U.S. policy toward Libya in the 1980s cast, subsequent allegations and events came to form an almost bizarre international drama, with the world's ranking superpower squaring of against a recently independent desert nation with a population of some 3.5 million persons. In the month following Chester Crocker's testimony on Libya delivered before subcommittees of the U.S. Senate's Committee on Foreign Relations, two key events occurred. On August 3, 1981, *Newsweek* published a report that the House Select Committee on Intelligence had protested in a letter to the president a Central Intelligence Agency "destabilization" plan directed toward Libya. The committee was concerned with reports that the C.I.A. was planning a disinformation campaign abainst Libya in the press, that an effort would be undertaken to organize Libyan counterrevolutionaries living abroad into a government in exile, and that support would be provided for guerrilla operations inside that country. The Reagan White House denied the existence of such a plan. However, a broad range of U.S. actions clearly designed to end the Qaddafi era in Libya were to be undertaken. These were justified by a continuing barrage of accusations, many couched in the language of "international terrorism."

Also in the month of August, 1981, the Reagan administration sent the Sixth Fleet into the Libyan-claimed Gulf of Sirte to conduct maneuvers and assert the right of "innocent passage" in international waters. The subsequent shoot-down of Libyan aircraft, the saga of Libyan "hit-teams," and a seemingly endless list of other accusations contributed to the high drama of terrorism through the 1980s. (Some of the more notorious of these were examined in Chapter 3 and need not be repeated here.) Libya and Qaddafi became prime players in the feared "Islamic Resurgence," puppets of the Soviet Unoin, a threat to Western civilization, major players in a terror network, and the new international version of Murder, Inc. The ideological linkage gave Libya star billing in U.S. demonology (Chomsky, 1986: 123–55 passim).

An ideological analysis of the official story of Libyan terrorism raises serious questions of credibility, as do the repeated failure of officials to meet the burden of proof, relying instead on *ad hominem* arguments and the legitimation of the office. Such appeals to prejudice, stereotypes, and selfish interests are especially troublesome when they speak to powerful underlying ideological currents. *Ad hominem* arguments are masterful devices for the subtle shifting of an argument away from the merits of logic and evidence and along the lines of national chauvinism. They are indications of the weakness of most political arguments that resort to "buzzwords" (both positive and negative) that relieve people from the burden of thought. With these cautionary notes in mind, we turn to two of the more credible allegations of Libyan political violence.

As noted in Chapter 3, Amnesty International attributed 14 killings of political opponents (four abroad) to Libya through 1985 (Amnesty International, 1985). It is clear that some Libyans lost substantial property and political power because of the revolution. Some have been widely suspected of collaborating with the U.S. C.I.A. to assassinate Muammar Qaddafi, or to form a government in exile, or to sponsor coups inside the country. (It should be recalled, that the very policies of the Reagan administration were designed to "remove" Qaddafi by virtually any means.) Nevertheless, it is clear that the killing of counterrevolutionaries can be termed a form of terrorism, even if done in the name of protecting the gains of the revolution. Still, as two reviewers of the Amnesty International study noted: "The striking feature of Libyan atrocities is that they are the only ones whose numbers are sufficiently limited that the individual cases can be enumerated (Haiman and Meigs, quoted in Chomsky, 1986: 127). The point is not that a low level of political killings are unimportant. Nor is it simply that U.S. client regimes have had far bloodier histories as cited throughout this work. The contrast is instead necessary to point up the possibility of larger forces at play.

In addition to political killings involving Libyan counterrevolutionaries, an episode at the Libyan People's Bureau (embassy) in London drew international condemnation. In 1984, a demonstration by Libyan counterrevolutionaries ended in tragedy, when shots fired from inside the Libyan People's Bureau took the life of a British policewoman stationed to provide protection for the demonstrators. The British government argued that the People's Bureau, and its personnel, under the immunity provisions of the Vienna Convention on Diplomatic Relations, were protected from a police assault, and consequently the assailants were not apprehended. However, as this act was carried out from inside the Libyan London embassy, it can arguably be considered an act of state terrorism, albeit of substantially smaller scale than most other attempts on the part of states to practice institutional domination through fear. Libya, as all nations, must accept political responsibility for what transpires in its missions, even when such acts appear to be reckless improvisations on the part of renegades.

With these episodes aside, it is possible to examine the question of Libya at a higher level of abstraction. Certain of the official allegations have a strong basis in fact, but are subject to far different interpretations when the world is viewed through a utopian prism. In the fall of 1986, a Public Broadcasting System special on *The Africans* drew a firestorm of criticism from conservative groups in the United States. Distinguished African scholar Ali Mazrui (who wrote and narrated the series) viewed events in African history through an indigenous prism. The negative response to two segments is quite instructive. In one, the tragedy of African life today is traced to the historical exploitation of the continent by the West. That history ranged from the slave trade to the introduction of modern technology that disrupted native patterns of self-sufficiency as well as native culture. In another segment, Libyan leader Muammar Qaddafi is presented in a very different light than most Americans are accustomed to. Generally presented as a statesman and visionary, in one graphic scene Qaddafi mourns Libyan children killed in the April, 1986 bombing raids while Ronald Reagan's voice was played for ironic effect (Clark, 1986). Once again, differing interpretations follow from the differing positions of parties in conflict.

Thus the charges that Libya and Qaddafi are persistent supporters of the cause of the Palestinian Arabs, as well as implacable opponents of the state of Israel are clearly true. However, from the Libyan side (and the side of the Arab and most Islamic countries, as well as most African states), the cause of the Palestinian Arabs is just and compelling. In their view, the Palestinian struggle is one of national liberation and it is the Israelis who, through the power of a modern warfare state, spread real terrorism. (We will examine the basis for such claims in Chapter 8.) That Libya has provided material and/or ideological support for other organizations and movements branded as "terrorist" by some is well known.

In addition to supporting the Palestinian cause, Libya has declared its solidarity with the Nicaraguan Sandinistas in Central America, with the Irish nationalist forces in Northern Ireland, and with the antiapartheid movement in southern Africa. There are many other examples of lesser known movements, and while it is an open question as to whether all of these qualify as legitimate national liberation forces, there is a pattern here.[1] Many of these movements lay claim to substantial internal support, and in some cases broad international sympathy. Taken in isolation, they seek the transformation of particular societies. Taken as a whole, they may be seen to threaten the interests of dominant states, or of existing global market relations.

Similar arguments concerning charges that are true but subject to different interpretations can also be made concerning Libyan relations with African states. Libya has been at odds with a number of states that have retained strong ties with the West. The episodic military intervention in neighboring Chad (a former French colony) is variously interpreted in the West as an attempt to subjugate the country to Libyan control, or to control the Aouzou Strip, a region reputedly rich in deposits of uranium, iron, and phosphate that Libya claims based on a pre–World War II treaty between Italy and France. However, as is usually the case in international affairs, the tale is a bit more complex.

Libyan military intervention in Chad came first in 1980 after a long and vicious civil war inside that North African state, and it came in support of a Chadian movement that took state power and signed an agreement uniting Chad and Libya. When asked to do so by the new Chadian government (under Goukouni Oueddei) and the Organization of African Unity, Libya withdrew its troops. However, with the opposition of the U.S. C.I.A., the new Chadian regime came under continuing pressure and ultimately collapsed. The successor government (under Hissene Habre) dissolved the unity agreement with Libya and, supported by French troops, fought Libyan-sponsored forces and Libyan military units in Northern Chad.

By late summer of 1987, the United States had doubled its military aid to Chad to $32 million, and was actively supporting Habre's stated intention of capturing not only the disputed Aouzou strip but the Aouzou base, about half of which is inside Libya. In opposition to the French position, which called for international arbitration to settle disputes, the *New York Times* reported on November 7, 1987, that the United States was supplying heat-seeking Stinger missiles to the Habre government. From the U.S. side, the Chadian conflict represents still another part of the strategy to contain Libya and destabilize the leadership of Muammar Qaddafi (Sinai, 1987). From the Libyan view, Chad is simply another arena where Western colonial powers continue to exercise their influence. Chadian conflict remains far from settled, and although there is no doubt that Libya has intervened in Chadian affairs, Libya is not alone.

The second example of Libyan military intervention is found in Uganda. Tripoli's early support for Idi Amin, the dictator of Uganda until he was deposed in 1979, appears to have put Libya at odds with much of Africa, especially Tanzania, a progressive African state on Uganda's border that intervened militarily in Uganda in 1972 and 1979. While Amin's regime fully qualifies as an example of state terrorism, the Libyan role once again cannot be understood in isolation. The actual role of the Libyan militiary in Uganda was small (with perhaps 400 troops involved in 1972, and approximately 2,000 troops in 1979, which did little more than pave the way for Amin's flight from Entebbe.) But it is not the scope of military involvement that is at issue. Libya's early support for Amin was prompted by regional politics. In an attempt to counter Arab-African ties in the continent, Israel had worked furiously to establish a diplomatic presence in 29 African countries between 1957 and 1967. During the sixties, Israel also sought to increase its volume of trade on the continent to acquire the new markets and raw materials necessary for its fledgling industries. The aid programs were modestly funded, but between 1960 and 1966 Israel signed technical assistance programs with 30 of 38 African states. Between 1958 and 1966, some 5,000 Africans were training in Israel, and during this era twenty bilateral aid agreements were signed between Israel and African nations. Then came two events that were to disrupt the Israeli agenda for Africa.

During the Arab-Israeli war of 1967 only six African states supported the Arab position, while the majority remained silent. However, in the aftermath of the war it became clear that the Israelis had no intention of returning Arab land. After the 1969 overthrow of the Libyan regime by forces led by Muammar Qaddafi, Libya became perhaps the one Arab state most staunchly opposed to the Israeli efforts to penetrate Africa. When Israel refused to return Arab land and declared that its occupation of the whole of Jerusalem was irrevocable, relations with the Organization of African Unity grew strained.[2]

In Uganda (which had only gained independence from British rule in 1962), the Israeli presence was strong under Ugandan Prime Minister, Milton Obote. After Idi Amin seized power in 1971, the following year saw the expulsion of the Israeli technical assistance team of some 470 persons. Shortly thereafter, it was Libya that sent aid and advisers, giving rise to the conjecture that a deal had been struck with Amin beforehand to remove the Israelis (Ishmael, 1974: 175–80). Whatever may be said about Libya's soiled relations with Idi Amin, they must be understood in the larger context of anticolonialism. This is because, from the perspective of Libya and many African, Arab, and Third World states, Israel's relations with a subject Palestinian Arab population, as well as its military strikes on Palestinian fighters, villages, and camps inside Arab states as far away as Tunisia in North Africa, render it an internal and international colonial force.

## THE SPECTER OF ZONAL REVOLUTION

With the consideration of the Chadian and Ugandan issues in hand, it is possible to consider the larger question of Libya. Why did Libya become the unlikely symbol of the War on Terrorism during the Reagan years? If Libya is too small to be a military threat to the continent, much less to the Middle East, if the involvement in terrorism as conventionally defined has been small in scale and basically indirect, then why the uproar, why the polemic, why the economic sanctions, why the military intimidation, why the use of airpower as a weapon of assassination? The critics of "terrornoia" in the 1980s were quick to argue that Libya was a target of convenience, only a step above Granada, and that the politics of state coercion (including the use of deadly force) presented little real risk to the U.S. administration. The portrayal of a superpower behaving as an international bully is plausible, and doubtlessly true in part. The probability of real threat (measured in attacks on U.S. citizens or other targets) must be assessed as insignificant, especially as the "terrorist" capability of Libya appears to have been constructed to a large degree by the administration and a compliant media. However, it is also plausible to ask whether there were more substantial forces at play in the shattering of U.S./Libyan relations in the 1980s.

## LIBYA AND THE MAGHRIB: SUCCESSIVE COLONIZATION[3]

In North Africa, a region transecting the nations of Libya, Tunisia, Algeria, Morocco, and Mauritania has been known historically to its indigenous Arabs as the *Maghrib*.[4] Commencing some seventeen centuries before the birth of Mohammed, a succession of colonizers including the early Phoenicians, Greeks, Romans, and Vandals established settlements and systems of rule and tribute there. The history of conquest continued through the mid-twentieth century, with Arab movements of national liberation bringing down French colonial rule. The Libyan saga will be examined more precisely, but it should be remembered that the peoples of the region share a common history founded not merely in culture and faith but in external domination. This realization compels the conclusion that change may not ultimately be confined to narrowly defined movements for national independence. Indeed, the authenticity of a revolutionary movement (measured in part by a potential to end dependency relations) must be judged by its potential to transcend national boundary lines, often arbitrarily drawn by colonizers. Liberation movements may be termed "national," but the European conception of nation may not coincide with indigenous definitions of a people.

The strategic significance of Libya in history is reflected first in geography. To the east are Egypt and Sudan, lands earlier colonized by the British. Former

French colonies include Niger and Chad to the south, and Tunisia and Algeria on the west. While the land mass of some 675,000 square miles is composed chiefly of the Sahara, Libya is bounded on the north by the great Mediterranean. It is this sea of power that from the time of the early Phoenicians has been vital to commerce and empire-building. It is on Libyan soil that the North African coastline makes a great curve to the south to form the Gulf of Sirte and the Sahara touches the Mediterranean.

In the sixteenth century, more modern forms of colonialism began to impact the region. Libya then became a prize in the conflict between Spain and the Ottoman Turks for control in the Mediterranean. The Turks ultimately prevailed when Barbarossa recognized the authority of the Ottoman sultan and was appointed his regent. Barbarossa's successors drove the Spanish from Tripoli and sought to control the Arabs in the region. Turkish colonialism brought the rise of regencies at Algiers, Tunis, and Tripoli. The regencies were routinely without consistent government, forgotten by the Turks, and largely dependent on income from piracy directed toward primarily European and occasionally U.S. shipping. As the "sick old man of Europe" decayed in the nineteenth century, the Ottoman regencies began to unravel in North Africa.

The dawning of a new century brought a new colonizer to the North African scene. Italy, a united state only since 1860, looked to join other European colonial powers. In 1911, the Italians declared war on Turkey in order to expand their commercial interests in North Africa. Their expeditionary force of 35,000 troops met fierce resistance from the indigenous Arabs and some 5,000 Turkish troops. However, the immediate interests of Turkey were more with the Balkans and in the 1912 treaty of Lausanne, the Turks granted "independence" to Tripolitania and Cyrenaica. These ancient lands were promptly annexed by Italy, marking the onset of a twenty-year colonial war with the indigenous Libyans.

From 1912 then, the history of Libya intersected that of a European colonial pretender on the other side of the Mediterranean. However, Italian internal history during this time was to reflect a momentous shift toward barbarism. Since the time of unification, Italian industrial development remained well behind that of England and France. In the south, larger owners staved off the land reform demanded by suffering peasants. The laws calling for compulsory, public supported education were not implemented, taxation remained regressive and government bureaucracy remained stagnant. As liberal democratic ideals withered in the dust of economic stagnation, the intellectuals grew disaffected and popular insurrections flourished. Then, on October 28, 1922, Benito Mussolini marched on Rome. The Italian colonial policy was now to bear the imprint of the new Fascist government.

Mussolini faced the fiercely independent bedouins with the new colonial policy anchored in brutish military pacification. However, pacification was easier said than done. Under the command of a middle-aged teacher, Umar El Mukhtar, a few thousand Libyan tribespeople mounted an impressive guerilla struggle against the mechanized Italian forces. In 1929, Mussolini sent his respected General

Graziani to Libya to expedite the stalled campaign. Graziani's pacification techniques included search and destroy missions, concentration camps, and a scorched earth polity intended to destroy popular support for Mukhtar's forces. In 1930, Graziani ordered the construction of a 200-mile-long barbed wire fence along the Egyptian frontier to cut Mukhtar's forces off from their sanctuaries. Still Mukhtar fought on before he was captured in September of 1931 and hanged before 20,000 of his people. In Libya still, the Lion of the Desert remains a well-known historical figure. More than this, Umar El Mukhtar was to become a symbol, fully integrated into a Libyan culture of resistance.

With the pacification of Libya now somewhat successful, Fascist Italy sought to develop its colony popularly known as the Fourth Shore. In classic colonial style, Mussolini sought to remedy unemployment at home by transporting settlers to the region. By 1940 there were over 100,000 colonists, all provided Libyan land and payments by the Italian Libyan colonization society. Then, in this crucible of conflict, came World War II—and with it, the defeat of Rommel by the Allies under the command of Montgomery at Al Alamein and the fall of the Axis powers in North Africa, Europe, and the Pacific. As a vanquished party, Italy renounced all claims to its African possessions.

Postwar Libya was governed by the British military until the United Nations implemented a directive calling for the establishment of an independent and sovereign state. In 1951, a federal monarchy was born with King Idris as chief of state. Thus the United Nations action brought the appearance of political independence. However, the Libyan people were to learn that political sovereignty is no guarantee of autonomy. King Idris, firmly in the Western camp, granted military bases to Great Britain and the United States in return for economic aid. He also provided concessions to the world's giant petro-corporations that began the search for oil. In 1959, Esso (now Exxon Corporation) confirmed the location of a major find at Zalton in Cyrenaica (American University, 1979).

During this period other forces were at play that would ultimately bring Libya into the path of the leading Western power. Also in 1959, the Eisenhower administration created a presidential committee to study the U.S. Military Assistance Program. The committee (somewhat ironically given the concern in modern capitalism with global markets) was headed by an investment banker by the name of William Draper. Its report, including annexes and supplements, reveals a familiar demon.

The Draper Committee saw the armed forces in the developing region as the dynamic agents of social reform which could be an effective counter of "Communist-extremism". ... Since the democratic forces in these Third World regions were ... generally weaker than the communist forces, the Third World armed forces were to be developed into a counterbalancing "political and social counterforce." The military officer corps [in such countries] could and should be used as "a major rallying point of the defense against Communist expansion and penetration." The corps will provide a "stable and efficient government." (Sono, 1984: 80)

More specifically, Annex C of the report featured two military assistance programs; for Brazil and Libya. Libya was deemed of strategic importance and its friendship with the West necessary to counter the growing popularity of Egypt's Nasser and the cause of Arab nationalism. Libya, if it remained under Western influence, could insure Western control of the southern shore of the Mediterranean, while holding the line against the spread of Soviet influence (not only in North Africa but the continent.) The United States had a $150 million investment in the Wheelus air base, and had subsidized the Libyan economy since "independence" in 1951. The Draper report noted that the Idris government was an ally but worried that the Libyan people appeared to fear imperialism from the West more than they feared communism. Thus, it was advised that the United States consider grooming a reliable military elite to govern the country after the death of Idris (Sono, 1984: 80–82).

The decade of the 1960s brought dramatic change in Libya. In 1961, the Sarir field, the largest in Libya, was discovered by a partnership composed of Hunt Oil (headed by Texas oil man Nelson Bunker Hunt) and British Petroleum. By the time Sarir was producing at peak capacity, some one-half million barrels a day, Bunker Hunt was taking home 30 million U.S. dollars per year. All of this was exempt from U.S. taxes because of the Foreign Tax Credit. Although the Hunt's style of freewheeling capitalism stood in sharp contrast to the Weberian style rationalism of modern transnational corporations, his anticommunist credentials were certainly impeccable. While Hunt was supporting the extreme right wing in what is arguably the ultraconservative core of the Western world system, more dramatic events in Libya were to occur. One consequence of these events was the loss of Libyan oil concessions to the Hunt dynasty (Hunt, 1981).

The specific plundering of the petroleum wealth of Libya by Nelson Bunker Hunt was only a more bizarre outcropping of the neocolonization of this North African society. The 1960s gave evidence not only of Western control of oil production (signaling in turn the unequal exchange that marks dependency relations), but a bloated and ineffective bureaucracy, the decline of agriculture and other industries necessary for self-sufficiency, the rise of an indigenous elite sustained through import consumption of luxury items, and negligible improvement in the conditions of ordinary people. Exported petroleum was an enormous bargain for the industrial world at $3.00 a barrel. But the quality and quantity of Libyan crude could have made a difference even at this price with more effective mechanisms of internal distribution. Yet, by the end of the decade, Libya was a rich land with a poor people.

## The Al Fatah Revolution

On the first of September, 1969, the Free Officer's Movement, consisting of some 700 young officers and enlisted men, carried out a painstakingly planned, nonviolent coup initiated in Benghazi.[5] On September 7, 1969, the Revolutionary Command Council, consisting of 12 members of the movement, announced that a 27-year-old Captain, Muammar El Qaddafi, had been promoted to colonel and made commander-in-chief of the armed forces. Ironically, there is some evidence that the U.S. C.I.A. saw in Qaddafi the potential for the installation of the reliable military elite that would defend Western interests in the region (Cooley, 1981). However, this forecast of Third World currents was to prove as accurate as the C.I.A.'s negative assessment of popular support for the Cuban Revolution in the early 1960s, and its failure to understand the instability of Iran's Mohammed Pahlavi in the late 1970s.

Qaddafi was born a bedouin, to a family of stockherders in 1942, and his biography was to intersect Libyan and Arab history at critical junctures. On the one hand, his conscience was seared by the social, political, and economic inequality of his native Fezzan. Indeed, conditions in the Libyan south were even more appalling than those of Tripolitania and Cyrenaica. At the same time, it was the bedouin life that nurtured egalitarian beliefs in the dignity and value of ordinary people, and strong opposition to all forms of elitism. Other intersections of history and biography were more specific.

Qaddafi was to inherit Nasser's dream of one great Arab nation, a vision necessarily rooted in anticolonialism. In this context, the founding and expansion of the state of Israel symbolized more than a blood feud between Semites or the clash of great systems of faith. Viewed through the ideological prism of pan-Arabism, the building of a Jewish state meant the continuation of Western-style institutions and culture in the Middle East. Thus the European founders of Israel, driven though they were by both the terrible and more subtle forces of marginalization, could only reproduce Western institutions in the region. This process flew in the face of the surging cause of Arab nationalism and decolonization.

The most charismatic symbol of Pan-Arabism in the decades of the 1950s and 1960s was Gamal Abdul Nasser of Egypt. It was his broadcasts over Radio Cairo that developed in the young Qaddafi an early commitment to the formation of one unified Arab nation. While in secondary school in Sebha during the late 1950s, Qaddafi organized student groups in support of Nasser (Habib, 1979: 81–86). These early attempts to build a larger consciousness in Libya spread, and during the Sebha demonstrations of October 5, 1961, thousands were involved in expressing their support for Nasserism. A later demonstration was planned in support of the Algerian resistance; engaged in a fierce struggle against the last remnants of the French colonial rule in North Africa. As a leader of these movements, Qaddafi was interrogated by the wali of Fezzan (Sayf al Nasr) who quite correctly feared that the most immediate target of anticolonialism inside Libya would be the Libyan regime itself. Qaddafi was ultimately expelled from Fezzan and barred from attending its schools. In 1963, he entered military college and continued to participate in secret revolutionary activities along with other army officers who came to form the Free Unitary Officers. Within six years, the infiltration of the military by revolutionary officers was complete, and the Libyan revolution began.

## Authentic Independence

Libyan history should be understood in specific terms, but certainly not in isolation. Libya is Arab, it is Islamic, it is African, it is Mediterranean, and it must be configured with those peoples who together comprise the Middle East. Its revolution must then be understood not simply in terms of its content but in terms of its implications for broader (at least regional and perhaps global) forces of change. The clash between Libya and the United States must therefore be moved to a higher plane of understanding. For in theoretical terms, the question of terrorism may disguise a symbolic war on the broader forces of authentic liberation at work on the periphery. In the long ideological history of the term, terrorism in the context of colonialism has been routinely used by existing regimes to delegitimate forces of national independence. However, in the Libyan case, the revolution is without borders.

Colonialism in formations old and new has been the source of a structural transformation in Africa and the Middle East. By means of its processes, indigenous peoples came to serve the metropole, with dependency and inequality reproduced both externally and internally. Yet it is clear that a shared history of imperialism has not, in and of itself, insured the emergence of new and authentic conceptions of development and revolution. Stated forthrightly, many states in this expanded region are nominally independent (in political terms), but they remain economically dependent; consigned to peripheral status as a provider of raw materials and cheap labor in an international market system. The continuing absorption of former colonial possessions into a transnational economy is thus a material fact that does not necessarily fade with the coming of new political identities. Conversely, the transformation of a society in ways that seem to jeopardize a larger zone within the periphery (for example, Africa and the Middle East) may raise that society's historical, material, and symbolic standing.

With this sense of global relations in mind, the question of conventionally defined terrorism becomes something of a side show. The center stage of history features instead the emergence of new institutional forms and alternative ideologies that may embody the essence of an authentic revolutionary movement. The word *authentic* is from the Greek *authentikos*, the roots of which are *auto* ("self") and *entea* ("instruments"). To embellish a bit, the authentic revolution involves placing the instruments of production and rule, as well as the means of cultural enhancement and preservation, in the hands of what has historically been a subject population. In world-system terms then, an authentic revolution means more than altering the internal relations of economic inequality, political domination, and social oppression. It means to begin to alter the relations of global dependency. Thus an authentic revolution cannot be confined to the level of one society, but must signify a broader movement for change.

It should be clear that the problematique of revolution requires a transcendent explanation. Neither the nation-state (including its narrowly conceived political factions and administrative units) or the personalities of leaders can be made preeminent. Despite the popularity of viewing conflict in national political terms, larger constellations of power are at work that signify alliances of global and historical proportions. States then reflect and dialectically reproduce these greater forces that embody international markets, an international division of labor and an international resource base. Also dangerous is the convenient thesis of the super-power chessboard, which reduces all emerging peoples to pawns, satellites, or poxies of the United States and the U.S.S.R. The simple if ignored reality of history is that national superpowers come and go. What remains are the age-old conflicts inherent in institutional responses to the imperatives of production, distribution, rule, and dignity.

Finally, a critical analysis must transcend nondialectic and deterministic conceptions of culture. Imperialism certainly has a cultural side, but culture should not be allowed to mask underlying material forces. Ironically, the issue of a misplaced causal analysis of cultural and superstructural forces is not simply a puzzle for intellectuals. Actual movements of resistance may appear to represent a revolutionary focus on the symbols of domination (modernization, westernization, etc.); when their role instead is one of *reactionary negation*. Symbolic crusades against imperial culture (see Chapter 8 on Iran) are often rooted in a call to traditionalism. In the sense of political culture, traditionalism embodies certain conceptions of rule and authority that may be out of phase with the historically specific requirements of a society in crisis. Thus a contradiction remains when, in the name of cultural purification, the energy of resistance movements is spent only in negating the customs of foreign masters and "infidels." Stripped bare, such movements legitimate the resurrection of archaic structures of authority that are timeless only in the minds of true believers. This focus, which seeks to find the future in the past, can only replace failure with failure. With the above caveats in mind, it is possible to consider the Libyan revolution.

### The Real Libyan Menace

In addition to supporting forces (whether authentic or not) asserting the cause of national liberation, and beyond its antizionist stance, Libya played an historical role in altering the relations of dependency involving petro-corporations and Western consumers on the one side, and the oil-producing states on the other. This role began to be played out shortly after the September 1, 1969, beginning point in the social transformation of this North African state. It illustrates quite clearly the regional implications of this revolution, and offers one more historical reason for the gathering storm in Libyan-U.S. (more generally, core-periphery) relations. In a review that is otherwise harshly critical of Libya and Qaddafi, we find the following:

In the view of many analysts, Libya played a crucial role in world oil affairs during the early 1970's by taking the lead in forcing prices upward and breaking the control of the major international companies. Libya's revolutionary leaders skillfully pressured the 23 oil companies operating in the country to accept their terms, using selective nationalization as a weapon. By 1974 the government had taken over about 60 percent of the country's oil production. (Berger, 1984: 192)

In a far more extensive study of the role of OPEC in the world economy, Abbas Alnasrawi notes:

Leadership had been provided (on increasing the price of crude) by the new government of Libya, when it achieved what seemed beyond the capability of one government— higher oil prices and tax rates. The Libyan breakthrough, which set in motion the events leading to the Tehran Agreement, was by all accounts a turning point in government-company relationships. (1985: 6)

It should be self-evident that a key-player in the alteration of the structural relations of the world petroeconomy would be defined by the defenders of that order as dangerous. But there is more to the international role of this small country. Libyan aid to Africa has not been limited to support for national liberation forces (generally called international terrorism in the Reagan era). Throughout its contemporary history, Libya has channeled aid through *multilateral agencies*, including the Arab Bank for Economic Development in Africa, the OPEC Special Fund, the Islamic Development Bank and the U.A.E.-Libyan Fund for African development. *Joint banks and development companies* financed by Libya have provided development aid to Togo, Chad, Uganda, Niger, and Mauritania. (Libyan contributed $5 million U.S. to the Libyan-Togolese bank.) Other structures for development include *joint holding companies* in Uganda (with a working capital of $50 million U.S.) and Burundi, and *jointly funded development companies* to finance projects in agriculture, mining, fishing, and industrial production in African countries such as Guinea, Gabon, Rwanda, the Malagasy Republic (Madagascar), Togo, Ethiopia, Mozambique, and Mauritania. A "soft loan" of $50 million to Guinea in 1978 to be applied to the construction of a dam and alumina plant, and a direct grant (of $128 million) to Burundi for a road development program represent examples of other African aid. In affirming its Islamic identity, which is an important international cultural identity, Libya has helped fund the U.A.E.-Libyan Commission for Islamic Cultural Centers in Rwanda, Gambia, and elsewhere. These centers include a mosque, but also schools, libraries, and dispensaries (Sono, 1985a: xi–xii).

Although many Arab states have contributed to the development of Africa, there is some evidence of a distinctive ideological imperative operating in the case of Libyan aid. Qaddafi has arugued that other Arab states offer government-to-government aid while Libyan cooperation is based on whether projects serve the "grass roots, the African citizen, the masses" (in Awan, 1985: 40). Whether this position has material (as opposed to ideological) significance is unclear, but it is at least suggestive of an understanding that aid may develop underdevelopment rather than foster authentic independence. Taken as a whole, aid and its underlying ideology, together with the other dimensions of Libyan international policy, may be suggestive of transnational revolutionary influence, bent on the altering of dependency relations in this zone of the periphery.

**Ideological Synthesis**

In an assessment of the brief history of the Libyan revolution, the focus cannot be on the international arena alone. Exporting a revolution means something quite different from anti-imperialism, however defined. Further, despite the official Western story, exporting revolution is not synonymous with military conquest and subjugation. If revolutionary Libya has entertained serious dreams of territorial expansion, and there is no historical evidence to support this view, its limitations are evident. What can be exported are: (1) material forms of aid, including arms, for what are defined through the Libyan prism as authentic national liberation forces; (2) ideologies of liberation grounded in, but not confined to, Libyan history, and (3) conceptions and practices of economic development and political organization that offer some substance to the recurring call throughout the Third World for collective self-sufficiency.

In the mid–1970s, Muammar Qaddafi went into seclusion with the task in mind of preparing an ideological treatise on the Libyan revolution. What emerged as the Green Book (1976) contains what Qaddafi termed the *Third Universal Theory*. It stands less as a set of formal explanations than as a number of broad ethical premises on political, property, and social relations, as well as a design for the political organization of direct democracy. The phrase *Third Universal Theory* is telling in that Qaddafi attempts to construct an alternative to the two opposing Western ideologies and systems. The form of utopian ideology expressed by Qaddafi bears the distinctive imprint of Libyan history, but it is conceived without regard to national borders.

Summarizing broadly, Third Universalism attempts a revolutionary synthesis that supercedes both the structure and ideology of bourgeois order and its Marxist negation. It offers a critique of what Qaddafi views as the factionalism of Western democracy, including its political forms that are seen to mask the theft of power. (Qaddafi dismisses both the parliamentary and party systems as divisive.) On the political side, Western forms (whether capitalist or Marxist) are to give way to the alternative instruments of people's congresses and committees designed to implement a political system founded in natural rule: that of direct democracy. Third Universalism also offers a critique of wage systems, whether private or state-controlled, opting instead for the establishment of a "Partners Not Wage Earners Economy." In idealized terms, units of production would be owned and operated by groups of workers. The ethical premise is one of economic equity without which promises of political liberty are seen as empty. Stated simply by Qaddafi, "in need freedom is latent."

Given the prominence of the term *national liberation* to describe various sorts of movements, Qaddafi's conception of nationalism is pertinent. For Qaddafi, the nation represents a higher (above family and tribe) expression of the social nature of human beings, founded in a common history, culture, and language. The negation of social being and the destruction of cooperative life ultimately gives rise to revolutionary forces (often misguided and unsuccessful) that seek to establish the economic, political, and social conditions of natural egalitarianism. The Green Book is not concerned with the causes of revolutionary movements; these are seen to be rooted in all forms of domination that deny freedom in its holistic sense. The Green Book is not a manual of revolutionary strategies and techniques. Its critique of the great Western dyad is joined by an alternative vision for the ongoing transformation of society by its members. Hence the conception of revolution is not bound to a particular time or place when power may be seized by liberation forces. From Qaddafi's vantage point, revolution instead involves the emergence of new institutions that are supposed to empower the whole people, and unleash their total human potential.

**Material Transformation**

On the material side, before revolution can be exported, it must be consolidated and institutionalized on an internal scale. What is the evidence for the social transformation of Libyan society? And what in its institutions and altered social relations may influence change elsewhere? In the aftermath of the First of September movement, planning and resources were committed to providing a vastly improved Libyan educational system. Certain of the more enduring features were to include vast expansion of adult education services to combat the pervasive problem of adult illiteracy; a deemphasis of the traditional patterns of religious education (reflected for example in the merging of Islamic University and the University of Benghazi); dramatic increases in the number of schools with care given to their geographical distribution to avoid an educational form of "uneven development"; moving the requirement of compulsory education from six to nine years; new emphasis on technical and vocational training; and a commitment to college and university education (especially in studies such as engineering, agriculture, medicine, electronics, and others that would eventually lead to greater self-reliance for the local economy). In 1969, there were a total of 1,454 schools with a combined enrollment of 361,648 (Deeb and Deeb, 1982: 32, 36). By 1982, there were 4,286 primary, public preparatory (intermediate), secondary, teachers' training, and technical schools with 1,049,000 enrolled, almost one-third of the total population (Europa, 1984: 1950). In the first decade of the revolution, enrollment at the major universities at Tripoli and Benghazi increased from 4,000 to 15,000 with many Libyans seeking higher education abroad. Despite such gains, in the late 1980s Libya still remained dependent on foreign contractors and imported labor, to provide a substantial portion of the technical skills to build and operate its economic infrastructure.

The reliance on foreign labor will not be addressed by education alone. In much of the Arab world, women are bound to family and home. Among the more educated, these strong cultural constraints have eroded significantly as the importance of women in economic development came to be recognized by Qaddafi and the Libyan government (Deeb and Deeb, 1982: 64). Mandatory education laws also apply to women, and by the mid–1980s the number of women in this country's two leading universities (Al-Fatah and Ghar Younis) was approaching 50 percent of the student body. Women are also in military service, a condition that represents an enormous break with a conservative past. All of this is not to say that women are liberated in a Western sense. In the Libyan ideological system, the "liberation" of women in the West is another word for abandonment, poverty, and the destruction of the family. This view is in part a concession to a lingering system of male dominance, but it also suggests the potential for a dialectical synthesis that transcends both Western and traditional conceptions of women's roles. Be that as it may, Libyan women in the 1980s were still being encouraged to have large families, as they were channeled into such occupations as teaching, nursing, social work, secretarial work, and such industries as clothing and textiles.

On another crucial front, at the beginning point of the revolution, the Libyan housing situation was among the worst in the Arab world with some 40 percent of the population living in tents or shanty houses (Sono, 1985: xii). On May 6, 1978, the law on property ownership passed that limited home ownership with few exceptions to one house. The law had a dual effect. First, renters became instant owners, required to make mortgage payments to the government based on their ability to pay for property that the government devalued by 30 to 40 percent of its worth. By September, the estimated one-third of the population living in both public and private apartments and houses had become owners of their dwellings. Second, urban landowners who were becoming wealthy through providing housing for the influx of foreign workers in the 1970s, were compensated by the government but lost economic power. One study of Libyan revolution interpreted the distribution of housing as a device to ward off the threat rich landowners represented for the regime (Deeb and Deeb, 1982: 117).

However, in economic terms, the rapid inflation in the cost of private housing for the imported labor force during the 1970s could only drive up the cost of housing for Libyan citizens. This condition in the market clearly ran counter to the ideological mandate in Qaddafi's Green Book, whereby the "house belongs to its occupant." Thus it was not simply the growing power of urban landlords that was at issue. As the private market in housing clearly made the promise of ownership empty for a substantial number of the population, a nationalization policy was implemented. With housing defined as a "basic need" to be met by the resources of the whole people, housing programs expanded rapidly. (Sono reports that 150,000 units were built in 1985 alone (1985a: xii).)

Since the 1969 transfer of power, free health care became a right for the total population (Deeb and Deeb, 1982: 6). During the 1970s, the number of physicians in the country tripled, the number of hospitals grew from 45 to 60, and the number of beds increased from some 7,600 to over 13,000 (Ezwai, 1980). In the vital area of agriculture, the objective (commonly expressed in Third World ideology) is self-sufficiency. Given the absence of great expanses of fertile ground in this North African state, vast reclamation projects were undertaken. Although the largest involves the Gefara Plain (where 1.5 million hectares of irrigated and dry cultivation were planned), vast projects in the interior (in Jebel Akhdar, Fezzan, Sarir, and Kufra) also represented a commitment to a national food production policy.

The Libyan variety of a "green revolution" has in part been successful with the U.N. Food and Agricultural Organization reporting in 1985 that Libya increased its overall agricultural output by some 50 percent during the previous decade (Abdrabboh, 1985: 15). Libyan agricultural policy thus seemed to recognize the necessary link between the problem of agricultural production and that of uneven development. In the 1970s a linkage was drawn between increasing locally grown crops and improving the rural standard of living through the systematic provision of schools, clinics, and housing. However, the disproportionate population growth of Greater Tripoli, owing in part to patterns of internal migration reflecting the labor demands of the oil industry, suggests that planned, even development continues to face strong obstacles.

In Libya, land is not privately owned but it may be privately held. This means that farmers must follow the economic objectives of society, embodied in agricultural planning. However, the public sector in turn has routinely contracted with farmers to try to insure a fair market, while instituting a policy of agricultural import substitution. When local produce is relied on in lieu of the customary range of imported foodstuffs, some shortages will result. All of this is not to imply the existence of chronic basic foods shortages in Libya, but the goal of agricultural self-sufficiency remains unrealized. Still, an interesting agricultural synthesis has taken root. It represents an attempt to join public sector marketing, vast reclamation projects and the ultimate societal ownership of land on one side, with private holdings, private ownership of what is produced, and inheritance rights (for family members to continue to hold the land) on the other.

Collective self-sufficiency in agriculture in the harsh Libyan climate is easier said than done. For example, in the Second Development Plan (1976-1980), it was anticipated that an investment of L.D. (Libyan dinars) 942 million would generate an increased output of L.D. 90 million. In actuality, the increase was only L.D. 16 million, and Libya was falling far short of the projections in its plan (Awan, 1983: 94). Accordingly, by 1983, a massive irrigation project known as the "great artificial river" had begun with a contract worth $3 billion awarded to South Korea's Dong Ah Construction Industrial Company. The pipes to be laid reach a diameter as wide as four meters and were designed to carry 700 million cubic meters of water from underground reservoirs in the desert to the coastal plains. A second phase of production had a two-billion-dollar price tag. When completed, the river is intended to provide water for an additional 450,000 acres, doubling the irrigated land. When coupled with the cost of the reclamation ventures described earlier, the total project could reach 25 billion (Abdrabboh,

1985: 17–18; Berger, 1984: 193). Such projects are of course imperiled by precipitous declines in the world market price of oil.

Whether this dream of agricultural self-reliance is brought to fruition by the great artificial river and the reclamation projects of Libya remains to be seen. However, it is important to make two observations overlooked by critics who see this only as a grandiose scheme. First, it is clear that vast resources that might be used in the short term to finance import consumption are being invested in self-sufficiency. Whereas by Western economic standards, it might be more cost-effective to import food, this is quite beside the developmental point. Should a North African state, composed chiefly of the Sahara, be able to feed its growing population, its claim to independence and influence would be immeasurably strengthened. The second point speaks to the culture of Arabic nomads and the Islamic faith for which plentiful water, for obvious reasons, is a symbol of paradise. If under the "Protestant ethic" material success is a sign of God's pleasure, what then would an abundance of water signify to the Arab world in particular, or more generally to the 250 million Moslems who make up half the population of the African continent?

In assessing economic performance overall, it must be remembered that the criterion of *equity* is at least as important in Libya as the standard of *efficiency* measured in investment/output ratios. With this in mind, one study published in 1983 offered a frank appraisal that still holds true as the decade ends. In it the author finds that the new socioeconomic system of Libya has been important in reducing inequality in this society. There is also evidence to support the existence of *collective self-management* in economic life. However, this new system has been less than successful on the efficiency side.

> Due to immense inefficiencies in key sectors, such as agriculture and manufacturing, the fundamental structural problems facing the economy remained the same. Dependence on the petroleum sector is still very high; reliance on expatriate labor is heavy and the share of imports in total supply of foodstuffs and consumer goods is very large. (Awan, 1983: 96)

Awan attributed the problem of inefficiency to the failure to place into practice the theory of "dual-ownership" evidenced in Libyan economic ideology. In other words, the implementation of a form of property relations in which successful producers benefit directly from their production while not exploiting others remains unsolved. In an interview published in September of 1987 in the Jamahiriya News,[6] Qaddafi argued that although the problems of power, administration, incentives, and ownership have been solved theoretically, the ownership features of the worker-partner economy were not clear practically, and *could not be exported*. The reality of the Libyan economy at present begs comparisons with the Yugoslavian system in which socialist ownership coexists with forms of self-management. However, this European system has as yet no ideological imperative calling for the passing of more direct forms of ownership to groups of workers. More important, Libya has avoided crippling levels of debt incurred in the name of development.

On the political side, there appears to be some substance to the attempts to institutionalize direct forms of democracy through an intricate system of congresses and committees that invite mass participation. However, there is also considerable power to be found in the hands of revolutionary committees whose members are committed to a course of activism and leadership in building and defending the revolution. These revolutionary committees (*lijan thawriya*) represent a concession to pragmatism, and an attempt to push the revolutionary agenda. However, their existence was and is an implicit admission that new structures do not quickly and easily negate the cultural and psychological residuals of powerlessness among an historically dominated people. Moreover, once in place, leadership on the part of a political elite may in turn retard the development of the "people's authority," which occupies such a central place in the Third Universal Theory.

## SUMMARY

What then are the prospects for the spread of Libyan-style revolution beyond national borders? On the material side, there are immense obstacles reflecting both the immaturity of the transformational process and the specific nature of Libyan resources. Certainly, full decentralization and direct forms of worker ownership have not ascended. Libyans have been asked to settle at present for social ownership (with its attendant problem of central controls), a general leveling in society, and some degree of self-management. It is also clear that petroleum wealth continues to be a blessing and a curse. Libya has sought to minimize the problems evident in other oil-rich states where wealth means increasing dependence on imported consumer goods and external technological monopolies. Still, the incredibly costly programs of irrigation and reclamation, along with huge investments in manufacturing, public services, and infrastructure cannot offer a working model to other nations without such resources. Ironically, Libya's wealth has enabled it to follow the road of capital intensive development. Other countries, especially those in the Third World with strong peasant populations and more fertile ground, may have to rely more on traditional practices while learning to refuse aid tied to the Western model of development, a model that reproduces the international linkages of dependency.

The ideological imperatives of the Libyan revolution are not without significance, however. The failure to conceive of truly new institutions and new ideologies, and the failure to affirm the social being of the species has doomed many would-be revolutionary movements in Africa and the Middle East, as well as elsewhere in the periphery. Seen through a utopian prism, revolutions founded only in the charisma of a leader fail. Revolutions that confuse formal political independence from former colonial masters with authentic self-sufficiency and self-determination fail. Revolutions that are ingrown, confined unto themselves, and which do not challenge the imperial strategy of "divide the world and conquer" fail. Revolutions that retain the old colonial forms and instruments of governing and wealth-making fail; they fail because such enduring colonial structures embody the forms of domination and subjugation of the old order. It is arguable that the ideological principles of the Libyan revolution represent a design for the transformation of the periphery of the modern world-system. Such is not to say that Libyan political violence, incompetence, and a failure to distinguish authentic liberation forces and authentic development are wholly fictional. But whatever the scope of valid criticism, the full mosaic of this revolution should not be obscured by the rhetoric of terrorism.

## NOTES

1. For example, Libya, as many other opponents of the shah of Iran, provided some support for the broad-based Iranian revolutionary movement that came to be primarily controlled by the forces of the Ayatollah Khomeini. This support cooled as the bloody border war continued, but the point remains that anticolonial movements may be reactionary (see Chapter 8).

2. The OAU was formed by 32 African countries (membership reached 51 by 1986) to coordinate cultural, political, scientific, and economic policies, to defend the independence of members, and to end colonialism.

3. This section is informed by my "Ideology and the Third World."

4. Excellent references on the history of the Maghrib include Abun-Nasar, Knapp, and Laroui.

5. A succinct history of Libya and the First of September movement is in Habib (1979).

6. Libya's official name is the Socialist People's Libyan Arab Jamahiriya. Jamahiriya means "state of the masses."

# 7

# *Settler Terrorism: Israel and the P.L.O.*

In confrontation, the rioters should suffer casualties and scars, so that they know it would not end with detentions.
>Defense Minister Yitzhak Rabin on Israeli policy in the wake of the Palestinian revolt that began in December of 1987, Israeli radio, October 8, 1988

They are like grasshoppers compared to us.
>Israeli Prime Minister Yitzhak Shamir, addressing West Bank settlers on March 31, 1988

By the year 2000, we will look in the mirror and we will see South Africa.
>Israeli political scientist Shlomo Avineri

In the tortured land called Palestine by the Arabs and Greater Israel by maximalist supporters of Jewish nationalism, the rituals of state and guerrilla violence embody both the greater terror of war and the specific deeds of vendetta. The structural and ideological ties between Israel and the West (more specifically the core states of Britain earlier in this century and now the United States) are complex. So too are the patterns of opposition that involve not only the Palestinians and the Arab world, but much of the Third World in general. It is tempting to reduce these complexities to terms that are not specific to history and globally founded relationships. It is appealing to cast issues in the language of anti-Semitism, culture-clash, religious intolerance, superpower rivalry, or a Semitic blood feud. It is seductive to speak in terms of moderates and extremists on both sides, and to identify personalities, parties, and factions who either advance or retard the quest for peace. It is even attractive to throw up one's hands and argue that the grievances are so deep that no *rapprochement* is possible (a position that implicitly leaves the field to military and other forms of deadly force). But to yield to such temptations is to obscure the more transcendent forces of order and change.

In the pages to come, the question of terrorism and the state will be placed in the context of the Israeli-Palestinian conflict. Once again, there are larger relationships here, historically grounded relationships that embody the dialectic of transnational and internal colonialism. These dynamics will be specified, not only with respect to the major parties, but as they reflect factional interests within Israeli economy and polity. That the power of the Israeli state has been used to control the Palestinian population is self-evident. However, not all colonizers are created equal. All Jews in the state of Israel, as well as Jewish settlers in the occupied territories, may enjoy certain caste-like advantages that come from living in a Jewish nation. But the claim to political rights should not be confused with claims to wealth and privilege for all.

It was the descendants of the Ashkenazim Jews, who settled in middle and northern Europe after the Jewish Diaspora, who waged a violent struggle to form and defend/expand the new state of Israel. However, it is the descendants of the Sephardim, who lived originally in Spain and Portugal before the Inquisition, and many of whom entered Israel from Morocco, that now represent a demographic majority in the Jewish state. Although both groups have been served by the state, it is the poorer, more recently arrived Sephardim who now seek to use its power to redress their categorical position as economic marginals. Thus to the internal colonial dyad of Jew and Palestinian, must be added the class divisions within the *chosen*; divisions that have both preserved yet altered the nature of colonial settlement.

Maxime Rodinson's analysis (1973, originally published in 1967) of the founding of Israel as a variation of European colonialism is useful, as it specifies the institutional ties between Israel and the West. However, to his portrayal of transnational settlement must be added the compounding dilemma of new waves of Jewish settlers seeking land and sustenance. Thus the dynamics implicit in the term "settler" must be explored on two levels. Consistent with Rodinson's thesis, the founding of a Western state in the Middle East embodied European colonial processes. This is not to equate the early adherents of political Zionism with the organized programs of empire building of Britain and other imperial powers. The oppression suffered by Jews in Eastern Europe and Tsarist Russia, and the systematic genocide at the hands of the Nazis, were terrifying and real. Such conditions represented fertile ground for an ideology of deliverance; one that merged the messianic promise of religion with a secular political vision. However, the historical point should not be obscured. The ideology and objectives of the Zionist movement merged quite easily with larger imperial forces, with routine disregard for the pattern of successive victimization directed at Palestinian Arabs.

At the second level, the settling of Israel is not confined to earlier transnational history. The support of settlers and settlements in economic, ideological and military forms has become fully institutionalized at the level of the Israeli state. That such patterns can only evoke resistance at the hands of the dispossessed should be clear to all, unless the structures and processes of internal settlement are obscured by ideological forces. And it is to these forces that we now turn.

## HOW THE WEST CAN WIN[1]

In an edited book entitled *Terrorism: How the West Can Win*, Benjamin Netanyahu, then Israeli ambassador to the United Nations concluded: "The terrorist challenge must be answered. The choice is between a free society based on law and compassion and a rampant barbarism in the service of brute force and tyranny. Confusion and vacillation facilitated the rise of terrorism. Clarity and courage will ensure its defeat" (1986: 226). Reasonable people would agree that there is indeed confusion on the question of terrorism. However, it is appropriate to inquire into the nature and source of such confusion.

The contributors to Netanyahu's book stand as a "who's who" of political leaders and journalists for the 1980s. They included leading members of the Reagan administration: U.S. Secretary of State George Shultz, U.S. Ambassador to the U.N. Jeanne Kirkpatrick, U.S. Attorney General Edwin Meese, and F.B.I. Director William H. Webster. There are articles by U.S. Senators Cranston, Laxalt, and Moynahan, journalists George Will, Paul Johnson, and Claire Sterling, Israeli ministers Moshe Arens and Yitzhak Rabin, and Israeli Chief Justice Meir Shamgar, among others. The contributors were participants in a second international conference on terrorism, organized by the Jonathan Institute, named for Jonathan Netanyahu, brother of Benjamin, who was killed in the raid on Entebbe. The Second Jonathan Conference and Netanyahu's book drawn from presentations by the participants can be said to represent an exemplar of long-standing and official U.S./Israeli views on the question of terrorism. Accordingly, it deserves careful study by those interested in the ideological problematique of terrorism.

Those whose pronouncements on terrorism were delivered in the Second Jonathan Conference offered concrete identities to Ambassador Natanyahu's "forces of barbarism." As might be expected by now, those movements, states and ideologies that have historically opposed Western world interests were labeled as "terrorist." For example, Israeli ambassador Netanyahu refers to the P.L.O. as the most perfect form of a modern terrorist movement (1986: 35). Paul Johnson alleged that: "Modern terrorism dates from the middle 1960's when the P.L.O. adopted terror and mass murder as its primary policy" (in Netanyahu, 1986: 31). To be sure, the *enemies to democracy thesis* did not stop with the P.L.O.

George Shultz discerned a "league of terror" including Libya, Syria, North Korea, and Iran, while arguing that "The Soviets use terrorist groups for their own purposes, and their goal is always the same: to weaken liberal democracy and undermine world stability" (in Netanyahu, 1986: 21). In a similar vein, another contributor argued that the use of terror is legitimated both by Marxism and the Soviet constitution. According to Wolfgang Fikentscher, Article 28 of the U.S.S.R. constitution, which calls for the "assistance of the peoples in their fight for national liberation and social progress," is actually a mandate for terrorism. Hence, in the Western view, Marxism and terrorism are wedded into a monolithic evil.

There is more than a permutation of anticommunism here. Three participants in the Second Jonathan Conference found that the political nature of the Muslim faith offered a justification for "Islamic Terrorism" (Lewis, Kedourie and Vatikiotis, in Netanyahu, 1986: 65–84). Another argued that terrorism drew "on the immense financial resources of the Arab oil states" (Johnson, in Netanyahu, 1986: 31); another added Iraq and South Yemen to Schultz's "league of terror" (Arens, in Netanyahu, 1986: 84); and still others identified Cuba and Nicaragua (Borchgrave, in Netanyahu, 1986: 119). In sum then, the socialist world, the Islamic world, and the Arab world are portrayed, along with national liberation movements that seek independence from the West, as terrorist. There is no troubling ambiguity here, no weighing of complexities, no recognition of the relations of domination and subjugation. The ideological world of terrorism is clearly cast, its characters act out a morality play of good and evil, righteousness and corruption, guardians and false pretenders.

Historically, those responsible for constructing and disseminating the dominant view give little thought to the proxy forms of terror that implicate Western states. Schultz declared: "The resistance fighters in Afghanistan do not destroy villages or kill the helpless. The Contras in Nicaragua do not blow up school buses or hold mass executions of civilians (in Netanyahu, 1986: 19)."[2] At a higher level, Israeli ambassador Netanyahu employed the example of a R.A.F. raid on Gestapo headquarters in Copenhagen in 1944, where bombs hit a children's hospital. But this deed by a Western state, he declared, was only an accident of war (1986: 9). By inference, when it is the state that strikes down the innocent, then the raiders are not responsible because they did not willfully and in premeditated fashion take the lives of specific victims. It is once again, the impersonal deadly force of the state that is held up to a different standard.

The ideological construction of terrorism also impinges on interpretations of international law. Yehuda Blum (in Netanyahu, 1986: 133–38), former Israeli ambassador to the United Nations, declared:

Armed reprisals have been repeatedly condemned by states and international organizations as a violation of international law. Let us examine, therefore, the alternative recourse, namely, self-defense. Admittedly, shifting emphasis from reprisals to self-defense may be considered by some as an exercise in semantics, which it probably is: yet given the indisputable potency of language symbols, there is no reason to disregard this aspect of international law. (Blum, in Netanyahu, 1986: 135)

Having declared an intent to redefine reprisal as defense, Blum proceeds to discuss the conditions under which a state may exercise armed attack and label it as self-defense. Under Article 51 of the U.N. charter, the right of self-defense may be exercised "if an armed attack occurs". Blum cites the *Nadelstichtaktik* ("tactics of the needle prick") argument, which holds that if a pattern of needle pricks occurs, then the injured state has the right to take military action, in his words as a "legitimate response in anticipation of the next terrorist attack (Blum, 1986: 136). There are two implications in this argument. The first is that the state or its agents not only have the right to self-defense (clearly recognized by the charter), but that the state can defend itself on anticipatory grounds. Second, Blum seeks to defuse the question of disproportionate use of deadly force on the part of a state by noting a pattern of provocation.

Moving on to the question of civilian casualties, Blum argues that a sanctuary state *whether acting willingly or unwillingly* is responsible for harboring "terrorists". In effect then, civilian casualties in such a sanctuary state are the responsibility of that state, an interpretation that transfers blame from the state whose forces actually inflict the casualties. And finally, Blum argues that "self-defense" (as he has now defined it) takes precedence over the right of "self-determination" calling "self-determination" in effect a legitimating guise of terrorists. This official view of state power is quite revealing. As "self-defense" is a right of states, and "self-determination" refers only to those movements that do not hold the power of the state, the legitimacy of the state is assumed to be preeminent. This ideology of statism also brands national liberation movements (whose utopian ideology routinely includes the language of self-determination) as "terrorist."

Of course, such expressions of *raison d'état* are not confined to Israel. The Reagan State Department also warned of "preemptive strikes" as a legitimate response in anticipation of terrorist acts, while asserting the unavoidability of civilian casualties. After the bombing of Tripoli and Benghazi, the official U.S. view included the "self-defense" and "proportionality" arguments that the Israelis developed in defense of the "iron fist". On this point, Prime Minister Thatcher of Great Britain had a precondition for her political and military support for the raid on Libya: justification under the self-defense provision of Article 51 (*Time*, April 28, 1986: 17–33). That Blum's position "fits" the nature of relations between the United States and its antagonist in North Africa is not accidental. Nor is this a case of the Israeli tail wagging the American dog. There is an ideological convergence here born of Western state policy, strategic considerations of Mediterranean hegemony, the future control of Middle Eastern petroleum, and the potential of authentic liberation movements to alter global relations. It is within this more general milieu that the real nature of the conflict between the state of Israel and its primary antagonist must be assessed.

## THE P.L.O. AND THE QUESTION OF TERRORISM

With the Palestinian cause virtually unknown in the West, the Popular Front for the Liberation of Palestine (a P.L.O. affiliate) devised and implemented a strategy for high visibility hijackings of international flights between 1968 and 1970. In September of 1970, three airliners were hijacked and their 276 passengers held at an abandoned airfield in Jordan. (One jumbo jet was too large to land and was taken to Cairo.) Ultimately the hostages were bussed to Amman, but the aircraft (valued at 30 million dollars) were blown up. After a subsequent conflict with the Jordanian army, the hostages were released. Other episodes of political violence did not end as well. Selecting a global showcase, the renegade Black September group took 11 Israelis hostage at the 1972 Olympic games in Munich. An attempt was made to trade these hostages for 200 Arab prisoners held in Israeli jails. However, a botched assault at the Fürstenfeldbruck airport resulted in the deaths of all eleven Israeli hostages and five members of the Black September group (Poland, 1988: 46–56). Other examples might be cited, including perhaps the most notorious of recent episodes: the aforementioned attacks on El Al in the Rome and Vienna airports in December of 1985 by the Abu-Nidal faction.

In reviewing these and other episodes of conventionally defined terrorism, certain distinctions are often lost. To begin, the P.L.O. has broadly based support that one would not expect to be accorded to a "terrorist organization." That support is not confined to the Palestinians or the larger Arab world. The P.L.O. has been recognized by more than 130 countries around the world, and has observer status at the United Nations where it is also recognized as the sole legitimate representative of the Palestinian people. The isolation of Israel inside the U.N. and its continued reliance on the U.S. veto in the Security Council is well known. In part, the support enjoyed by the P.L.O. inside the United Nations reflects the changing composition of the member states of that organization. The U.N. began as something of a Western-dominated international club in the post–World War II era. Its General Assembly, however, has provided a forum for many nations that have emerged from a colonial past. It is within this context that the support of the P.L.O., and the opposition to Israel, must be judged.

All of this is not to imply that the U.N., the Arab world and the Palestinian people have sanctioned political violence of the Abu-Nidal type described above. Neither is it possible to somehow attribute these and similar acts to some omnipresent P.L.O. The P.L.O. is not a monolith that embodies the organization and efficiency of the modern state. It consists of a coalition of nine fronts (Amos, 1980) that are united strongly on the question of the establishment of a Palestinian state, and differ widely in ideology and tactics. The largest and better-known Al Fatah organization of Yasir Arafat features a nationalist ideology, in which political independence is central. The P.L.A. (Palestine Liberation Army) is a standing army, consisting of perhaps 15,000 fighters, under the command of Al Fatah. A clear ideological contrast is found in the Popular Front for the Liberation of Palestine (P.F.L.P.) of George Habash. The P.F.L.P. rejects the existence of a state of Israel as historically bound to Western interests, and destined to reproduce the class formations of a capitalist global order. In contrast to the political solution of independence common to many liberation movements historically, the ideology of the P.F.L.P. is informed by an analysis of political economy and features a call for the social transformation of Palestine.

"Splinter" groups that have evolved from the P.F.L.P. include the Popular Front for the Liberation of Palestine-General Command (P.F.L.P.-G.C.), whose most widely recognized leader has been Ahmed Jibril; and the Popular Democratic Front for the Liberation of Palestine (P.D.F.L.P.) formed by Nayaf Hawatmeh. The Palestine Liberation Front (P.L.F.) emerged from the P.F.L.P.-G.C., to seek an alliance with Iraq. These offshoots have retained the P.F.L.P.'s insistence that armed struggle cannot be confined to Israeli soil. Ideologically, it may be true that they are less sanquine about the prospects of a class-based revolution. Another P.L.O. affiliate is the Syrian-aligned Al Saiqa, second in size to the Fatah group, which emerged in the aftermath of the 1967 war. The Palestine National Front (P.N.F.), formed after the 1973 war to carry out operations inside the occupied territories (primarily the West Bank), and the Iraqi-aligned Arab Liberation Front (A.L.F.) conclude the list.

Certain of the more spectacular acts of conventionally defined terror attributed to the P.L.O. have been actually carried out by renegade groups. For example, it was Black September (an organization named for the month during which the Jordanian army drove the Palestinian people from Jordan in 1970) that carried out the Munich operation. This faction split off from the P.F.L.P. in 1970. Other P.L.O. fringe groups have broken with Al Fatah. In 1985, it was the faction lead by Abul Abbas that carried out the sea jacking of the *Achille Lauro*. (These episodes pale of course when compared to the bloody trail of Abu Nidal considered above.) However, in the murky world of conventional terrorism, where the state is a key player through its intelligence and special forces units, responsibility for random acts of repugnant violence is not easily assigned.

It is more than ironic that Yasir Arafat has come to personify terrorism in the U.S. media. It was at his initiative that the P.L.O. National Council decided in 1974 to seek a political solution to the question of a Palestinian homeland through negotiation and diplomacy, while not abandoning the right to armed struggle. Specifically, this strategy assumed that the new state would be formed from the West Bank and Gaza territories occupied (and increasingly settled) since 1967 by the Israelis. This decision led to the international recognition of the P.L.O., while the P.F.L.P., the P.L.F., and the A.L.F. withdrew from the P.L.O. executive committee in protest.[3] Further, in the Cairo Declaration of 1985 Arafat renounced "armed struggle" outside Israel and the occupied territories (Curtiss, 1988: 4). Given such events, the political consequences of applying the terrorist label to the major leader and front within the P.L.O. are clear. Such labels represent a rejection, not merely of vendetta violence; nor of the employment of armed struggle on the part of a resistance movement; but of diplomacy and negotiation. Further, given the international recognition of the P.L.O., the refusal to bargain with this organization is tantamount to a refusal to negotiate in any substantive fashion on the question of a Palestinian homeland. The ultimate result is to keep the conflict on a military plane.

It is not possible to understand the emergence of the Palestinian nationalist movement in isolation. From the utopian view, the drama of nonstate terror is a theatrical production staged for the benefit of an international audience of the deaf. Almost a generation passed from the establishment of the enlarged boundaries of the state of Israel in 1948 until the founding of the P.L.O. in 1964. During that period, and for four years or so later, the Palestinian struggle had been largely political. It had also been ignored. The formation of the P.L.O. confirmed that the Palestinians must have independent political institutions that would represent them as a people. Although the question of a Palestinian entity *al-kiyan al-filastini* was formerly raised by the United Arab Republic in the context of Nasser's dream of Pan-Arabism (Shemesh, 1984), it was clear that the Arab states could not take the lead in a Palestinian struggle for self-determination. It was also clear that this movement and its political wing would not be content with refugee doles and U.N. resolutions (Ahmad, 1986).

Political violence, even employed circumspectly when all other methods fail, can be a two-edged sword. In the words of Eqbal Ahmad, "today, no one denies that there is a question of Palestine (1986: 5)." However, the resort to random violence, no matter how provoked, may retard the development and use of creative tactics of nonviolence, while discrediting commando attacks directed at military targets. At a quite different level, the misdirected rage of vendetta terrorism signifies the absence of a mature revolutionary ideology. To point out that the rage is a consequence of victimization; that oppression is an incubator of vengeance would be termed mitigating factors by those trained in law. However, vendetta terror against targets of convenience can only bring scorn to a movement and raise questions about the ability of a people to form a new society.

Still, it can be argued that between 1968 and 1972 the P.L.O. made the deaf to hear again. P.L.O. hijackings ended when the organization gained a base in Lebanon and world recognition. But the *symbolism* of Palestinian skyjackings, seajackings, and international operations against Israeli, U.S., or other Western targets, no matter how repugnant and whether or not they involve disciplined forces or renegades, cannot be ignored. On the one hand, these are tactics without boundaries employed by a people without land. On the other, the targets signify the connection of the Israeli-Palestinian conflict to wider global patterns. And it is to these global patterns that we now turn.

## THE JEWISH STATE

Although Jewish nationalism has older roots, its emergence in more formalized ideological and political forms took shape in the late nineteenth century (Rodinson, 1973: 35–78). The 1881 wave of eastern European anti-Semitism directed toward Jews was a precipitating factor. However, it is also true that the formation of this ideology borrowed liberally from the broader context of an age of Imperialism. Leo Pinsker (1831–91) in *Auto-Emancipation* questioned the practicality of restoring ancient Judea, calling instead for establishing Jewish self-rule wherever a suitable territory could be found (1944, originally published in 1881). North America, Palestine, or Syria were offered as possible sites for what Pinsker called a "colonial community."

Theodor Herzl, in the Zionist manifesto *The Jewish State* (1896), noted that Jewish colonization had some roots by late century in Palestine and Argentina. He also held that the latter country was rich in resources, but that Palestine by its very name would offer a unifying symbol to would-be settlers. Thus the Zionist Organization, founded at the Congress of Basel (August, 1897), settled on Palestine as the place for a Jewish "homeland." The selection of the term "homeland" is a revealing exercise in political symbolism. Although state sovereignty was the ultimate objective, it could threaten the support of powerful nations with other clients. And too, the vision of a homeland could be expected to neutralize opposition by the religious interested only in a spiritual center, and assimilationists who held fast to their existing national identities.

For his part, Herzl depended less on the will of God and more on temporal power to secure eventual sovereign rule. That early Zionists sought to negotiate the fate of Palestinian Arabs first with Turkey, and later with Britain and other Western powers was simply an extension of the objective conditions of imperialism. Moreover, Herzl understood that Jewish colonization was bound to take a different form that other patterns of European expansion. Unlike settlers attached to a specific nation-state, Jewish settlers were imagined to someday come from all over the continent. The colony they would establish must then be fashioned from other than national-imperial cloth. Instead, a Zionist state would serve more global and transnational interests. More specifically, Herzl argued that such a state would "constitute a bulwark against Asia," and "the advance post of civilization against barbarism," with its existence guaranteed by "all of Europe (Herzl in Rodinson, 1973: 43)."

It is clear that the appeal of Palestine would be founded for some in messianic visions of return granted by God to the chosen. But the broader and sustaining ideology of imperialism conferred upon European powers and their populations a conviction of selection not limited to orthodox Judaism. Thus it is common to find in the specific ambiguities of faith, *rapprochement* with specific ideologies of domination and resistance. Religion, in dialectic relation with the more mundane processes of secular expediency, may be refined to offer sacred legitimations for the material forces of this world. Clearly, the form of the message varies with the social position of its makers and believers. Zionism in its European context offered pride and deliverance to an often victimized population. Transferred and reconstructed to fit the objective conditions of a new settler state, it was to offer legitimation for the reproduction of the colonial relations that build and maintain permanent marginalization for an indigenous population.

It was 20 years after the establishment of the Zionist Organization in Basel, in the context of world war, that Lord Arthur Balfour offered a declaration (1917) pledging support for a "Jewish national home" in Palestine. In 1919, the same Balfour noted in a memorandum that the four great powers (Britain, the United

States, France, and Italy) were "committed to Zionism and Zionism, be it right or wrong, good or bad, is rooted in age-long tradition, in present needs, in future hopes, of far profounder import than the desires and prejudices of the 700,000 Arabs who now inhabit that ancient land" (in Chomsky, 1983: 90).

Rodinson (1973) argues that the League of Nations granted the postwar mandate to Britain in part because of an agreement negotiated at the Peace Conference in Paris between the Zionist leader Chaim Weizman and Emir Faisal, the son of Sharif Hussein (and thus a representative of the Hashemite dynasty). Despite the value of Rodinson's detailed account, there were broader forces at work in these negotiations. Britain at the time was not only an imperial nation state, but a *systemic exemplar* of the global market order. Its national interests cannot be isolated from its core role in the maintenance of that system. It was within the context of this higher role that the British assumed dual responsibility, first for the oversight of Jewish immigration into Palestine, but also for supporting a particular form of Arab nationalism.

What the British recognized was the political independence of monarchal governments and feudal systems; systems that represented continuing dependency on the economic side and potential allies against the forces being unleashed in the Russian Revolution. Moreover, Arab nationalism was historically destined to proceed in accordance with the *territorial* restrictions of colonial lines drawn on maps. Thus the dream of ONE Arab nation would be thwarted in the future by the enduring legacy of colonialism: the geographical, political, and administrative factionalism of the Western model of the nation-state.

At the same time, Jews bringing capital, technical skills, and a European conception of the world could be expected to serve as a colonial outpost, or in Herzl's words as a buffer. But the real buffer, paradoxically, consisted of both Jewish settlers and Arab monarchs. The buffer was to be less a shield against specific nations, and more a force of negation directed against the uncertain future of the Arab masses in particular and the vital Middle Eastern region in general. Thus the Peace Conference of 1919 represented a convergence of systemic interests mediated through Western core states, indigenous feudal orders, and an outpost colony. This alliance of historical roles, sometimes with a changing cast of national players, has proven remarkably durable over time.

By the beginning of the mandate, and after almost three decades of independent Zionist effort, the Jewish population of Palestine in 1922 stood at only 11.1 percent of the total. Under the mandate, the percentage grew to 17.7 percent in 1931 and 28 percent in 1936. As the terrifying specter of the Third Reich grew in Germany, additional immigration pressure brought the Jewish population by 1943 to some 539,000 of 1,676,571, some 31.5 percent of the total. Despite the "push" factors behind the immigration, this dramatic reconstitution of the population could only have occurred under the mandate, with British support expressed not only through the acceptance of settlers, but through its *de facto* intimidation of Palestinians and other Arabs preoccupied with their own national independence (Rodinson, 1973: 57–58). However, as the immigration of Jews accelerated between wars so did the opposition from Palestinian Arabs.

With the failure of the Munich agreement becoming ever clearer, it was evident that Britain would not have the military force to continue to police Palestine. In May of 1939, the British Government issued a White Paper seeking to limit its problems by restricting Jewish immigration and declaring its belated opposition to the goal of a Jewish state. However, this course came too late. Under the mandate, the Zionists had gained sufficient strength and numbers inside Palestine to mount their own campaign. Nazi terror and postwar displacement meant more people would seek to flee from Europe, while Zionists inside Israel and the United States worked hard to direct the flow of that immigration toward Palestine (Chomsky, 1983: 90–93).

Thus, by the beginning of the postwar period in Palestine, the historical stage was set for the emergence of two interrelated processes. The first was the supersession of British-style colonialism through a pattern of revolt by strongly established Zionist settlers eager to set their own agenda. The second was the fashioning of a protectorate alliance with the new core state in a postwar transnational capitalist system. Each of these processes has implications for the question of terrorism and the state. But it is their interdependence that must be kept foremost in mind, even when *intra-system* revolt emerges.

Whatever the British may have come to hope for in the way of a bicultural, Western-oriented state in Palestine, the Zionist leadership viewed the mandate as a framework to guarantee the settlement that would lead to a Jewish state (Weizmann, 1949: 290–91). Thus the execution by the British of their global role, until the eve of the Second World War, proved consistent with the specific objective of Jewish statehood. When the British sought to limit settler immigration, there were consequences. What was tacitly understood within the Zionist movement became real. David Ben-Gurion (president of the Executive Committee of the Jewish Agency and later first prime minister of Israel) recanted his earlier "objections" to acknowledge the goal of statehood (Lucas, 1974: 192). A far greater consequence came in the form of a revolt by Zionist settlers against the British. However, the British role was to be assumed by a new core.

The United States survived World War II with its industrial infrastructure intact, and (paradoxically) without the stress on its resources represented by national liberation movements in the colonial world. It also emerged as the key player in a design for the postwar international economy that began with a meeting of the allies in 1944 at Bretton Woods, New Hampshire. The United States (and its currency) came to play a central role in the modernization of market relations, which took the form of new institutions of global reach such as the International Monetary Fund, the World Bank, and the General Agreement on Tariffs and Trades (Debt Crisis Network, 1985: 17–34.) It also acted to restore the European economies through the Marshall Plan and nurtured during the occupation period the rebirth of Japanese production. But in this epoch of postwar modernization, complete with new and more sophisticated relations of power and forms of dependency, the defense of the West still meant the defense of resources and influence in regions of *le tiers monde*.

Although much has been made of the role of supporters of Jewish nationalism inside the United States, their program cannot be isolated from this larger historical role of the new core. Despite the considerable influence of American groups committed to "Israeli interests," the success of such lobbying is a superstructural phenomenon. There is, as many Israeli supporters have argued, a commonality of interests that joins the two states. But the nature of that commonality is secondarily one of politics and culture. The underlying base on which the Israeli-U.S. connection was to be built is that of *world-system convergence*. The nature of that convergence is one of guardian and outpost.

The nature of the relationship between the United States as the successor core and Israel as an outpost in the periphery is evidenced in a number of particulars. Through *FY87*, total U.S. aid to Israel since statehood amounted to more than $38 billion (Washington Report, 1986: 2). Much aid has been directed toward the Israeli military-industrial complex, the exports of which grew from a value of $10 million in 1972 (U.S. Arms Control and Disarmament Agency, 1984: 61) to $1.8 billion in 1985 (SIPRI yearbook, in *U.S. News & World Report*, 1986: 37). The United States funded virtually all of the 1.5 billion dollar Lavi fighter, finally urging Israel to give up the project because of escalating costs (Fisher, 1987). In a familiar replay, workers and managers at the Israel Aircraft Industries strongly reacted to the potential loss of thousands of jobs. The cultivation by the United States of the Israeli arms industry has had several manifestations in the international arena.

Israeli arms deals in Latin America are a case in point (Bahbah, 1986). In Central America, Israel has supplied military hardware, technology, and other counterinsurgency aid to "anti-Communist" Central American regimes and movements (Jamail and Gutierrez, 1986). During its era of the Generals and the "disappeared," Argentina became one of Israel's major arms customers. Other arms clients and vendors for Israel have been Khomeini's Iran and the Union of South Africa (Beit-Hallahmi, 1987). An arms for export economy is an expected consequence of the Israeli outpost role. That the overall economy will feature stagnation, inflation, uneven development, and dependency on external aid (both public and private) are costs paid by settlers, who in the history of colonialism have often found themselves to be expendable.

## SACRED TERRORISM

The diary of former Israeli Prime Minister Moshe Sharett describes the military force of that state as "Israel's Sacred Terrorism" (Rokach, 1986). The process by which the practices and ideology of sacred terrorism have been institutionalized in modern Israel begins with the revolt of Jewish colonists against the British. Although the guerilla tactics of resisters are routinely termed "terrorist" by representatives of a threatened system of rule, two Zionist groups were noteworthy for their attacks on civilian populations. One of these was the Irgun and the other was its off-shoot Lehi, commonly known as the Stern gang.

The Irgun Tsvai Leumi, one of whose leaders was Menachem Begin, blew up the King David Hotel in Jerusalem with a loss of over 90 lives. Lehi was willing to collaborate with the Nazis against the British, and in the winter of 1941 drafted a proposal calling for the establishment of a Jewish totalitarian state that would seek relations with the Reich. The chief of operations for Lehi, who was later an official in Israeli Intelligence (Mossad) was Yitzhak Shamir (Curtiss, 1986: 4).[4] Of course, both Begin and Shamir went on to become prime ministers of the state of Israel.

The United Nations General Assembly (in its early years a Western-dominated organization) voted to partition Palestine into an Arab and a Jewish state in November 29 of 1947. At the time, some 1.3 million Arabs owned 90 percent of the land, and 600,000 Jews owned 7 percent. After partition, 53 percent of the land was given to the Jewish state (with some 590,000 Jews and 497,000 Arab inhabitants), and the remainder to the Palestinian Arab state (Curtiss, 1987: 3). Violence intensified, some of it designed as a symbolic eviction notice. On April 9 and 10 in 1948, Irgun-Lehi carried out a well-organized and systematic massacre in the village of Deir Yassin. The death count was 254 persons with some 40 percent of the casualties women and children. The Irgun-Lehi lost four members in the attack. The flight of the already terrified Arab population from land to become the state of Israel was accelerated by this deed (Rodinson, 1973: 114–15). In the ideological tradition of "sacred terrorism" old and new, the Irgun command offered a message of congratulation. "As in Deir Yassin, so everywhere. . . . Oh Lord, Oh Lord, you have chosen us for conquest" (in Chomsky, 1983: 96). Such conceptions of sacred terror both reflect and interact with the objective conditions of domination, offering flexible legitimations that grow stronger in the face of resistance.

The weary British withdrew in May of 1948 as the state of Israel was declared independent on May 14. In the context of massive population transfer (already amounting to some 300,000 persons, which could only mean trouble for Arab states) and the presence of a European outpost at Palestinian expense, a poorly integrated Arab military force, out-numbered and divided, attacked. The Israelis easily defeated the volunteers from Egypt, Jordan, Syria, Lebanon, Iraq, and Saudi Arabia. In the 1948 war another 700,000 Palestinians took flight from terror, some helped along by Israeli programmatic expulsion. At the end of the war, half of the territory designated as a Palestinian state by the U.N. had become part of Israel. The West Bank of the Jordan River was annexed by Jordan, while Egypt and Israel took control of the Gaza Strip. Nineteen years later, Israel in another war of "national survival" took the West Bank, Gaza, and Sinai from Egypt, and the Golan Heights from Syria. (Egypt was to recover the Sinai "wilderness" as a consequence of the Camp David accords brokered by President Carter of the United States. The treaty agreed to by Anwar Sadat for Egypt and

Menachim Begin for Israel split Egypt from the Arab League but led to increased aid from the United States, for this most populous of Arab states, as well as to development loans and a staggering 32.5-billion-dollar debt by 1985 (Walker, 1985: 101).)

Israeli journalist Tom Segev, in a 1986 book based on Israeli declassified official documents and other archival material, argues that during the first year of Israel's existence, the leadership of the new state decided to expel Arab residents (as at Haifa) and to destroy villages (such as Ikrit and Bir'em). Those who had fled were denied return, as new Jewish refugees from both Europe and now the Arab world left the squalor of detention centers to seize Arab homes and property. Armed Israeli forces, described by Segev as lacking in military discipline, were also clearly responsible for rapes, murder, and massacres of unarmed Arab villagers.

Of course, to place the blame for violence on refugees and the ill-trained and undisciplined military in 1949 may offer backhanded support for a recurring theme emanating from Israeli higher circles. The official story on state violence has routinely denied any *systemic* and *programmatic* attempt to intimidate Palestinians, and to force their expulsion from their lands. Argued thusly, military violence directed toward a civilian population is depicted as an isolated and unofficial response on the part of beleagured forces who suffer periodic lapses in discipline under stress.

The ideological norm for military conduct is *tohor haneshek*, or "purity of arms." This is an extension of the legitimation constructed by Israeli leaders from Ben-Gurion to Peres that Israel's survival was dependent not merely on strength but on *righteousness*. The claim of moral authority for the appealingly named Israeli *Defense* Forces, of course offers legitimation for the state, whose leaders decide the conditions under which military force can be used. Further, if holy warriors are required to eschew violence directed toward civilians and the innocent, then new legitimations may be required to account for such unrighteous terror when it occurs. It is within this context that the responsibility for violence may be expected to pass from inherent structural forces to other factions that do not so centrally implicate the state.

A case study in terrorism and its ideological reformulation is evidenced in the assault by paratroopers of Ariel Sharon's Unit 101 on the Jordanian village of Qibya, mounted in October of 1953. The occasion for the attack was the murder of three Israeli settlers (a mother and two children), although there was no known relationship between the killers and Qibya. U.N. military observers described the scene.

Bullet-riddled bodies near the door-ways and multiple bullet hits on the doors of the demolished houses indicated that the inhabitants had been forced to remain inside until their homes were blown up over them.... Witnesses were uniform in describing their experience as a night of horror, during which Israeli soldiers moved about in their village blowing up buildings, firing into doorways and windows with automatic weapons and throwing hand grenades. (In Chomsky, 1983:383)

The massacre at Qibya claimed 70 lives, including dozens of women and children. However, Prime Minister Ben-Gurion (remaining consistent with the righteousness theme) disavowed official military involvement. Instead, he blamed Israeli settlers consisting of refugees from Arab countries and Nazi concentration camps (Chomsky, 1983:383). The material facts of Qibya are clear, as evidenced in the subsequent condemnation of the raid by the U.N. Security Council. However, Qibya also starkly reveals something of two recurring ideological themes that legitimate Israeli policy on the use of deadly force. The first theme is that of *reprisal*, which can be considered the ideological genesis for what in the Likud era came to be known as the "iron fist." The second addresses the ideological transformation of terrorism, by which zealots and extremists (in this case, settlers on the border), motivated by vendatta, are portrayed as independent of the state.

With the coming to power of Likud in 1977, under the real and ideological leadership of Begin, Shamir, and Sharon, official Israeli pronouncements began to feature an escalation of the language of grandeur and force. The new symbols were those of nationalism, complete with eschatological pronouncements on Judea, Samaria, and the Greater Israel. Some saw in this rhetoric a substantive political realiance inside Israel, a realiance that marked a drastic departure from Israel's civilized and civilizing role in the Middle East. However, this *departure from righteousness* thesis, by which forces of moderation inside the Israeli state (notably the Labor Party) are seen as pitched in battle with terrorists who have simply moved up in life, is misleading. Stated simply, the shift from "righteousness" to "iron fist" represents no great ideological shift. Taken together, these are the components of *sacred terrorism* alluded to earlier.

Thus argued, it should come as no surprise to find the forces of righteousness clearly aware of the power of state terror. It was none other than David Ben-Gurion, often remembered as a proponent of Israeli purity of arms, who in a January 1, 1948, entry in his Independence War Diary wrote: "Blowing up a house is not enough. What is necessary is cruel and strong reactions. We need precision in time, place and casualties. If we know the family—[we must] strike mercilessly, women and children included. Otherwise the reaction is inefficient. At the place of action there is no need to distinguish between guilty and innocent" (in Chomsky, 1983: 182). As documented in the diaries of former Israeli Prime Minister Moshe Sharett, in the 1950s Ben-Gurion and Moshe Dayan (another moderate voice) were clear concerning a vision of the "Greater Israel." Such would involve the seizure of additional lands in Jerusalem, the West Bank, Lebanon, and Syria (Rokach, 1986). The institutional point, of course has little to do with personalities.

The ideology of righteousness implicitly condemns the behavior of the "Israeli Caesar," Ariel Sharon (Benziman, 1985). It was Sharon who led Unit 101 in the destruction of Qibya. It was Sharon who moved his "war on terror" to the Gaza in the early 1970s, where the houses of suspected enemies of the State were blown up, where bulldozers were driven through the camp to divide it into more easily controllable sectors, where "terrorists" were methodically killed. It was Sharon who, as agriculture minister from 1977 to 1981, presided over the settlement of the West Bank. It was Sharon who, as defense minister, commanded the 1982 invasion of Lebanon, ostensibly designed to wipe out P.L.O. terrorism. And it was Sharon who, as reported by the Associated Press on January 29, 1989, called for the death of Yasir Arafat.

In the course of this invasion, according to the Lebanese police, the Israeli Defense Forces (I.D.F.) killed over 19,000 people, including 6,775 in Beirut alone where some 84 percent of the casualties were civilian (Ball, 1984: 47). However, the invasion of Lebanon was directed at something greater than the guerilla capabilities of the P.L.O. Between 1968 and 1982, some 300,000 Palestinians in Lebanon had developed powerful political and economic institutions and a resurging cultural identity (Rubenberg, 1983). Some Lebanese saw that presence as a threat, but others discerned a potential ally. It was against the larger threat of the P.L.O. ministate; its achievements and its potential for a growing Lebanese alliance that the I.D.F. struck (Khalidi, 1984).

It is of course within this wider theater of total war that the real terrorism lies, for Israel as for all states. But the most dramatized event of this invasion occurred in Sabra and Shatila, undefended Palestinian camps under the absolute control of the I.D.F. Here, in September of 1982, 700 to 800 persons were brutally killed by a force of 100 to 150 members of the Israeli allied Phalange and Haddad militia, given entrance into the camps by the Israeli forces who stood idly by. These Lebanese Christian units had a history of atrocities directed against Palestinians; a history well known to all parties in the region. When the predictable happened, it could not be kept secret—except, somehow, from the Israeli military.

Despite the presence of Israeli tanks standing guard outside the camps when the militia entered (Campbell, *in Chomsky*, 1983: 366); despite the presence of a main observation post providing a clear view of one killing ground with its mass grave (Jenkins, 1982); despite the hysteria of Palestinian women who escaped the camps and begged the soldiers to stop the killing (Campbell, in Chomsky, 1983: 366); despite the knowledge of the international press (claimed by the I.D.F. to be the source of their knowledge on the massacre) (Claremont, 1984), the Israeli army claimed not to know. The U.N. General Assembly voted 147 to 2 to condemn the atrocity. Those opposed were Israel and the United States (*Christian Science Monitor*, Sept. 27, 1982).

The fact that Sharon and his allies have continued to enjoy power confirms that what they symbolize is an enduring force. Moreover, the coexistence of the bold use of state violence, with its condemnation by more "rational" voices inside the government may have allowed Israel to have it both ways. On the one side is the terrible expediency of the "iron fist." On the other is the criticism of that use of force (which is no doubt comforting to believers in righteousness.) Whether such a symbiotic arrangement is consciously understood by actors is beside the point. The consequence of this political symmetry is to place the iron fist inside a velvet glove.

For those who respond to the near conspiratorial drama of special forces and "low intensity conflict" (L.I.C.) there is the organizational and tactical descendent of Unit 101 known as Sayaret Matkal. In the plentiful L.I.C. literature from U.S. military sources, the elite 200-member Sayaret Matkal is presented as a "counter-terrorist" organization.

They use the Uzzi, the Israeli invented machine pistol. . . . They also use the Kalashnikov. . . . They are trained on the Galil, another Israeli-made automatic weapon. . . . Pistol shooting ranks high in the curriculum and here the Israelis use an unusual weapon, the 22 Beretta pistol. They train with this pistol because some of them move on to become members of the hit teams which eliminate Israel's enemies abroad and the '007' squad who fly with El Al. The technique when used by the hitmen is for them to get as close as possible to their victim and then pump a full magazine into him at the closest possible range. (Dobson and Payne, in *Low Intensity Conflict* (P31):168)

It was the Sayaret Matkal that struck deep into Egyptian territory twice in 1968; that in the same year blew up 13 Arab aircraft in a raid on the Beirut airport; and that attacked a hijacked passenger plane in Lod (while Israeli negotiators were supposedly cooperating with the Red Cross to bring a peaceful solution to the crisis). It was Sayaret Matkal that struck Beirut in 1973 killing scores of Fatah leaders, Lebanese police, and bystanders. And it was Sayaret Matkal that precipitated a slaughter by attacking the Palestinians holding hostages in the cadet school at Ma'alot when the Israelis refused to release 26 prisoners. It is at the least ironic that a leader of the Sayaret Matkal, virtually from its inception until his death at Entebbe was none other than Jonathan Netanyahu, brother of Israeli ambassador Benjamin Netanyahu, in whose name the Jonathan Institute on antiterrorism was established.

In a more recent scenario, Israeli special forces have responded to the rising that began in the occupied territories in December of 1987. In February of 1988, the P.L.O. sought to sponsor the sailing of their own "ship of return" from Limassol, Cyprus, as a nonviolent demonstration of the plight of exiles. The ship was crippled by an explosion while still in port, and a few hours later Israeli Defense Minister Yitzhak Rabin declared in Tel Aviv that "The State of Israel decided it was compelled not to let them achieve their purpose, and we will do that in whatever ways we find (*Spokane Spokesman-Review*, Feb. 16, 1988: A2). The following April, a commando team assassinated high-ranking P.L.O. deputy Khalil Wazir at his home in Tunis in front of his wife and child. The U.N. Security Council adopted a resolution on April 25 implicitly condemning Israel for the killing (*New York Times*, 1988: 6). These events cannot be isolated from the immediate question of revolt and the larger objective conditions of settler terrorism and internal colonialism. It is to these conditions that we now turn.

## SETTLER TERRORISM

For Israel, settlement is an ongoing process now rooted in the structural and ideological formations of the society. The welcoming of Jewish in-migration, expressed ideologically and politically in the *law of return* and *dual nationalism*, goes beyond the portrayal of Israel as a safe haven. On the one hand, such conceptions seek to strengthen the state by creating transcendent ties with a globally dispersed population. On the other, the process of settlement has meaning both for population increase and the continuing economic, political and social integration of newcomers into the social order. Given the material need for land and other resources, and the ideological message of the "Greater Israel" (by which the West Bank is redefined as Judea and Samaria and thus belongs to the Jews), the implications for conflict are clear.

If the settlement process has been the means by which the state of Israel was born, then it is also the means by which its frontiers have been expanded. Settlers are routinely described as "extremists" and it is certainly true that these 70,000 Jewish occupiers are among the most nationalistic of Israelis. The Gush Emunim (Block of the Faithful), for example, represent one of several Jewish sects who have sworn to keep the West Bank under Israeli control. Devoutly committed to the concept of a chosen people on a promised land, the Gush envision the expulsion of all Arabs from the West Bank (Newman, 1982: 27–30). However, to dwell too long on the fanaticism dimension of the settler phenomenon is to miss the larger context. The settlements in the occupied territories, whether paramilitary outposts or extensive residential and agricultural complexes, did not emerge *ex nihilo*. The Israeli state has provided the planning, the resources, the subsidies, the low mortgages, and the military support (including army-issued Uzi submachine guns) for its heavily armed settlers. And it is those Israelis who are subject to unemployment and relative poverty who are most susceptible to such inducements.

One of the ideological meanings of settlement is pacification. This reflects the long-standing colonial assumption that the land is wild and its occupants are savage. Thus the role of settlers is not merely to establish permanent homes but to advance "civilization." As settlers come to define the land as their property, it is clear that others with claims must be increasingly dehumanized. Settlement then, wherever practiced, implies a process of expulsion, whether legitimated by claims of God's favor for the powerful or by complementary visions of the less-than-human standing of the indigenous inhabitants. Expulsion need not be achieved through force and confiscation, although the symbolism of state violence should not be overlooked. The long standing tactic of blowing up the houses of Palestinians suspected of rebellion is a metaphor of negation. It signifies the destruction of home and abode, but more than that—it is an eviction notice served by a would-be landlord.

More sophisticated forms of expulsion involve the imposition of conceptions of law and private property on a traditional culture where such have little meaning. It was by these methods that much "Indian land" fell into the hands of whites who "settled" North America. So it was with Palestine, with even Palestinian citizens of Israel (15 percent of the total population) occupying an inferior social, economic, and political status, often victimized by discriminatory land legislation (Sabri, 1976; Rodinson, 1973: 86–87) such as the Absentee Property Law. It is expulsion, whether by force or "market forces," coexisting with the attempts by the expelled to acquire the political or armed strength to take back some of what they have lost, that is at the root of much state and commando terrorism.

Although the terrorism of armed Israeli settlers is well-documented (*Palestine Human Rights Campaign*, 1986), the theoretical point of isomorphic interests should not be obscured. Certain tactics may be officially condemned, but the ends to which those tactics are directed may be structurally consistent with those of the state. Violence and counterviolence in the occupied territories are logical consequences of a state-driven settlement imperative. Thus vigilante methods are to be understood as a continuation of the politics of state expansion by other means.

Other dimensions of the relationship between settlers and state remain instructive. In April of 1988, a group of hikers from the ultranationalist settlement of Elon Moreh, went to the outskirts of the Palestinian village of Beita for a picnic. In a confrontation, a 15-year-old Israeli girl was killed and the story spread throughout Israel that she died from Palestinian stones. After much of Beita had been destroyed by the Israeli military, an army autopsy revealed that Tirza Poret had been killed by an armed settler guard who accompanied the group, a guard who had been involved only six months earlier in a vigilante shooting in Nablus (*Newsweek*, 1988: 32). The other guard had been convicted in 1984 of the destruction of evidence in the killing of an 11-year-old Palestinian girl by a settler (Lewis, 1988a). Despite this, both were allowed to play their paramilitary role.

This "picnic," like the 48 other outings mounted by settlers on the same day (*Newsweek*, April 18, 1988: 32), can only be described as expulsion theater staged to assert Israeli proprietorship. Had the Israeli army not released the results of the autopsy, the result might well have been to unleash uncontrollable forms of reprisal, leaving the state of Israel on the sharpened horns of its continuing dilemma: how to use the settler vanguard while reigning in excesses that threaten the claims of democracy. To sum up this and earlier points, the relation between the military and settler/vigilantes encapsulates the dialectic of convenience between the forces of occupation and the forces of annexation. Thus understood, the settlers on the frontiers of the "Greater Israel" serve to expand the limits of state power.

## Intifadah: The Revolution of Stones

On December 8, 1987, a sustained revolt began in the occupied territories that provides the clearest evidence to date of the "permanent" nature of the settlement crisis. Just as Israeli settlement must be considered a process, so to is the Palestinian movement. Over a generation after the founding of the P.L.O., a new stage in the resistance appears to have taken form. A broadly based pattern of revolt emerged from inside the West Bank, Gaza, and Jerusalem and gained support from within Israel's Arab population (Hazo, 1988; Collins, 1988). (As of winter 1989, the uprising showed no signs of abatement, but should the violence subside, enduring ideological and structural changes in the resistance movement would continue to have sociological implications for the future of Israeli-Palestinian relations.)

This new stage offers a change in the roles played by Palestinian nationalists inside the occupied territories, from that of political support and/or sympathy for the P.L.O. to active demonstration and rebellion. This means a new definitional stage for self-determination, in which responsibility is no longer solely vested in the political, economic, social, and guerilla forces of the P.L.O. located in other lands. The development of indigenous forces of resistance from within the 1.5 million Palestinians living under conditions of military rule means increased potential for a sustained rebellion. As the meaning of self-determination is reformulated in ideological institutions (specifically in the mosques and schools) and as new cadres emerge (as with the clandestine Unified National Command), new and more generally based tactics of resistance can be expected to strain the resources of state control.

Further, as resistance escalates, an increased level of state violence can be expected to spur Palestinian solidarity at various levels. The sense of family and tribe, which facilitates a "divide and conquer" strategy of rule, may be expected to give ground to other collective identities embodied in such terms as "nation" or "people." The unexpected support for the resistance from the Israeli Arab population represents another level of solidarity, underscoring the dilemma implicit in reconciling the tenets of democracy with the more exclusionary assumptions of a Jewish state. At the tactical level, in 1988 more sophisticated forms of nonviolent civil disobedience emerged to buttress mass demonstrations, with strikes, shop closings, boycotts, the refusal to pay taxes, and other means of supporting the rising.

In keeping with the mandate of the "iron fist," as the Palestinian revolt escalated arithmetically, the Israeli response escalated geometrically. Military authorities halted the education of almost a half-million Palestinians in February, when some 1,200 schools in the West Bank and Gaza Strip were closed for three months, reopened, and then closed early for the year. Jerusalem born Mubarak E. Awad, a Palestinian who took American citizenship before returning to establish a Center for the Study of Non-Violence was ordered deported by Prime Minister Yitzhak Shamir in May. As reported by the Associated Press on January 29, 1989, 370 Palestinians and 15 Israelis had died in the 14 month period. On October 9, 1988, the Associated Press reported that 7,000 Palestinians had been wounded and 18,000 detained, with some 5,600 still jailed and 2,000 serving sentences of up to 6 months without benefit of trial. Al Haq put the Palestinian death toll at 400 with an estimated 20,000 injured.[5]

In the context of the "revolution of stones," the Palestine National Council (the P.L.O.'s parliament in exile) met in Algiers on November 12–15, 1988. The P.N.C. endorsed U.N. Security Council resolutions 242 and 338 (implicitly recognizing the right of Israel to exist) as the basis for convening an international conference on the question of Palestine. The conference would be organized under U.N. auspices, with the five permanent members of the Security Council and all parties in conflict (including the P.L.O.) participating. It further declared the establishment of the state of Palestine with its capital in Jerusalem (P.N.C. documents in Curtiss, 1988: 6). Subsequently, the United States triggered a firestorm of international protest by refusing to grant Yasir Arafat a visa to address the United Nations on the familiar grounds of P.L.O. terrorism. In spite of a 121 to 2 General Assembly vote calling for the granting of the visa (with only Israel and the United States opposed), the U.S. State Department refused. The General Assembly then shifted its session to Geneva in protest, underscoring that global isolation had become one of the costs of the core-client form of imperial formations mystified by the ideology of terrorism. Driven by events having their genesis in the intifadah, on December 14, 1988 the United States agreed to enter into cosmetic low-level talks with the P.L.O. (Greenway, 1988: A6).

As demonstrated, this is only the most recent chapter in an historical record of state violence. On the other side, documentation assembled by the Israel Defense Forces (1985 and 1986) (and made available through the Israeli embassy in the United States) details the attacks on Israeli targets both internal and external. One summary covers the period June 1967 to October 1985, and the other July 1968 to July 1986. A careful reading of these accounts makes it clear that the I.D.F. has included attacks on military personnel as well as civilian; makes no distinction as to whether the "civilian" targets were armed; includes the attack by Japanese terrorists at Ben-Gurion airport in May of 1972 that took 26 lives (claiming they were working "on behalf of" the P.F.L.P.); and takes no responsibility for deaths pursuant to its iron fist policy of no negotiation. (Recall that the death toll of 24 civilians and one soldier at Ma'alot in 1974 (I.D.F., 1985: 7) followed a rescue attack by Sayaret Matkal. According to Said (1979: 172), the Ma'alot incident followed weeks of Israeli napalming of Palestinian camps in southern Lebanon.) All this aside, the total Israeli death toll owing to terrorism (as defined by the I.D.F.) in these two surveys covering almost two decades appears to be fewer than 400 persons.

**Maximal Zionism and Apartheid**

An increasing number of authors, some already cited in this inquiry, have sought to identify cultural, political, and economic similarities between South

Africa and Israel. Such attempts are necessarily limited when they remain at the level of analogies. What is necessary is the construction of a conceptual framework that addresses the *parallel development* of settler economies. By this I mean to identify a set of structural and ideological forces common to the internal relations between settlers and their descendants on the one side and indigenous peoples with prior claim on the other. Such relations defy simple conceptions of ethnicity, faith, or forms of national identity; nor do they coincide with lines drawn on maps.

Internally, the conflict in ancient Palestine is not a simple matter of Jews and Arabs. The objective conditions of Arab citizens of Israel differ from those of Palestinians living in the occupied territories, which differ in turn from those of Palestinians dispersed in other lands. So it is within the Jewish caste inside Israel. It is the Sephardim, and other newly arrived settlers and marginals, who have sought to rectify their material disadvantage through the Likud bloc. The connection with the Afrikaners in South Africa in this respect is not circumstantial. As evidenced in Chapter 6, the state has also been the vehicle for the less-favored members of South Africa's white caste to alleviate their standing as marginals. That the most adamant supporters of apartheid have the most to lose from surrendering the patronage and labor advantages offered by the state is axiomatic.

Yet to hold the more recently arrived Sephardim responsible for the Palestinian dilemma is to ignore the total history of the Zionist movement. More important, it is to ignore two theoretical aspects of the settler economy common to both Israel and South Africa. First, the existence of caste conditions may *alter*, but does not *negate*, class formations within a dominant caste. However, those conscious of their intracaste marginality may seek to rectify their disadvantage through seeking state influence. It is their marginality, not their ethnicity that is at issue, although demographic and organizational factors are relevant for electoral success. This form of *caste consciousness* can only retard the formation of a class consciousness that must necessarily transcend the boundaries of birth, faith, and culture.

Once institutionalized in the laws and policies of the state, this consciousness of caste becomes a real force. The emptying of that population's land, labor value, and other resources serves the immediate interests of caste marginals (whether Afrikaner, Sephardim, or their functional equivalent), without severely disrupting existing patterns of privilege. In the process, the system as a whole is maintained. It is at this theoretical level of system-maintenance, with its dialectic reproduction of societal and global relations, that the larger questions of internal colonialism must be joined.

It comes as no surprise to find state representatives in both South Africa and Israel asserting that the indigenous populations they control are materially "better off" than their counterparts in Black African or Arab societies in general. Such claims were not invented by these states of course but are common to imperial ideology whether expressed in the "white man's burden" of Kipling or the *mission civilisée* of the French colonialists. It is clear that such legitimations completely miss the point of self-determination. However, on a less philosophical plane, they also fail to address the material dynamics of internal colonialism. For example, the occupation of Gaza by Israel is not confined to a military presence. It represents instead a process of economic absorption and reverse development that benefits the more privileged (Roy, 1986).

Palestinians in Gaza do not control their land, labor, technology, or consumption. At least one-third of the strip has been *de facto* confiscated by Israel with most of this designated for settlement. Israel controls not only land allocation but access to water, agricultural production, and trade. Given military restrictions on planting and replacing trees, land loss and water diversion to settlers, Gazan citrus production declined from 243,700 tons in 1975 to 175,000 tons in 1984. The pattern of reverse development is also evidenced in the Israeli imposition of land taxes, value-added taxes, and taxes on exports, which in concert with restrictions on trade thwart authentic economic development. Bans on exports to Western markets, and on exports to Israel of products that compete with Israeli goods coexist with virtually unlimited access to Gazan markets for Israeli producers. On the industrial side, Palestinian manufacturers endure the restriction of credit, the denial by Israel of export subsidies and tax breaks, as well as restrictions on markets.

The uneven exchange that marks the dependency of the periphery in general is evidenced in the Gaza in particular with its trade deficit in 1985 of some $164.5 million, most of that owing to the dumping of Israeli products. On the side of labor dependency, Gaza residents officially registered with the Israeli Employment Service as working inside Israel grew from some 5,900 workers in 1970 to 41,700 in 1985, a number that does not include the illegals in the labor reserve. What is interpreted by Israel as job creation for Palestinians may better be interpreted as labor dependency. Claims of job growth are further suspect as the consumption made possible by the wages paid this absentee work force is channeled toward Israeli markets. The structural parallels with South Africa are clear, and they are more than analogies.

On the administrative side, social control necessitates the cultivation of an indigenous elite that in turn legitimates the claim of self-rule, while representing a counterinsurgency agenda. Israel (as South Africa) has appointed "moderate" Palestinian leaders, who (as their bantustan and township counterparts) have enjoyed power, privilege, and systems of local patronage. In the context of the December 1987 rising, these appointees came under increasing threats and pressure from Palestinians who accused them of collaboration. In Beit Sahur (a largely Christian village on the Israeli-occupied West Bank), Bicharra Qumsaya resigned as the head of the Village League for the entire West Bank in March of 1988. The league had been created by the Israelis in the hope of offering an alternative to the P.L.O. In the same month, the Israeli-appointed mayor of Gaza City, Hanza Turkamni, stepped down. The rising also saw the resignation of hundreds of Palestinian tax collectors and police (Kifner, 1988).

When the institutions of indigenous control fail, more direct forms of population control will be placed in force. Certain of these have already been discussed, but again the theoretical construct of structural parallelism is apropos. These involve restrictions on the press, mass detention, curfews, and the ready resort to deadly force or highly dangerous riot-control technology (including the introduction of plastic bullets by the I.D.F.). The consequences of the iron fist, as the parallel ideology of *collective responsibility* used by the French in Algeria, can only be to build national solidarity among resisters.

If the exponential recourse to force is insufficient to prevent the emergence of a "permanent" state of revolt against the formations of internal colonialism; and if settlement is in fact *institutionalized*; what may then be predicted for the future of the Israeli-Palestinian conflict? To begin, if settlement is institutionalized within the Israeli state, it follows that the popular liberal solution in the West (and within the Israeli Peace Now movement) is suspect. That solution, which is to trade land for peace, is contrary to the material forces of open immigration and natural increase by which the Jewish population has grown from some 600,000 at the point of statehood, to 3.2 million today. It is contrary to the history of Israel's geographic expansion, ever spurred by the need for new lands for new settlers. It is contrary to the ideological forces that take religious form in the conception of chosenness, and politically in the conception of dual nationalism. It is contrary to the more social-psychological forces by which a people, well-conscious of their historical victimization, are imbued with the imagery of the warrior and the purging process it symbolizes.

Viewed structurally and historically then, the Palestinian question is less about the Palestinian problem than about the nature of a maximal Zionist state. The extension into the future of past and existing forces and counterforces is at best an imprecise exercise. However, the forces of maximal Zionism ascendant in Israel have not emerged in a vacuum. Rather they are consistent with and build upon a history of settlement. Should internal Palestinian resistance to this process intensify and grow more effective, the resort of the state to repression will increase and, in keeping with the legitimations of the iron fist, increase exponentially. In this context, extremism may well be redefined, and the forces of absolutism come to dominate the state.

The settlement imperative aside, some consideration must be briefly given to the militarization of Israeli society. The establishment of a permanent warfare state, engaged in a permanent state of war has already been alluded to. That Israel spent 29 percent of its G.N.P. on "national defense" in 1983 (*World Almanac*, 1987: 582) (compared to less than 7 percent for the United States, and the constitutional limit of 1 percent in Japan) cannot be dissociated from the development of its arms industry and its role as an arms exporter. Thus in objective terms the Israeli version of a military-industrial complex has been taking form. This traditional alliance of the military bureaucracy, job-holders, international arms dealers, and politicians seeking to please constituents both reflects and reproduces the higher-level material and ideological forces described above.

On the international scene, future relations with the United States may grow strained as the Israelis pursue interests not precisely coincidental with those of the Western world system or its core. If Palestinian revolt and the specter of intensified Israeli state repression do not undermine U.S. support, then it is altogether possible that the now paranoid fear of waves of conventional terrorism both inside and outside Israel may acquire a real basis in fact. Essentially nonviolent tactics among Palestinians in the occupied territories may develop mass support, but should patterns of brutal state repression continue this can be transformed into more active support for armed insurrection.

At the very least, the 1.2 billion (1984) Israeli tourism industry (*World Almanac*, 1987: 582) will continue to be disrupted and P.L.O. proscriptions on striking targets outside Israel may be rescinded. As the British four decades ago, the United States may find its burden an increasingly heavy one, with its Middle Eastern policy increasingly mired in strategies of "low-intensity conflict" (see Chapter 9). And remembering the history of the British imperial role may serve notice inside Israel that even the United States is not to be trusted to stay the course. It is within this context that the Jonathan Pollard scandal, in which Israel engaged in espionage against its patron state, must be understood (Al-Abed, 1987: 4).

Given such conditions, relations between Israel and South Africa will continue to grow in importance, a symbiosis born of common historical forces. The pattern of cooperation in industry, trade, intelligence, and nuclear weapons development (Beit-Hallahmi, 1987) is a logical outgrowth of the settler imperative at work in both societies. The racial exclusion grounded in religious fundamentalism has marked both maximal Zionism and apartheid, and attempts to more than cosmetically alter the relations they represent will loosen increasing waves of ultranationalism. Both states must continue to resort to military force and the arming of reactionary states or counterrevolutionary organizations within neighboring states. Such tactics of *regional* destabilization are designed to weaken the forces of insurgency inside Israel and South Africa and to further fragment already-fragmented opposition from without.

Before there is peace in southern Africa or in the Middle East, a transformation of these two surviving settler states appears mandatory—a transformation that brings more authentic forms of power sharing, economic rights and reparations, demilitarization, cultural pluralism, and an end to state domination. And as in all such struggles, the lead role will be played by the colonized themselves. Once again however, these flashpoints in history represent the clash between the forces of order and change, the privileged and the dispossessed, the state and mass movements of liberation.

## NOTES

1. This section is informed by the author's "The Selling of International Terrorism" (1988).

2. Such declarations fly in the face of reality. Armed with U.S.-supplied stinger missiles, the Afghan Mujahideen have brought down civilian aircraft on at least two occasions, and their missile attacks on civilian urban neighborhoods in Kabul and elsewhere are well known (*Spokane Spokesman Review*, April 11, 1988: A–3). As for the Contras, their internal war has routinely targeted schools, clinics, and civilians (see Chapter 9).

3. For an exceptional study of the organizational history of the P.L.O., see Alain Gresh (1985).

4. For an account of prestate terrorism on the part of these groups, see Levi Brenner's *Zionism in the Age of Dictators*.

5. Al Haq is an Arab human rights organization, affiliated with the International Commission of Jurists based in Geneva. (The Associated Press reported on its findings on December 6, 1988.) With a West Bank/Gaza Palestinian population of 1.5 million, 20,400 casualties represent a casualty to population ratio of 1:74. Extrapolating to the United States, such a ratio would mean 3.3 million American casualties, including 65,000 deaths. Israeli casualties suffered in war, invasion, population control, battles with guerillas, and vendetta terror are certainly far fewer than those they have inflicted, but clearly reveal the enormous price of maximal Zionism.

# 8

# Holy Terror: Iran and Irangate

I have tasted poverty and still feel its bad taste.... [Khomeini] is the representative of the Mahdi and the echo of God. Like Abraham and Muhammed, he is also a destroyer of idols. Never abandon his path. Remember that if you do not resolve the problems of the deprived masses, you will be defeated.

> The Last Will and Testament of Martyr Ahmad Musaie,
> who fell in the Iran-Iraq War in 1981

I cannot believe, I do not accept that any prudent individual can believe that the purpose of all these sacrifices was to have less expensive melons, that we sacrificed our young men to have less expensive housing.... No one would give his life for better agriculture.

> Ayatollah Ruhollah Khomeini

The tradition of all the dead generations weighs like a nightmare on the brain of the living. And just when they seem engaged in revolutionising themselves and things, in creating something entirely new, precisely in such periods of revolutionary crisis they anxiously conjure up the spirits of the past to their service and borrow from them names, battle slogans and costumes in order to present the new scene of world history in this time-honoured disguise and this borrowed language.

> Karl Marx, *The Eighteenth Brumaire of Louis Bonaparte*

On Sunday morning, November 4, 1979, the U.S. embassy in Tehran was occupied by Iranian students loyal to the Shi'ite Moslem holy man, Ayatollah

Ruhollah Khomeini. What apparently began as a demonstration planned to last some three to five days quickly escalated into international political theater. Hostages, including over 60 Americans were taken, as students demanded the return to Iran of the deposed Shah Mohammed Reza Pahlavi. Most remained in captivity on U.S. "soil" for 444 days with their official release to come on January 21, 1981, at 12:05 P.M., Washington time, five minutes after the single term of President Jimmy Carter ended (Sick, 1985: 197, 341). This taking of hostages, which fits well conventional conceptions of terrorism, was not in the ordinary. The symbolic defiance of a superpower, long supportive of the shah, was played out on a world stage. When in April of 1980, a force of army Green Berets and Rangers (called Delta) were forced, because of the mechanical failure of helicopters, to abort their rescue mission in the Iranian desert, the appearance of American impotence hardened (Ryan, 1985: 1–2). Before the hostage crisis (called by its creators the "second Iranian revolution") ended, forces supportive of Khomeini's conception of an Islamic republic further consolidated their grip on the immediate Iranian future.

The coming of the Islamic Republic of Iran represented more than internal war, hostage-taking and other symbolic confrontations with the "Great Satan." On September 22 of 1980, Saddem Hussein reasserted long-standing Iraqi claims in the area of the crucial Shatt al-Arab waterway. As always, the complexities transcend geography. The two nations represent exemplars of conflicting material and ideological forces in the Middle East. Iran, embodying the dream of Islamic universalism, stood in opposition to the Iraqi forces of Ba'ath Arab socialism, committed to the eventual emergence of one Arab nation. Long-standing Iranian support for the Kurdish minority fighting Iraqi rule, together with the fact that Shi'a Muslims were a majority in Iraq, contributed to an Iraqi fear of "Persian expansionism (Ishmael, 1982: 1–40)." Hussein perhaps anticipated a quick victory over a clerical movement seeking to exercise other than spiritual power. Iraq (and many observers) were to be surprised, as the ensuing border war brought carnage to both sides over the decade to come. Iran expended the massive war machine built by the Shah and employed its three to one population advantage against Iraq with its long-term equipment superiority and better-trained armed forces. In this war, the ideologization of Islam by Iranian clerics subordinated Qur'anic injunctions against suicide to new and terrifying conceptions of martyrdom on battlefields, conventional and new.

In the wake of the 1982 Israeli invasion of Lebanon, suicide squads tied at least ideologically to the Khomeini movement, came to synthesize a maximal doctrine of intentional martyrdom and conventional terror in attacks on U. S. and other targets in Beirut. On April 18, 1983, 50 people were killed in an explosion at the U.S. Embassy. On October 23, 241 U.S. and 58 French soldiers died in separate bombings (Wright, 1986:15–25). (These were only three of a number of such episodes in the Middle East that fit conventional conceptions of terrorism.) In the midst of this turmoil, the Reagan administration traveled a confused course. In 1982, it declared an arms embargo against Iran; in 1984, it designated Iran as a state sponsor of terrorism; and two years later, then Director of the C.I.A. William Casey argued that "more blood has been shed by Iranian-sponsored terrorism during the last few years than by all other terrorists combined (1986:6)." But in a bizarre turn of events, this most "antiterrorist" of administrations became involved in the sale of weapons and spare parts to a state branded by President Ronald Reagan as a leading member of an international "Murder Incorporated" (see Chapter 1).

Viewed superficially, the Irangate affair[1] stands to be dismissed as the work of an inept administration, seeking to trade arms to Iran for hostages held by pro-Iranian kidnappers in Beirut to provide out of channels funding for anticommunist contras fighting in Nicaragua. (This described by U.S. National Security Council functionary Col. Oliver North as a "neat idea.") But there is something of an historical gossamer thread that runs throughout these tangled affairs, a thread often obscured by the political language of terrorism. That thread can only be understood when the structural and ideological forces that underlie the Islamic resurgence in Iran begin to be uncovered.

## WHOM THE GODS WOULD DESTROY

Given the stereotypical conceptions of Islam that abound in the West, the title of this chapter may carry unintended ideological implications. It is true that the Iranian revolution from the late 1970s has featured first antistate and then state violence bent on intimidation through fear. Terrorism was thus in evidence as the forces of Ayatollah Ruhollah Khomeini first deposed Shah Mohammed Reza Pahlavi to establish the Islamic Republic of Iran. It is also true that the new order moved ruthlessly to crush internal opposition, that it inspired and supported (at least through teachings, example, and deed) distorted conceptions of revolution and *jihad* among splinter groups within the long repressed Islamic Shi'ite minority, and that the Iran-Iraq war has added unique dimensions to the given terror of state warfare. However, the misnamed Iranian revolution as well as the complexities of political terror are not well-understood when viewed through a Western ideological prism, a prism that deals glibly and concretely with what is loosely called an *Islamic resurgence*.

In the early stages of the formalization of Islamic state power in Iran, an event that appeared to provide some historical credibility for the old dream of Pan-Islamism, Ali Dessouki complained that accounts of the broader Islamic resurgence in the media were marred by sensationalism, denial, and retrogression (1982). By the late summer of 1988, cease-fire talks began in Geneva, with hopes high for ending the protracted border war between Iraq and Iran. But the sensational images of a fanatical and violent Islam will not easily pass. Also to endure is the ideological generalization that social movements in Islamic societies can only be dogmatic and reactionary. This of course denies the historical specificity of such episodes, with very different movements, parties, and persons grouped together simply because of their faith. Westernized views of Islamic resurgence may be expected to continue to obscure the real divergencies of such as the Islamic Republic of Iran, the fronts constituting the Palestine Liberation Organization (see Chapter 7), and the Libyan Jamahiriya (see Chapter 6).

This chapter is guided by several premises intended to transcend the reified conceptions that distort the nature of change. To begin, it is important to place the religious factor in something of a material context. Movements for change that claim sacred inspiration or legitimation are not driven solely by a desire to propagate the faith and convert the nonbeliever. Beneath the language and rituals of the supernatural are the real concerns of the natural realm. When the practitioners of an indigenous faith rise up to smite the infidel or the corrupters of faith, it is not surprising when the infidels happen to represent the forces of imperialism. These representatives are held responsible for transgressions that diminish not only the faith but the conditions of this life. Put simply, at the base of what superficially appears to be a holy war can often be found the materially "profane" relations of dependency. Such do involve, at least in a derivative fashion, the despoiling of native culture and the psychological assault on dignity. But central to dependency status are the control of resources, the imposition of models of unequal development, and the recurring questions of state power. However, such relations are not distorted by imperial ideology alone. Also crucial to the mystification of domination are the ideological forces of reaction.

Within the movements that claim the inspiration of God, material forces are also at play. That believers may aspire to the power of the state (whether for themselves or kindred spirits) is clear. That the faithful may interpret religious principles to fit earthly exigencies should also be clear. There is nothing sinister about this, but it does mean that one must look beyond the holy writs to find political truth. Happily for those who seek guidance for this world, articles of faith are ordinarily ambiguous when it comes to social, political and economic systems. Exponents of liberation theology in Latin America and Africa find in their faith a legitimation for changing real systems of structural inequality, and are informed by Marx as well as Jesus. Christian fundamentalists in the United States laud free enterprise and anticommunism. The rising pentecostal movement in Central America is favored by landlords and offers the escape of episodic rhapsody to struggling *camposinos*. Devout believers in Islam who have helped to fashion the Libyan revolution see no need for rule by clerics (though Muammar Qaddafi argues that the Jamahiriyan state of the masses embodies the principles of social justice found in Islam). But in Iran, Khomeini and his followers found in Islam (as some others before them) legitimation for a *theocratic* state with its indivisible merger of sacred and secular authority.

It follows therefore that movements whose utopian ideologies feature the symbols and imperatives of religious faith are not created equal. Some may seek the authentic transformation of society along new lines; others may seek to find in tradition old answers to new problems. Still others may be content with a "changing of the guard" by which old colonial institutions are retained under the control of an indigenous elite. Because all of these may employ the language of anti-imperialism while rejecting the established order, the term *revolutionary* is often applied to each. Yet a religious movement founded in *cultural purification*, a fundamentally superstructural reaction that seeks to resurrect traditional clerical authority and elevate it to state rule, faces the past. It is this question of historical direction that is central, as there is something more to a revolution than a reaction to domination. Such distinctions may be lost, however, if one insists on reducing broader historical forces to a superficial treatise on supposedly irrational emotion.

That religious conviction may fuel the forces that challenge established systems of rule is true, but not true enough. When conviction is portrayed (rightly or not) as fanaticism, something is lost in explanation. The word itself is from the Latin *fanaticus*, the root of which is *fanum*, or "temple." Thus, fanaticism refers to an inflamed, essentially spiritual form of inspiration. To the Western mind, fanaticism signals the triumph of emotion over reason, of zeal over restraint. It marks the loss of control, and of the ability to make calculated decisions in which pleasure is counterbalanced against pain and costs weighed against benefits. Other than its reductionism, there are some essential problems with this ready recourse to the fanaticism label to explain movements for change in Islamic societies.

One might begin by noting that fanaticism is no respecter of religion. To this point, the phrase *holy terror* can be assigned to all sides of the Irangate episode that rocked the second term of the Reagan administration. The religious legitimations of maximal Zionism, the erstwhile anti-Communist vision of the U.S. National Security Council "born-agains," and the confusion of state-inspired violence with martyrdom in Iran, all bear the seal of state terror conducted in the name of purity and faith. But there are more important arguments to be made. Islamic societies and peoples in the Arab world, Africa, and the Indian subcontinent, as elsewhere have traditionally ranked among the historical victims of colonialism, old and new. The imagery of fanaticism (even when well-deserved) not only delegitimates anticolonial movements (which may or may not be authentic attempts at collective self-determination) but forestalls closer examination of the real forces at play. So it has been with Iran where the "rule of the Ayatollahs" cannot be isolated from the history of Western intervention.

## THE GREAT SATAN

With such caveats in mind, we return to an analysis of the Islamic resurgence in Iran. On November 2, 1978, the Carter White House received two messages from William H. Sullivan, U.S. ambassador to Iran (Sick, 1985: 3–4). One was a routine account of his most recent meeting with the shah. The second contained an explosive message suggesting a wholly unanticipated seachange—in Iranian-U.S. relations, in the balance of power in the Middle East, and in the internal nature of the Iranian state and society. Shah Mohammed Pahlavi, considered a fast and secure ally of the West, was thought to be considering abdication.

Although signs of insurrection were abundant throughout 1978, U.S. foreign policy experts and the C.I.A., as well as Sullivan himself, had failed to comprehend the gravity of the gathering storm. Perhaps this is because the threat to the shah came from conservative mullahs not defined as a political force. Indeed, the condemnation of Western-style modernization by the *ulama* (plural of *alim* meaning men learned in religious "science") could easily have been dismissed by those predisposed to think only in terms of a threat from the left. But on January 16, 1979, the unthinkable happened. The shah left Iran and exiled religious leader Ayatollah Ruhollah Khomeini named a provisional government council in preparation for his return.

Throughout the year, internal conflict raged within the swelling insurrectionary movement. SAVAK, the shah's secret police, and his well-regarded army proved little match for a people divided along class, ethnic, and ideological lines, but generally united in their opposition to the dynasty. It proved to be the clerics, and above all Khomeini, whose movement ideology effectively synthesized the political language of anti-imperialism with the indigenous language of faith, that emerged. The leap from theology to sociology was not so great as some might think. Quite contrary to what has emerged in the West as separation of church and state, a recurring conception of Islam among certain of its scholars is that it is "a religion, a state and a whole social system suitable for all times and all societies (Aroua quoted in Merad, 1981:45)." Viewed thus, Islam is belief and law (*aqida wa shari'a*), religion and state (*din wa dawla*), and a value system that holds the spiritual and temporal world to be indivisible (*din wa dunya*). So conceived, Islam is a "set of principles which should guide the general organisation of the community" (Merad, 1981: 38).

Within this general matrix, however, the question of the temporal expression of political power remains to be resolved. When in 1979 the new Islamic constitution vested power in the *faqih*, it legitimated Khomeini's view that a "supreme overseer, judge and guardian" (Enayat, 1983: 160) should rule over the administration of the Islamic state. The underlying conception of the "guardianship of the jurisconsult" (*wilayat-i-faqih*) holds that the *faqih*, as the exemplar of Islamic jurisprudence, had the duty to "administer and rule the state and to implement the laws of the sacred path" (Khomeini quoted in Enayat, 1983: 163). The doctrine of an obligatory Islamic state had been advocated by other modern fundamentalists including Rashid Rida of Syria, Muhammad al-Ghazzali of Egypt and the Abu'l-A'la Maududi of Pakistan. However, where Maududi envisioned a gradual spiritual and peaceful revolution, Khomeini's focus was temporal, abrupt, and receptive to violence as a means to both spiritual regeneration and political justice (Enayat, 1983).

The designation of Khomeini as supreme *faqih* of the new Islamic Republic of Iran came in 1979 at the beginning of Islam's fifteenth century. This action added a distinctive political role and the legitimacy of state power to his spiritual position as Imam. The spiritually infallible Imams, as successors of the Prophet according to Shi'i tradition, already enjoyed authority of the first rank in spiritual affairs and in the application of principles of faith to temporal issues. But the definition of *wilaya* to mean the supervision of the state by the *faqih* added formal structures of power and governance to the duties of this particular imam. This interpretation of power also conveniently disposed of the objection that spiritual infallibility does not insure political competence. In his treatises Khomeini dismissed the argument that the inheritors and successors of the prophets lack technical or administrative training, arguing that the *faqih* could avail themselves of the skills of others when science or technique is required.

Khomeini's movement ideology also offered a particular interpretation of *asala* ("authenticity") quite at variance with structural/material interpretations that stress new institutions and a more secular view of self-reliance. His appeal to authentic Islamic *values* simultaneously condemned the corruption associated with modernization, as well as the degradation of the spiritually inclined Muslim personality. And as argued by Ali Merad, it induced recall of a "past golden age of Islam when the community had presumably lived the Qur'anic message in its completeness and truth" (1981: 39). Such distinctions aid in the understanding of the particular *problematique* of the ideology of Islamic popular resistance in Iran and elsewhere. They also help us grasp the importance of the historical directionality of movements and their ideals.

But the construction of an ideology of popular resistance requires more than the legitimation of faith. The clerics, whose position of authority could only be undermined by opposing forces (whether those of creeping Westernization, a Marxist negation or a new synthesis in Iran), were also able to articulate misery and shame in the language of the faith. From 1963 when he led the vigorous antishah demonstrations that resulted in his exile, Khomeini (1982) proved masterful in interpreting doctrinal imperatives in political terms; in transforming the quest for spiritual righteousness into a struggle for rule. Thus, the protection of Islam meant an anti-imperial and territorial command, not a matter of prayers, fasting and the purification of the soul. He also transformed Mahdism, a major tenet of popular Shi'ism, into a mandate for activism.

The anticipation of the Mahdi (*intizar*) meant that cosmic, social, and juridical justice was conditional on the return of the Twelfth or Hidden Imam at a point after the world is "filled with injustice." While not abandoning the doctrine of Mahdism, Khomeini sought to negate the passivity implied by a concept of "deliverance" to argue that justice would prevail when believers established an Islamic state (Enayat, 1983: 174). Despite this modification, it is clear that the charismatic appeal of Khomeini did not suffer from the popular belief among Shi'ites that God would send a deliverer. Also, for Khomeini, the traditional call for unity took the form of a temporal Pan-Islam, to be built through the exporting of the Iranian revolution. The expressed purpose was not territorial ambition but Muslim unity.

Political opponents, at home and abroad, were also subject to this ideological transformation. According to Khomeini, monarchs should be deposed, not simply because they rivaled the rising tide of clerical power but because they claimed sovereignty belonging only to God. Marxists and other materialists, who held that an obsession with religious values could only hinder authentic economic development, were of course open to the charge of heresy or infidelity.[2] After the invasion by Iraq, Khomeini drew from the Qur'an the inference that Saddam Hussein represented the backsliding Muslim that "rebels against God (Khomeini, 1982:16)." In this context, *jihad*, a necessarily ambiguous term calling for effort or struggle in the cause of God, came to mean a total war to remove Hussein, and martyrdom emerged as a sacred slogan which found terrifying expression on the modern battlefield. To this point, Khomeini (1982:55) asked: "Is it not true that martyrdom has been inherited by our martyr-nourishing nation from our Imams who regarded (eternal) life as a manifestation of 'belief and jihad' ... and safeguarded the dignified school of Islam at the cost of their own blood and that of their beloved youths. . . . Many youths come to me and ask me to pray for them to become martyrs for the sake of Islam." And in the course of such ideological progression, the U.S. government became the "Great Satan" (Khomeini, 1982: 55).

## THEOCRATIC REACTION

The attempt to reconstruct the past, and more specifically, to strengthen the rule of traditional leaders through the conferral of the power of the modern state, typifies what can be termed the theocratic reaction. Although such movements dot the landscape of Muslim history, they are by no means restricted to Islam. However, there are three exemplary Islamic movements, that while emerging in Arab lands, are in some ways instructive for understanding the contemporary cleric-led insurgency in Iran.[3] These include Wahhabism, led by Muhammad Ibn Abdel-Wahhab that began in late eighteenth-century Arabia and after a period of dormancy was resurrected in the early twentieth century; the Sanusi, identified with Muhammad Ibn Ali al-Sanusi in Cyrenaica, which spanned the period from 1840 to 1931; and the Sudanese Mahdist led by Muhammad Ahmad (whose title was Al-Mahdi) lasting from 1881–98.

Eighteenth-century and later Wahhabism holds in common with the other Islamic theocratic movements a militant and temporal focus. This revolt, advocating a return to the purity of the first century of Islam, opposed mysticism, the worship of saints and the cult of Muhammad as the perfect man. It was successful in the establishment of an Islamic state based on the Shari'a (the law of Islam, literally the "path to god" or more strikingly "path to a water hole") and it grew to oppose the imperial (though Islamic) political and administrative order of the Ottoman Turks. Early in the twentieth century, a new birth of this movement occurred when the British were present in eastern Arabia. However, this resurgence did not feature a clear anti-European focus. It is instructive to note that since the 1920s, the Saudi Arabian regime has featured the institutionalization of a strict Wahhabi interpretation of the faith (perhaps without its ascetic demands). But the ideological point to be made is that the insistence on *moral reform* in Wahhabism has coexisted quite well with Saudi accommodationist policies toward the West during this century, whether directed toward the British or of late, the Americans.

The Sanusi movement that emerged in what is now eastern Libya was distinctive in that Ali Al-Sanusi's missionary effort to convert the bedouin of Cyrenaica had other than purely spiritual consequences. His missionaries did not establish so much a state but a network of trading routes and pasture rights under the judicial and political coordination of the Sanusi sheikhs. This movement relied as much on the divine blessings bestowed by its founder as on military force, and grew radical in the late nineteenth and early twentieth century context of foreign domination. Still, the Sanusi movement was originally lacking in militance and its later insistence on insurgent action was more a reaction to imperial force than a design to materially transform social institutions.

Perhaps the most instructive case for the Islamic Republic of Iran is the Mahdi movement of the late nineteenth century. In it, the anti-imperial focus was clearly tied to the messianic concept of popular Shi'ism. By 1881, the Sudanese government had been formed in accordance with European criteria and was increasingly an employer of European officials and agents. However, the Mahdi seemed to focus their *jihad* more on the Turks (or more precisely, the khedivial government of Egypt), who were deemed to have corrupted the Muslim faith. Al-Mahdi Muhammad Ahmad sought to establish a new, messianic-ordained kingdom of justice before the millennium ushered in the final battle between God and the false Messiah (al-Dajjal).

The Mahdist conception of utopia was clearly founded in eschatological doctrines, an appeal to the purification of the faith, and the conviction that a golden age was destined to be established before the Day of Judgment. Such conceptions of messianic deliverance were sufficient only to unify tribal forces in reaction. The Mahdi did defeat the Egyptian forces under "Chinese" Charles Gordon at Khartoum, and established a short-lived Mahdist state. That state was overthrown by the British with the victorious Kitchener coming to be called the Dajjal. However, any triumph of evil over good was defined by the faithful as only temporary, and some twenty other insurgencies followed.

From these early forces of Islamic opposition may be abstracted the recurring dilemmas of theocratic movements. In each, resistance took the form of a temporal militance that served to negate a more detached spiritualism. In each, the revival of traditional faith was to be the basis for realizing societal objectives. Also for each, the context for resistance featured some degree of foreign domination. On the other hand, theocratic movements offered evidence less of historical action than reaction. They built on opposing enemies of the faith and sought no new historical synthesis at either a material or ideological level. What was revived was a version of "once upon a time," perhaps retold in the language of contemporary crisis, but always bent on redirecting the forces of change toward a lost world. Finally, though an imperial power was routinely identified and resisted, the material and global nature of a system of imperialism was not well understood. Portraying the foe as an infidel or corrupter of the faith was sufficient to rally believers, even though such shibboleths had little to do with the relations of dependency. However, the very *absence* of a competing ideology, together with a clerical organization used to mobilize the faithful, made a politicized faith a powerful force.

One should be careful not to draw a simple connection between Islamic zeal and reaction. The great moral principles that speak of reverence, morality, integrity and sobriety simply do not speak in historically specific terms to such contextual matters as the organization of health care, illiteracy, uneven development, the structure of governance, and the questions of ownership and distribution of wealth. Yet movements of national liberation in Islamic countries have often come to terms with Islam without surrendering state power to clerical forces. In early nineteenth-century Algeria, during the first stages of French colonial rule, the indigenous Islamic opposition was led by Abdel Qadir. He designed and used a green and white flag signifying independence from French rule. That dream was not be be realized until the French were finally forced out in 1962. However, the adoption of Qadir's flag in independent Algeria by nationalist forces represents a symbolic tie between earlier examples of Islamic resistance and more contemporary nationalists.

From the 1930s, a revived Islam was important in the cultivation of Algerian national identity. A central role was played by the Association of Reformist *ulama* in the development of this anticolonial popular ideology (Vatin, 1983: 98–121). Thus the principles of the faith embodied in a history of resistance may be used to legitimate political struggles for independence. However, it is the precise form of material and political expression that is at issue. In Algeria, Islam was defined as compatible with a modernized, indigenous socialism. Moreover, the F.L.N. used the language of Islam as a means of promoting national unity; it did not surrender state power to teachers of the faith and to interpreters of religious law. Such was not to be in the case in Khomeini's Iran.

In Iran, the Shi'a *ulama* have always represented greater authority than the clerics of the more independent-minded Sunni, often emerging as leaders during periods of crisis (Jansen, 1979: 103–4). Historically, the Shi'a have constituted a minority sect that split from the Sunni mainstream some thirty years after the death of the Prophet Mohammed to follow Ali, his cousin and son-in-law. Sociologically, the Shi'a derived from the *mawali*, Muslims not born to an Arab tribe who became economic and social marginals under Arab regimes (Lewis, 1973: 220–21, 240–41). Their minority status, defined not simply in terms of population but in powerlessness and economic inequality remains in place after thirteen centuries. Ideologically, the tenets of Shi'ism reflect earlier Persian and Judaeo-Christian forms of messianic deliverance, the clearest example of which is the Mahdism reviewed earlier. Compounded by the forces of external domination, this double minority found dignity in their faith, recompense in maximal conceptions of *jihad*, and power in intentional martyrdom. Shi'ites today represent a majority of the population only in Iran and Iraq, though they are approaching a majority in Lebanon. As of the late 1980s, it was only in Iran, where they constitute 95 percent of the population, that a Shi'ite state prevailed.

It would be simplistic, if dramatic, to attribute the real Middle Eastern terrorism to these points of faith. However, the poverty and humiliation of Shi'ites in Lebanon have rendered some susceptible to an ideology of deliverance. The largest Shi'ite movement in Lebanon in the 1980s was Nabih Berri's Amal, which gave little support to the Iranian insurgency. Other groups emerged including Hizbollah (Party of God) which, although loosely forming around local Shi'a clergy, represented more a state of mind than organizational being. Still, some of the more dramatic acts of violence and hostage-taking have been attributed to its influence. Hizbollah appeal grew especially among the young and peasant poor. The Islamic reaction it symbolized, took root in fertile soil. It was nurtured in a layered context of (1) the Israeli attempt to prop up the Maronite Christians and destroy the P.L.O. in Lebanon; (2) of a U.S. "show of force" that ultimately meant the landing of a marine detachment and the shelling of Lebanese villages by U.S. warships; and (3) of an attempt by displaced Palestinians to form a ministate of their own inside Lebanon. Thus conditions of marginality and humiliation bonded again with the message of delivery through sacrifice.

## THE NEOIMPERIAL CRUCIBLE

To this point, analysis has centered on the directive influence of ideology and its corresponding potential to build solidarity and inform mass movements. However, ideas cannot be understood purely in relation to other ideas. The structural crucible of the Iranian revolution is still to be explored. It was U.S. President Franklin Delano Roosevelt who called Iran the "bridge to victory" in World War II. A similar description by Richard Nixon in 1973 noted the strategic position of Iran, "between the East and West, between Asia and Europe and for that matter Africa." In the postwar Persian Gulf, Iran's vast oil reserves, together with its position on the Strait of Hormuz, became increasingly vital as the dependence of the West and Japan on imported oil grew (Ramazani, 1975: 7). However, the geopolitical significance of Iran is perhaps more clearly evidenced in the specific national identities of its neighbors. It is bounded on the east by Pakistan and Afghanistan (severed from Iran by the British in 1857), on the west by Iraq, on the northwest by NATO member Turkey, and on the north by the U.S.S.R. The geography is both symbolic and substantive. Iran in the modern era has been the locus of complex historical forces, often reduced by Western analysts to the simplicity of the "Soviet threat" or "Communist expansion."

Twentieth-century Iranians have found themselves impaled on the horns of a dual dilemma.[4] On the one hand, the structures of feudalism featuring the archaic social relations of royalty and commoner, landlord and peasant, traditionalism and modernization were to vie with the forces of supercession. What early Iranian critics in the first decade called "oriental despotism" and a "feudal ruling class" faced new currents of national independence, state organization and social reform. The *ancien régime* of Muzaffar al-Din Shah (1896–1906) came to be shackled by constitutional forces.

On the other hand, Iran chafed under the threat of Western imperialism. The Anglo-Russian Agreement of 1907 recognized Iranian "zones of influence" for the competing powers. Thus, before the First World War, the alliance that had brought down the shah was fractured along the more enduring lines of class and status interests. The (Social) Democrats who opposed both external capital and feudal institutions found themselves locked in a struggle with the Moderate party whose deputies included "thirteen members of the 'ulama, ten landlords, nine merchants, ten civil servants and three tribal chiefs" (Abrahamian, 1982: 105). This alliance of cleric, landed aristocracy, and merchant has proven especially resilient, often impowered more by the design of foreign capital and Western state power than by its own mastery of events.

The programs of the two early twentieth-century parties remain instructive today. The Democrats held out a vision of universal education (with special emphasis on the needs of women), the separation of religion and politics, free, direct, and secret elections, industrialization, progressive taxation, labor reform, the distribution of land to those who tilled it, and other secular reforms. The Moderates called for strengthening the constitutional monarchy, the preeminence of religion including religious education, and the protection of family life, private property, and the *petite bourgeoisie* of the bazaar (Abrahamian, 1982: 104–6). In a prewar context of escalating urban conflict involving these real (yet symbolic) forces, as well as rural tribal revolt against central government, the British landed detachments in October of 1911 and the Soviets dispatched an occupational force one month later. By 1914, Iran was an occupied territory.

The October Revolution brought an end to the tsarist era. Imperial Britain moved swiftly to fashion the 1919 Anglo-Iranian Agreement, promising to loan Iran two million British pounds and other assistance in return for a monopoly over administrative advisers, arms, and military training. This attempted extension of the British empire was followed nine months later by a small Red Army incursion into Enzeli. In 1920, the Democrats of Azerbaijan called for a republic and the Justice Party Congress meeting in Enzeli became the Communist party of Iran. By late 1920 political chaos ruled in the land. In this context, Colonel Reza Khan, who headed the Cossack Brigade in Qazvin, marched on Tehran.

Reza Khan's *coup d'etat* saw the fashioning of a new structure of power. Agreements were fashioned by which the U.S.S.R. (in return for a promise that Iran would not be used again as a staging area for attack), cancelled tsarist era debts and concessions and evacuated Soviet troops. The Anglo-Iranian Agreement was symbolically abrogated, but British advisers were asked to remain. Reza Khan moved quickly to strengthen the Western alliance through appointing Arthur Millspaugh of the U.S. State Department as treasurer-general, while offering a petroleum concession in the north to the Rockefeller family's Standard Oil.[5]

Reza Shah formed alliances with the more secular-minded conservative forces, and appeased the clerics through declaring his dedication to the laws of sacred Islam and specifically those concerning moral conduct. Taking the ancient name Pahlavi, he convinced his supporters in the Constituent Assembly not only to confer upon him the title of shah but to restore the power of the crown. He established his power first and foremost in a costly modern army whose officer corp enjoyed elite status, but he rooted it also in an extensive state bureaucracy and a system of court patronage by which he amassed estates of some three million acres and a personal fortune of three million British pounds (Wilber, 1975: 243–44).

In service of his absolutism, Reza Shah banned trade unions, closed newspapers, destroyed political parties, and brutally repressed not only the Communist party but those peasant tribespeople whose aspirations for land and water threatened large landowners. He shared the British fear of Bolshevism, a fear that was more than ideological. For Iran's vast oil reserves remained largely under the control (since 1909) of the Anglo-Iranian Oil Company, with Iran under a 1933 agreement receiving only a 20 percent share of the profits. Reza Shah's British connection thus left his regime open to criticism and ripe for anti-imperial forces both left and right.

Through his reign, Reza Shah facilitated the production of counterforces that would ultimately negate Pahlavi rule. Monopolistic practices alienated the merchants of the bazaar. The emphasis on education insured the development of an intelligentsia that could only chafe under absolutism. The growth of oil production and refining, as well as something of an industrial infrastructure insured the emergence of a working class. The preference for European dress, the support of Western conceptions of women's rights (including abandonment of the traditional veil and chador), and the diminished influence of the clergy under secularized rule threatened traditionalists. The massing of great personal fortunes could only set the stage for those who would make political capital out of an ascetic life style.

On the economic side was the *hydrocephalic development* that juxtaposed urban growth and agricultural neglect in a classic pattern of uneven development. To finance Western-style growth, the Pahlavis were dependent on taxes (which especially alienated the landlords) and on the West to market Iranian oil. In the early stages of the Second World War with the shah increasingly relying on state violence to maintain power, a joint British-Soviet invasion was mounted to "forestall the growth of German influence, to secure the oil fields of Iran and to acquire a route for the transport of supplies to the Soviet Union" (Sick, 1985: 5). Reza Shah abdicated and the forces of occupation brought his son, Mohammed Reza Pahlavi, to nominal power.

The Anglo-Russian occupation demonstrated once more the pawnlike standing of Iran and only insured more generalized resentment of foreign domination. However, specific constellations of resistance could not fail to emerge in the postwar period. They shared a common symbolic root in Reza Shah, and a common trunk in the similar excesses of his son: that of a *splendid dependency*. However, the expression of collective political will reveals underlying class and other categorical formations. Upon the abdication of Reza Shah, the Tudeh ("masses") party emerged, led by the leaders of a group of 53 activists who had been labeled "Communist" in 1937 by the occupant of the Peacock Throne (Ramazani, 1975: 92–94). Espousing a democratic centralism, the party drew its strength from university-educated intellectuals, industrial workers, artisans, and craftspeople. As Marxists they sought to fit theory to the specific exigencies of national struggle.

The Tudeh party was opposed by an alliance of the *ulama*, merchants from the bazaars and tribes that came to form the National Will party. Its structure was rigidly autocratic, and its platform called for the protection of the guilds (especially the shopkeepers), religious instruction in the schools, and the right to private property. It's leader was Sayyid Ziya ("sayyid" is a religious title for those claiming descent from the prophet Mohammed through his daughter, Fatima), who opposed the old structures of royalty and was vividly opposed to Westernization. The National Will party was willing to cooperate with the British, yet Britian, along with other members of the Iranian middle classes, feared not only the left but also the forces of reaction. Certain members of the traditional middle classes, specifically merchants and guild elders who had prospered through acquiring land through the confiscation policies of Reza Shah, formed an alliance with the royalists (Abrahamian, 1982: 193–98).

### Mossadeq, Nationalization, and Operation Ajax

In the postwar period, the United States expanded its oil concessions in the southeast and began to compete with the British in part through providing assistance for the growth of the Iranian military. Divisions in the Iranian parliament (the Majles) saw the emergence of royalists and others who favored a continuing alliance with the British. However, opposition forces began to rally around the charismatic person of the Western-educated aristocrat Mohammed Mossadeq. When an assassination attempt was made on the life of Shah Pahlavi in 1949, the ruler resorted to martial law, blamed the Tudeh party (without firm evidence), and moved to imprison or exile its leaders. Such methods, together with the shah's enduring alliance with British oil interests, led to the creation of Mossadeq's National Front. The Front was unified in opposition, but divided by divergent class formations and ideology. It was supported by well-educated professionals, government employees, women, and university students on the one side and some disenchanted bazaar merchants, ultranationalists, and clerics on the other.

The Majles in 1950–51 continued to be dominated by royalist/British forces, but strong popular demonstrations of support for Mossadeq (much of it coming from the suppressed but not destroyed Tudeh forces who organized both oil industry and general strikes) resulted in the nationalization of the Anglo-Iranian Oil Company in April of 1951 (Ramazani, 1975: 181–218). What had taken political form was the popular ideology that Iranian oil should belong to Iranians. The shah, in the face of nationalist forces, had little choice but to appoint Mossadeq prime minister (Sick, 1985: 3–7). However, Mohammed Pahlavi's allies proved formidable. The British countered through organizing a boycott of Iranian oil in the global petroleum market. In this context, Mossadeq's attempts to gain the support of the World Bank in funding oil company operations predictably failed, as the banks' "terms" would have divested Iran of direct control (Ramazani, 1975: 220–21). Despite immediate damage to the Iranian economy, nationalistic fervor remained high and Mossadeq remained in power. Shah Mohammed Reza Pahlavi was forced to flee to Rome on August 16, 1953. However, unlike his deposed father, he was to be brought back to political life.

In what has been a recurring theme in the centers of Western power through this century, the Eisenhower administration feared the loss of Iran to Soviet influence, and its C.I.A. became a key-player in the British proposed operation "Ajax" (Roosevelt, 1979). C.I.A. agents assisted in the orchestration of "pro-shah" riots (Copeland, 1969:51). But it was a military coup by forces loyal to General Zahidi that brought back the shah. Ironically, the army was in the streets to put down the Tudeh, under the orders of the anti-Communist Mossadeq, having been persuaded on this course of action by the U.S. Ambassador to Iran (Abrahamian, 1982: 324–25). The Mossadeq government fell on August 19, and the shah returned three days later courtesy of "an American operation from beginning to end (Tully, 1962: 96)." After his trial, Mossadeq was placed under house arrest. Having doomed the aspirations of a nationalism feared too much on the left, the West and its shah went busily about creating the precipitating conditions that could only resurrect the dormant forces of theocratic reaction in the years to come.

**Iranian Regime Terror: 1953–79**

In the decade following Mossadeq's ouster, the shah moved internally to suppress the Tudeh party and the National Front (Ramazani, 1975:326). One crucial event was the formation in 1957 of the National Security and Information Organization, the acronym for which from the Farsi language is SAVAK. SAVAK was created with the aid of the U.S. C.I.A. and F.B.I. and the Israeli Mossad (Abrahamian, 1982: 419). Although its duties included the screening of candidates for state positions and media censorship, SAVAK was to become a hated and feared arm of regime terror. Its more than 5,000 agents made ample use of torture to identify and brutally suppress political opposition from the left or right. Two other intelligence organizations, the Second Bureau and the Royal

Inspection Organization (Imperial Inspectorate), were formed to watch SAVAK and the military (Afshar, 1985: 179–80).[6]

It was, however, the new imperial ties with the United States that implicated a superpower in the excesses of the court and the economic violence visited on the poor (Pesaran, 1985: 15–50). Ironically, with the decline of the Iranian economy in the short-lived oil-nationalization period, it had been Mossadeq who had turned to the United States for technical assistance. The result was the Point IV program, which, with Mossadeq's demise, became part of the shah's First Plan. U.S. assistance in economic development was evidenced in agriculture, industry, public health, education, and administration. By means of the Mutual Security Act of 1954 and the Law for the Attraction and Protection of Foreign Investment in Iran (1955), Western (and particularly, U.S.) hegemony was assured. Foreign investors were offered guarantees against losses owing to nationalization, and between 1950 and 1970, U.S. military and economic aid to Iran amounted to some 2.3 billion dollars.

Under U.S. tutelage, Iran was absorbed into a Western model of development marked by several distinctive properties. A preference for a few large-scale projects (ranging from factories to the construction of dams and intercity transportation) disguised economic fragmentation and the continued neglect of the agricultural sector. Iran devalued its currency, increased its money supply and lent huge sums to the private sector. The resulting "boom" coexisted with inflation and deficits, leading to International Monetary Fund (I.M.F.) "stabilization" in 1960 with its standard austerity measures: control of private sector credit, import-controls, cuts in government services and higher interest rates. A Western-style *White Revolution* (a clear historical reference to anti-Red forces in the Russian Revolution), called for reforms ranging from female suffrage to literacy, profit-sharing to land reform and the privatization of state industries. These in concert with I.M.F. austerity measures began to revitalize the clergy/bazaar opposition, soon joined by the landed upper class. Iran responded to its recession by increasing oil exports, and appeared to have an opportunity to resolve its crisis of development through the fortuitous developments in OPEC. Oil that brought revenues of only 80 cents a barrel in 1960, and 86 cents a decade later, produced $9.49 by 1974.

However, massive growth in Iranian oil revenues proved only to fund its splendid dependency. At the international level, in the classic sense of "boomerang capitalism," the shah used petrodollars to support Western export industries, including vast expenditures on modern armaments. In 1977 alone, Iran purchased arms worth 2.3 billion, out of a total 6.5 billion exported by the United States (United States Bureau of Census, 1979: 367). Military sales from the U.S. alone for the five-year period 1973 to 1977 amounted to 15.2 billion (Halliday, 1979: 95). The "development" of Iran was in keeping with the shah's commitment to convert Iran into a "Great Civilization" and the world's fifth-ranking power. Internally, the inequality of dependency relations was reproduced with wealth concentrated by class and in the cities. The expansion of wealth, as well as its concentration, meant price inflation and growing reliance on imports as the domestic economy was unable to meet demand.

Parallel events on the political side marked the simmering potential of an anti-imperial reaction. The riots of 1963 (referred to by Khomeini (1979: 34) as the beginning point of the misnamed revolution), were not only a reaction to the growing authoritarianism of the shah but of the strengthening alliance between Tehran and Washington, D.C. The Kennedy administration in 1961 had pressured the shah to appoint as Prime Minister Ali Amini, former Iranian ambassador to the United States and a member of a wealthy land-owning family. Amini was dismissed 20 months later (only to appear in 1978 as a key adviser to the embattled monarch), but his influence together with the emerging of the White Revolution further convinced the Iranian people that the shah was a U.S. puppet. Khomeini, who had been conspicuously absent during the Mossadeq campaign, now began to denounce the Westernization of Iran, and the exemption of U.S. military personnel stationed in Iran from the jurisdiction of Iranian courts. When riots followed his arrest on June 4, 1963, the Pahlavi forces killed hundreds of dissidents. After a series of conflicts and imprisonments, Khomeini was exiled to Turkey in October of 1964. He was not to return for fourteen years. However, his very exile, added to his credibility as a symbol of resistance and paved the way for a dramatic return.

Although the Johnson administration added to the shah's military strength, it was in May of 1972 when Richard Nixon and Henry Kissinger negotiated a sea change in U.S.-Iranian relations. The United States offered to meet the shah's obsession for sophisticated military hardware, technicians, and advisers. The shah in turn agreed to use the armed force of his state to defend Western interests in the Persian Gulf. This political alliance revealed more concretely the real power behind the Peacock Throne. But the relationship born in splendor was to end in ironic ruin. When the shah and his entourage left Iran in 1979, he became *persona non grata*. However, the Rockefeller brothers Nelson and David gave personal expression to the tie between Iran and Standard Oil that had existed since the time of Reza Shah. With the aid of Henry Kissinger, they prevailed upon the Carter administration to admit the shah to the United States to receive medical treatment for his advanced lymphoma. Despite a warning from Tehran that there would be serious consequences to pay, the shah was admitted on October 22, 1979 (Sick, 1985: 9–13, 68, 180).

Thus history, from the side of the Khomeini forces, must have appeared to come full circle. The hated shah was on the soil of the nation whose C.I.A. had engineered his return to power in 1953, and that had presided over the international construction of its modern dependency. It was in this context that students loyal to Khomeini took the U.S. embassy in Tehran on November 4, and provided the Imam with one tool to seize control of a potentially authentic revolution. At a global level, the lead nations of the West had acted to preserve the Peacock Throne for over a half-century, while effectively dooming the Mossadeq nationalist movement in the early 1950s. Yet, when the external forces of imperialism combined with the indigenous conditions of royalist rule, faith, and reaction inside Iran, a new era was indeed born. Only in this case, terror begat terror.

## THEORETICAL CONCLUSIONS

A number of theoretical conclusions can be drawn from the Khomeini reaction. At the level of global forces, it is clear that the material prize of resources (particularly the "world petroleum economy" mentioned in the *Tower Commission Report*, 1987: 117) and markets, essential to the maintenance of a system of world-market trade, have dominated relations between Iran and the West. These are at the root of Western state international policies, including attempts under the U.S. Nixon administration to play the Iranian card to project surrogate military power in the gulf. They are also the base for the ideological forces of anticommunism, which found contradictory expression in support of a monarchy-imposed program of modernization. Yet the immense Iranian oil revenues proved only to fund the institutional terror of dependency and uneven development while making even more pronounced the class divisions between rich and poor.

The role of anti-Bolshevik/anti-Communist/anti-Soviet ideology, evidenced early on in British relations with Iran, even more strongly impacted U.S. policy *after the fall of the shah*. In December of 1984, the "C.I.A. Deputy Director of Operations considered the Marxist Mujaheddin E Khalq to be well organized, influenced by the Soviets, and likely to succeed Khomeini." In May of 1985, the Fuller Memorandum to C.I.A. Director William Casey argued that anti-Khomeini policies "may now serve to facilitate *Soviet* interests more than our own" (Tower Commission, 1987: 105, 113).

Concern with hostages (held by pro-Iranian groups) notwithstanding, the Tower Commission (charged by the Reagan administration in 1986 with the review of the Iran/Contra affair) thus inadvertently offered evidence that the Reagan administration was traveling another tributary of the same historical river. This obsession with negating the left, earlier generalized to Mossadeq's nationalism, had first blinded the United States to the prospects for the emergence of an antishah reaction, and now prompted the Reagan administration to support that movement. With the added need for "out-of-channels" funding for the Nicaraguan Contras, a second tributary joined the first. Thus the Irangate bridge between the Middle East and Central America was in itself a reaction, albeit a paranoid one, to the Marxist nemesis.

The global nature of the forces at play in Irangate is further evidenced in the role played by Israel. In a narrow sense, Israeli policy was to "insure a stalemate of the conflict with Iraq" (Tower Commission, 1987: 137), which may be translated to mean equipping Iran with the means to continue the war. Indeed, Defense Minister Ariel Sharon admitted as early as May 1982 that Israel was arming Iran (Alavi, 1988:5), while the Israelis also played a central role in the six arms transactions in 1985–86 between the United States and Iran (Tower

Commission, 1987: 438–49). The Jerusalem Post reported on December 6, 1986, that from the outset of the Iran-Iraq war, Israeli intelligence "supported the policy of backing Iran because Iraq has taken part in every war against Israel and is an integral part of the Eastern Front, whereas Khomeini's fundamentalism is first and foremost a threat to the Arabs themselves" (cited in Alavi, 1988: 6).

However, there is more at work here than cold political calculus in service of national interests. The Israeli role transcends national expansion and intersects Western hegemony. It must be understood in terms of global systemic forces, both material and ideological. Viewed through this prism, the Iranian Islamic reaction is far less a threat to Western imperialism than it is to the still-scattered forces of Pan-Arabism and to the emergence of more authentic forms of development within the periphery. In this sense, the Khomeini reaction is an appropriate (though ironic) successor to the Pahlavi dynasty. Put metaphorically, the specter of Khomeini now vies with the spirit of Nasser for the destiny of the region.

At another level, to comprehend the structural contradictions that brought down the shah's regime in general terms is to understand the clash between the powerful vestiges of a still feudal order and the nascent forces behind the "modernization" of Iran. Such involve several layers, with emerging patterns of horizontal as well as vertical conflict. To begin, the attempt to hurl a society into the industrial age meant even greater dependency as the shah was forced to import technology, infrastructure, advisers, and workers. With development focused in the urban areas, young migrants flooded into the cities, living in urban slums. With predictable growth (or at least greater visibility) of prostitution, alcohol abuse, delinquency, and crime, the clerics pointed to moral decay and laid it at the feet of westernization. However, there was more at work than too-rapid change. That royal/dynastic/aristocratic forces contend for power with the forces of organized religion is not unique to Iranian history. But it is ironic that the shah and his Western advisers were blind to this antagonism. Here, the arrogation of real power, together with the defilement of traditional culture and influence could only alienate the *ulama*. In political terms, westernization could only bring the *secularization* of Iranian culture, with clear consequences for the diminution of clerical power. And it was the clerics who had the ear of the people.

The traditional merchant class of the bazaar also had reason to be apprehensive concerning their role in the to-be-transformed economy. In characteristic fashion, the shah used the broadsword of state power in the early 1970s to control price inflation by fining or closing down some 250,000 "profiteering" merchants (Zabih, cited in Pesarin, 1985: 46). The resurrection of the historical alliance between the bazaar and the clergy could only follow. In the meantime, the shah's support of the educational improvements necessary to build a "modern" economy meant a growing intelligentsia, not willingly confined to technical knowledge. Thus came the bonding of professionals, intellectuals, and students who were well aware of the anachronistic nature of the Peacock Throne. And finally, to the outrage of the growing industrial working class, the shah's complaints against high wages and low productivity in 1978 came in the context of severely declining purchasing power and rising unemployment (Abrahamian, 1982: 511–12). Thus in the universities, the seminaries, the bazaars, and finally the streets the movement grew, flourishing on brutal retaliation by the military and the police.

On the question of movement ideology, the Islamic reaction in Iran demonstrates the pitfalls that follow the ideologization of religion. The abiding tension between sacred and secular paths to revolution is well-evidenced in the work of Ali Shariati, a sociologist educated at the Sorbonne, who combined a holistic call for revolution in the Third World with Islamic reform. However, he opposed the conception of a state dominated by the clergy. Believing that a cultural regeneration was fundamental to societal transformation, Shariati called on believers in "true Shi'ism" to develop a social faith, fitted to the temporal conditions of this world (Bayat, 1980: 100–4). However, his emphasis on cultural roots, including the faith, as a necessary condition for the building of authentic revolution proved to be a two-edged sword.

Shariati's works were widely read and his imprisonments under the shah added to his credentials, especially among disaffected students. However, with his death in 1977, it appears that the *culturalist focus* of his critique was too easily absorbed into the appeal of the charismatic Khomeini. Those sympathetic to Shariati may miss an important ideological point. While his focus on an Islamic cultural identity (while by no means exclusionary) offered an "enlightened" view, it proved *more compatible than not* to Khomeini's attempt to synthesize power and cultural purification. If a politicized faith was to be a revolutionary force (as Shariati argued), then, in the minds of the faithful, who better to lead the movement and the state than the Imam? That Shariati strongly opposed clerical rule does not alter the fact that the influential position of men of God could be used to claim the secular political authority, conferred by a transformed Shi'ism.

And finally, the Iranian reaction provides a theoretical lesson in the legitimation of the theocratic state. Following the thesis of Claus Offe, any state requires an input of loyalty and confidence from the people to support its output of autocratic administrative decisions (Perdue, 1986: 383). Earlier in this chapter, the doctrinal forces of messianic deliverance, of Islamic universalism, of maximal interpretations of *jihad*, of Mahdism, and of martyrdom were identified. The theocratic state thus gathers its legitimacy *only in part* from the ability of its principals to transform such spiritual symbols into a political, economic, and social agenda. But the premise of the theocratic state after all was that its creation would usher in a "golden age." Given this, offering legitimations that appeal only to the blind devotion of the faithful has its limits. As with any other state structure, the Iranian republic must ultimately produce results. As with any other state structure, it must balance the imperatives of economic growth and distribution against the demands of military expenditures and public services. The struggle against external symbols of imperialism may buy time, as has the border war with Iraq. (Even the woeful shootdown of a civilian aircraft by the U.S. Navy over the Persian Gulf in July of 1988 could only temporarily build a unity of outrage.) But sooner or later, the theocratic state must face its own legitimation crisis. As the breakout of peace voids the promise of martyrdom, and the threat to national survival subsides, the real Iranian revolution may emerge from the settled political dust of formations of reaction.

## NOTES

1. The Irangate "story" was actually broken by the Lebanese publication *Al-Shiraa*.
2. In the summer of 1981, after the ruling Islamic party had declared President Abolhassan Bani-Sadr unfit, a new wave of executions began. Perhaps 2,000 people, mostly members of the Mujaheddin Khalq and smaller Marxist-Leninist groups, faced revolutionary firing squads (*World Almanac*, 1987: 581).
3. General references for this section include Lewis, 1973: 237–52; Jansen, 1979: 87–120; and Humphreys, 1982.
4. General references on modern Iranian history include Abrahamian, 1982 and Ramazani, 1975.
5. As considered below, this was the beginning of a tie that was to resurface in the U.S. Embassy hostage crisis almost six decades later.
6. Under Khomeini, a new secret police (SAVAMA), together with the revolutionary guards, continued the tradition of SAVAK by using its torture chambers to protect the new theocratic state. Amnesty International reported in January, 1982, on the escalating resort to political executions.

# 9

# *Surrogate Terrorism: The United States and Nicaragua*

Our goal must be a day when the free flow of trade—from the tip of Tierra del Fuego to the Arctic Circle—unites the people of the Western Hemisphere. . . .
Ronald Reagan, State of the Union Address, January 25, 1988

I never learned to read. Now my children are learning to read, and the Yankees send the contras to burn down the school.
Peter Davis, *Where Is Nicaragua?*

The National Security Council is, in essence, the president's staff. . . . We worked on the development of a concerted policy regarding terrorists and terrorism. . . .
Lt. Col. Oliver North before the Iran-Contra hearings, July, 1987

When they had wiped out or driven off El Coco's defenders, the contras raped two women and a sixteen-year-old girl, then shaved their heads and cut their throats. The men captured by the contras were executed. Between sunup and noon, Senora Polanco lost her husband, two sons and two grandchildren.
Peter Davis, *Where Is Nicaragua?*

One of the extraordinary chapters of the Reagan years involved the creation of a "stand-alone" organization within the National Security Council of the executive branch, designed to carry out covert operations in defense of (and in isolation from) the "democratic process." One such operation was the Iranian arms sale, which (after duly enriching the arms merchants involved) provided some out-of-channel money to forces seeking to overthrow the Sandinista government of Nicaragua. This was not the only ingenious way in which the counterrevolutionaries (Contras) were to be funded. As the U.S. Congress could not always be depended upon for allocations, the administration turned to wealthy private citizens, somewhat notorious for their anti-Communist zeal. In speaking of the latter in the fall of 1986, Assistant Secretary of State for Inter-American Affairs Elliot Abrams told the Washington Post: "What has kept the (contras) alive has been private help. Some members of Congress accuse us of approving this with a wink and a nod. A wink and a nod, hell! We think it has been fine" (in Reston, 1986: 4).

Although it is tempting to attribute bizarre episodes to bizarre administrations, such attributions deny the past and distort the present. Relations between the United States and Nicaragua have historically turned on intimidation and intervention. Earlier, such patterns featured the use of armed force by a hemispherically dominant state. However, the structural ties of domination have traditionally been more subtle. They have bonded indigenous Nicaraguan elites with the more powerful external interests of the core exponent of a global market economy. From the perspective of ordinary people, these forces are not abstractions. They take the form of grinding privation and perennial fear; subjugation at the hands of real players who stand in for others on the stage of history.

## MANIFEST DESTINY AND NICARAGUA: THE ROOTS OF TERROR

Ironically, Ronald Reagan's 1988 call for free hemispheric trade was only an echo of older changes in capitalist market forces. Until 1821, what is presently the Republic of Nicaragua was part of a vast colony of Spain (the Captaincy General of Guatemala) ranging from Costa Rica to the southern Mexican border (Booth, 1982: 11–15). Spain's Bourbon monarchs were forced as early as the seventeenth century to free trade by easing their control of concessions and monopolies. The landholders and new commercial elite who stood to benefit from this new "liberalism" opposed the conservatives of the day who favored the old order. It was to be the liberals of the Central American provinces who, in the aftermath of the successful Mexican war of independence from Spain, broke with Mexico in 1823, to establish a federation. The internecine struggle between ascending and traditional elites turned, and by 1838 a conservative resurgence fashioned a Nicaraguan secession from the United Provinces of Central America. However, the conflict was neither ended nor confined.

Spain was not the only Western imperial power interested in Central America. From the early 1800s, Great Britain (with its immense naval and commercial power) sought successfully to control Central American Atlantic shipping, establish mining interests, and influence through loans the fledgling republics of the region. As the British looked West, they considered the linkage of oceans by means of a Nicaraguan canal. Toward that end, they seized San Juan del Norte in 1847. But the British were not alone. To the north, another set of imperial designs were taking ideological form. Eager for new territory, the United States looked not only westward but southward toward Mexico and Central America. The fervor of *manifest destiny* led to a reinterpretation of the Monroe Doctrine, transforming the warning to European powers into a legitimation for intervention at will.

This ideological synthesis both followed and stimulated commercial and territorial expansion, as by 1846 the trumped up war with Mexico had added Texas, New Mexico, and California to the new American empire. However, the takeover struggle between Britain and the United States was given particular impetus by the discovery of gold in the Sacramento Valley. Between 1843 and 1849, San Francisco was transformed with its sleepy population growing from a few hundred to some 25,000 (Selser, 1981: 9). Some came overland, but most seized by gold fever sought a faster route. Thus it was that the general rivalry between Britain and its upstart rival took specific form over the question of a transisthmus passage through little Nicaragua. In 1850, the warship U.S.S. *Cyane* bombarded San Juan del Norte, and in keeping with the shape of things to come, landed a detachment of marines to burn the British stronghold. Occupied in the Crimean, the British responded to the increasing pressure by dropping territorial and protectorate demands in Central America by 1859 (Booth, 1982: 16–17).

## The Rogue and the Tycoon

The race to the gold through Nicaragua was to bring together two exemplars of bawdy nineteenth-century capitalism, a rogue and a tycoon. The voyage round Tierra del Fuego and Cape Horn was a more judicious way to the gold, but for the truly greedy, a shorter passage could be had across the Isthmus of Panama or through the waterways of Nicaragua. By 1849, five companies with capital in excess of one million pounds sterling, were registered in London; all offering the interoceanic path to riches. However, it was the American Cornelius Vanderbilt, of the legendary steamship and railroad empires, who established the Accessory Transit Company. For some $300, Vanderbilt took lesser opportunists by ocean to the San Juan, upriver to Lake Nicaragua, by stagecoach to the Pacific, and then on by his Pacific Line to San Francisco. By 1853, his profits amounted to $11 million (Selser, 1981: 9–20; Davis, 1987: 50–51). Then came the struggle for control for the Accessory Transit Company, a battle that helped bring the rogue William Walker to Nicaragua.

One of Vanderbilt's partners in his trans-Nicaragua venture was Cornelius Garrison. Although Garrison's takeover of the Accessory Transit Company failed, he sought local favor through recommending the services of Walker to the Nicaraguan Liberals who sought his help in their continuing war with the Conservative opposition. Walker's zeal for "manifest destiny" coexisted well with the promise of land grants. With a force of mercenaries, and advanced rifles, he joined with liberal forces to take the Conservative city of Grenada. Supported heavily by Vanderbilt's former partners, as well as by proslavery

American recruits, he sought external support through advocating both slavery and the annexation of Nicaragua. In time, Walker was also to make the mistake of revoking the charter of Vanderbilt's transit company. Vanderbilt-supported anti-Walker forces, consisting of Nicaraguan conservatives, and the British-financed Central American republics, beseiged Walker's army.

In July of 1856, William Walker declared Nicaragua a democracy and staged a rigged election to make himself president. Now playing desperately to *El Norte*, he legalized slavery, offered land to supporters, made English the official language, and sought to appease the appetite of landowners for peasant labor through the passage of vagrancy laws. Faced with military disaster, he fled with his mercenaries from Nicaragua under the protection of the U.S. Navy in April of 1857. Attempting to return to Nicaragua, he was captured by the British in 1860. William Walker was given over to the Hondurans who tried and shot him. Cornelius Vanderbilt who helped turn U.S. policy against the agent of his rivals, abandoned the Accessory Transit Company. He became instead, a major shareholder in the Trans-Panama railroad (Woodward, 1976: 139–45; Booth, 1982: 18–20).

The saga of Vanderbilt and Walker may seem obscure to those lost in the here and now. But they are well-known to educated Nicaraguans, both for what they were and for what they symbolized. Here, biographies intersected the structural forces and ideological currents of the time, and foreshadowed the shape of Nicaraguan-U.S. relations to come. Although Cornelius Vanderbilt has major standing in history, his outmatched rival seized the imagination of expansionist America. In July of 1856, Purdy's National Theatre of New York staged a musical entitled "Nicaragua, or Gen. Walker's Victories" and the *New York Evening Post* referred to his campaign as evidence of the "irresistible law of modern colonization" (May, 1973: 77–78). The *New York Times* (a more enduring part of the institutions of ideology) devoted an entire front page to his exploits four times during 1857 (Bermann, 1986: 51). On a superficial level, such episodes may be perceived as melodrama and sensationalism, designed to sell tickets and newspapers. But against the larger backdrop of history, William Walker personified the expansionist ideology of manifest destiny, fitted particularly for the dream of a Central American/Caribbean empire.

## Beachheads Old and New

The U.S. "special relation" with Latin America meant the formulation of a hemispheric enclave within a preexisting global market system, where isolation from European powers yielded advantage to the ascendant power in the New World. Ultimately, the U.S.-headed hemispheric empire was to be a place where republics took the place of monarchs, and colonial charters gave way to entrepreneurial commerce. Essential to this vision was a canal route across Central America that, along with other commercial routes, would facilitate transoceanic trade. The lands to the south also represented new resources, cheap labor, and markets—in short, fertile ground for investment capital. But it was more than immediate opportunism that fashioned these ties. In 1895, Secretary of State Olney in a note to the U.S. minister to Britain noted the preeminence of the United States in the hemisphere, and wrote a prescient description of the "beachhead" argument that has endured through most of two centuries. Should European competitors gain a foothold, he wrote, the consequences would be disastrous. "The loss of prestige, of authority, and of weight in the councils of the family of nations, would be among the least of them. Our only real rivals in peace as well as enemies in war would be found located at our very doors" (in Bermann, 1986: 291–92).

In the third of a century following its Civil War, the United States grew as an industrial and commercial power. The conquest of Spain led to the domination of Cuba, expressed economically in foreign investment and politically in the Platt Amendment. This called for the withdrawal of occupation forces provided Cuba agreed to adopt a constitutional amendment giving the U.S. the right "to supervise Cuban foreign policy and to intervene in Cuba's internal affairs whenever it saw fit" (Bermann, 1986: 167). Later, at the request of the Nicaraguan Diaz regime, Woodrow Wilson agreed to the extension of the Platt Amendment to Nicaragua. The salary of Diaz, a member of the indigenous mining and sugar elite, was paid by the National Bank of Nicaragua, a U.S. corporation incorporated in Connecticut.

The birth of the National Bank of Nicaragua was a condition of an interim loan by North American bankers of $1.5 million, most of which went into the pockets of Diaz and his allies. These Conservatives had come to power with the aid of U.S. weapons, warships, and marines, displacing the Liberal government in 1910. (The Liberals under Jose Santos Zelaya had incurred opposition from the North by their insistance on Nicaraguan sovereignty, the regulation of concessions of U.S. companies, negotiating a loan with a British-French syndicate, and building an Atlantic railroad with aid from a German company.) Loans, then as now, tied the neocolonial state to the core in the new forms of financial imperialism. In fact, the terms of U.S. recognition as specified in the State Department's Dawson Pact required that no Zelayista be allowed in the Nicaraguan government, that a new constitution protect the rights of foreigners, and that the U.S. government arrange for a loan to be secured by Nicaragua's customs duties.

Teddy Roosevelt's "big stick" had already claimed for the United States the duty to police the hemisphere (Bermann, 1986: 140–59). The financial side, for those on the receiving end of the Big Stick, was "dollar diplomacy," another dimension of the relations of dependency for Nicaragua. Historically, dollar diplomacy and the big stick stand as superstructural permutations of the Monroe Doctrine at the level of state policy. In the new hemispheric century, however, colonial-style domination no longer required formal territorial possession. Instead, changed structures of dependency featured more sophisticated formations of remote economic control (as with absentee loans and investment); the reproduction of indigenous class formations (binding the local elite to the hemispheric core); the support of these elite through the regime terror of the neocolonial state (always in the name of opposing revolutionary threats to order); with the permanent threat or occasional practice of military intervention from the hemisphere's most powerful state.

## SANDINO AND SOMOZA

The U.S.-supported conservative faction presided over the uneven development of the Nicaraguan economy from 1910 until momentous events took shape in the 1920s (Booth, 1982: 32). Insisting on private investment and loans (in lieu of direct aid), the U.S. government intervened to be certain that Nicaraguan public revenues were spent on debt retirement and on inflated foreign damage claims attributed to civil disorder. Hence, public services shrank and civil unrest increased. The U.S.-controlled from 75 to 80 percent of trade, while its private investments rose from $1 million in 1908 to $17.3 million by 1929 (this in a poor society of 600,000 persons) (Booth, 1982:33). It had also negotiated exclusive canal rights by 1916. However, the Panama Canal was already under U.S. control, as Teddy Roosevelt and the canal company in 1903 had instigated a revolution to "free" Panama from Columbia (Paterson, 1977: 222). Thus, canal rights in Nicaragua were negotiated to keep other countries (notably Germany and Japan) from building. That a canal might have benefitted Nicaragua was not a question.

In the 1920s, Nicaragua's financial dependency coexisted with an embarrassingly long occupation by U.S. Marines, who since 1912 had been stationed there to preserve its Conservative government (Bermann, 1986: 183). In the United States, the 320,000 casualties suffered during the 19 months of World War I (*World Almanac*, 1987: 337) helped to rekindle opposition to the naked forms of imperialism evidenced in military intervention. Thus, in 1924, a State Department plan for an election in Nicaragua was implemented. However, this particular election brought some nationalists to power, bent on securing financial independence from the United States. The marines were indeed withdrawn, but the new government was brought down by a coup headed by Emiliano Chamorro, an old Conservative ally whose excesses in power had embarrassed the United States. In a context of growing Liberal revolt, the United States insisted that the Nicaraguan Congress replace Chamorro with the more palatable Conservative, Adolfo Diaz. However, the nationalist forces (heavily supported by the Liberal party) that had been displaced by the coup were not through. They were recognized by Mexico, leading Diaz to resort to an early version of the "communist threat" to legitimate continued U.S. intervention. He accused the Liberals of having "allied themselves with the forces of communism" while Chamorro charged that the opposition was "in direct communication with Soviet Russia through Mexico." President Coolidge ("the business of America is business") in the meantime cited that this "revolution" threatened "large investments in lumbering, mining, coffee growing, banana culture, shipping and also in general mercantile and other collateral business" (cited in Bermann, 1986: 188–89).

Although such rhetoric may have supported the reintroduction of marines, the class composition of the Liberal forces made the allegations of Bolshevism absurd. Many of the leaders were wealthy coffee growers and exporters whose "populism" was a device to strike at their old elite rivals. Many of the Liberals were not "nationalists" seeking independence but were opportunists looking for political office. One of these was Jose Moncada, the commander of the so-called constitutional forces so successfully pressing the Diaz forces. Moncada, in "negotiations" with Coolidge envoy Henry Stimson, agreed to U.S. guarantees of Liberal representation in the Nicaraguan cabinet, supervised elections, and the formation of a U.S. trained national guard (already in place in Haiti and the Dominican Republic). The alternative, Stimson assured Moncada, was to face the armed force of the United States (Stimson, 1970 (1927): 78–79). Moncada went on to lead the Nicaraguan government, but his capitulation had two more important consequences. One was to create the conditions for the emergence of an historical figure of authentic resistance. The second was to put in place an instrument of regime terror that preserved a pro-American Nicaraguan dynasty for a half-century.

Augusto Nicolas Calderon Sandino was born in 1895, the son of a smallholder and an unwed *campesina* mother, and was once cast into debtor's prison with her as a child (Booth, 1982: 41). In 1921 he left Nicaragua after wounding or killing a man in a fight for reasons not known to his biographers (Selser, 1981: 63). He worked in Honduras, then for United Fruit in Guatemala and finally for the Doheny-owned Hausteca Petroleum Company in Tampico, where he encountered the revolutionary ideology and nationalism at large in Mexico, especially among the oilfield workers. At this time, the giant U.S. petroleum concerns (Sinclair, Doheny, Mellon), through the State Department, were seeking to stave off Mexican control of Mexican resources. To achieve their ends, the oil companies halted operations in Mexico, wringing concessions from the Mexican government. Taunted by workers who ridiculed Nicaragua for its failure to resist, and witnessing first-hand the heavy hand of economic intervention, Sandino returned to Managua. To survive, he went to work in the San Albino Mines, also owned by U.S. interests. But here, from wretched miners paid in "company-store" script for fifteen-hour days, he recruited his first revolutionaries (Selser, 1981: 62–65).

When Moncada made his bargain, it was Sandino alone among the rebel commanders who refused to lay down his arms. The first Sandinista army consisted of 29 men, but the fires of resistance against "gringo forces" were fanned and that number grew. In his first manifesto he declared, "Seeing that the United States of North America, lacking any right except that which brute force endows it, would deprive us of our country and our liberty, I have accepted its unjust challenge, leaving to History the responsibility for my actions" (quoted in Selser, 1981: 77). Although Moncada sought unsuccessfully to quash the rebellion, it was G. D. Hatfield, Commanding Officer of the U.S. Marines, who delivered an ultimatum on July 12, 1927. In it he declared that Sandino should surrender with honor or suffer an "infamous death" as a "criminal who deserves to be shot in the back by his own followers." Hatfield also promised that "Nicaragua has had its last revolution (cited in Selser, 1981: 79)." The Marine was to be proven wrong on all counts.

Sandino's guerrilla forces employed hit-and-run tactics, using mountainous terrain to their advantage and avoiding battles where they were outmatched. The untrained *campesinos* who rose in their support in El Ocotol (July, 1927) were not so fortunate. Seven aircraft, summoned by Brigadier General Feland, bombed and strafed the peasants. Three hundred *campesinos* (men, women, and children) died, along with one U.S. Marine. From that point forth, the Marines warred not only on Sandino but indiscriminately by means of a scorched earth policy and summary executions against the *campesinos* (Selser, 1981: 74–101). However, the cruel face of colonial warfare was yet to come, as through a pattern of "Nicaraguanization" the battle against Sandino was turned over to the U.S.-trained Guardia Nacional.

By 1930, the forces of the indigenous elite, wearing U.S.-style uniforms, with heavy armament and machine guns, and backed by U.S. aircraft, fought the tenacious Sandinistas in their own sanctuaries, using their own guerrilla tactics. With the coming of the Guard, the growing Marine casualty lists, and in deference to the growing diplomatic debacle of its peasant war in Nicaragua, the United States decided on a troop pull-out in 1933 ending 20 years of occupation (Paterson, 1977: 355–57). With the withdrawal of U.S. forces, Sandino immediately began peace negotiations with the newly elected Liberal government. But a new player had quietly slipped upon the stage of Nicaraguan history.

The choice of U.S. Minister Matthew Hanna to lead the National Guard was Anastasio Somoza Garcia ("Tacho"), from a *petit bourgeois* family in the Liberal party. An astute politician whose superb English served him well, he had ingratiated himself with the U.S. diplomatic mission, as well as the Liberal higher circles (Booth, 1982: 46–48). When Sandino negotiated peace with President Juan Sacasa (who acted in good faith), he was convinced that Sacasa could and would regulate the National Guard. On February 21, 1934, after dining and negotiation in the presidential palace in Managua, Sandino and two of his generals left to spend the night elsewhere. They were intercepted by Somoza's Guard and murdered (Booth, 1982: 51). One of those responsible was Lt. Abelardo Cuadra. Cuadra had attended a meeting of National Guard officers in Somoza's home in which the plot to kill Sandino was hatched. According to Cuadra, Somoza declared that U.S. Ambassador Arthur Bliss Lane had assured him "that the Washington government supports and recommends the elimination of Augusto Cesar Sandino, considering him as it does a disturber of the country's peace" (quoted in Selser, 1981: 1974).[1] After the murder, the Guard surrounded Sandino's disarmed men and their families at their cooperative farm, slaughtered them, and left their bodies unburied. And "the crows, dogs and swine of the neighborhood treated themselves to a prolonged feast of human flesh'' (in Selser, 1981: 178).

There is a parallel between the early Sandinista movement and that headed by the forces of Zapata and Villa during the Mexican Revolution. Both movements were hampered by more or less spontaneously occurring ideologies of popular resistance. These were constructed from a burning sense of injustice, emerging under charismatic leadership from the privation and misery of peasant life. But just as the peasant revolutionaries in Mexico failed to press their advantage, so did Sandino fail to fight on against the new institutions of colonial domination. Each failed to understand the importance of seizing state power, both as a means of insuring and implementing the land reform so crucial to authentic agricultural development and to set about the task of societal transformation. Sandino (admittedly weary) agreed to disarm, defining the withdrawal by the Marines as victory. He believed that the Sacasa government could control the National Guard, and guarantee the continued existence of the cooperative farm worked by his people. He was wrong. But in killing him, Somoza did more than create an enduring legend. He insured that the ideology of the future Sandinistas would transcend a narrowly constructed anti-imperialism.

The creation of a National Guard to maintain internal order was not original with the Nicaraguan question. The United States had traveled a similar road with Rafael Trujillo in the Dominican Republic. Tacho Somoza used the guard to support his internal rule, but he always understood the broader hemispheric relations of power. In the latest permutation of the ideology of hemispheric domination, the new administration of Franklin Delano Roosevelt had declared a "Good Neighbor" policy (though the phrase was that of Herbert Hoover's), intending to avoid direct intervention in Latin America. It was in this era that Tacho Somoza took the power of the state. He consistently played the anti-Communism theme while offering the Guardia Nacionale as a buffer to mediate between the Liberal and Conservative parties. He continued to use the Guardia to massacre former Sandinistas and their families, to imprison critics without trial, and to conduct a war on the press. He ignored civil authority, and ridiculed the Sacasa administration in his own newspaper. He appointed the leader of Camisas Azules, an indigenous Fascist movement, minister of education after using his group to create the civil disturbances that undermined nominal civilian rule.

By now aware of his precarious position, President Sacasa asked Washington for support in regulating the guard. The State Department refused to comment on the "reorganization" while declaring U.S. support for the continued existence of the Guardia Nacionale. With the 1936 elections in the offing, Somoza's forces surrounded the presidential palace and executed a *coup d'état*. Later, when Sacasa and other (by now) exiled former presidents (Emiliano Chamorro and Adolfo Diaz) came to the United States to protest the seizure, Washington responded. The U.S. minister attended the inauguration of Tacho Somoza as president of Nicaragua on January 1, 1937 (Berman, 1986: 221–26). Thus, in dialectical fashion, direct intervention created the surrogate, and the surrogate negated the need for the heavy use of imperial force.

Thus the political reality of the "Good Neighbor" policy becomes apparent. The core state of the hemisphere would leave the role of hemispheric policeman to friendly local forces. The big stick for Nicaragua had been transformed. It took the form of clubs for the Guardia Nacional. But perhaps above all, it was Tacho Somoza who clearly understood the enduring Monroe Doctrine, and the material forces it embodied. At the outbreak of World War II, he quickly aligned Nicaragua with the Allied forces and moved to confiscate German- and Italian-owned properties in Nicaragua (buying the best at auction for himself at distress prices). In this context, F. D. R. said of Tacho Somoza, "He's a sonofabitch, but he's ours" (Christian, 1985:24). This perhaps is the ideological essence of the "Good Neighbor" policy.

By the end of World War II, Tacho Somoza's commitment to free enterprise was legendary. He received a 2.25 percent surcharge from U.S. mining companies, which at $175,000 per year supplemented the earnings of the San Albino gold mine he owned himself. He owned 46 coffee plantations and 51 cattle ranches. He owned half of those factories producing cement and matches (he barred lighters). Somoza's other enterprises included most of Nicaragua's sawmills, electrical companies, and a monopoly on the distribution of tallow. His international holdings included Miami apartments and Swiss bank accounts. At the time, the Nicaraguan *campesino* earned 15 cents, and miners 65 cents a day. Tacho Somoza did not keep everything for himself, however. Nicaragua's mining, coffee, cacao, and forest products industry were controlled by U.S. concerns. And, as a foreshadow of things to come, Nicaragua proceeded to alter its agricultural economy to meet U.S. consumption demands. Self-sufficiency in basic foodstuffs (notably corn and wheat) gave way to import-dependency (Selser, 1981: 183–85).

Tacho Somoza weathered some political storms in the immediate postwar period, resorting to imprisoning hundreds of demonstrators on the Corn Islands, under lease to the United States. Under pressure from an increasingly embarassed United States, he agreed to step down hoping to rule through a hand-picked successor. With the aid of Somoza's Nationalist Liberal Party, Leonardo Arguello was elected. However, when Arguello proved uncooperative, Somoza arrested him and charged him with mental incompetence. With the coming of the cold war, Tacho Somoza began once again to appeal to the "national interests" of his ally. Striking once again at the Communist menace, he arrested socialists and rival business leaders alike, and warned Washington of the red threat in Guatemala and Costa Rica. More important, Somoza made a deal with the old Conservative party and its wealthy elite, promising patronage and one-third of the congressional seats for the minority party. This demonstration of pluralist politics was to be superceded by the anticommunism of the early 1950s. The C.I.A. used the Managua airport, Somoza's estate and some of its Guardia Nacional to mount its overthrow of the reformist Jacobo Arbenz government of

Guatemala. With the elimination of organized political opposition, there appeared to be but one threat to Somoza. On September 21, 1956, he was gunned down by a young poet by the name of Rigoberto Perez (Bermann, 1986: 228–43).

## SANDINISTA NATIONAL LIBERATION

Luis and Anastasio Somoza followed their father to power, with older brother Luis winning another demonstration election in February of 1957, but with the real power of the National Guard vested in Anastasio. A wave of regime terror followed in the wake of Tacho Somoza's assassination, as the act of a single gunman became the pretext for the arrest of some three thousand persons. Leaders of the opposition suffered a range of torture, from the yanking of a cord tied to the genitals to imprisonment in coffins. Many spent time in the Somozas' private zoo, caged near wild animals. Such episodes served to harden general opposition to the Somoza dynasty, producing in their wake the formations of resistance (Booth, 1982: 71–72). Still, the expressions of Nicaraguan regime terror were rooted in larger forces.

In the ideological context of the Cold War, U.S. aid to Nicaragua was designed to promote stability and anticommunism. It is impossible to separate the questions of stability and investment climate. More important, anticommunism became a generic label promiscuously applied to any agents of change. When in July of 1959, the Guardia Nacional killed four demonstrating university students in Leon, the U.S. Ambassador, Thomas Whelan, issued a statement labeling them as "reds" (Alisky, 1960: 27). As had their father, the younger Somozas made Nicaragua available for attacks on social alternatives in the hemisphere. The C.I.A. used the country to train and launch the Bay of Pigs invasion. Nicaraguan troops also supported U.S. forces in the occupation of the Dominican Republic in 1965, and joined with Guatemalan forces to intervene in El Salvador in 1972 (Booth, 1982: 76). However, a new permutation of the Monroe Doctrine took shape during the Kennedy years, congenially called the Alliance for Progress. Although it was a specific reaction to the Cuban revolution, for Nicaragua its programs represented business as usual.

All types of U.S. assistance to Nicaragua grew steadily from 1953 through 1975. Military aid rose from an average of about $200,000 yearly for the 1953–61 period to $1.8 million per year for 1967–1975. Overall economic assistance for the same periods grew from an annual average of $1 million to $17.3 million. The biggest shift in both military and economic assistance to the Somoza brothers' regime occurred with the beginnings of the Alliance for Progress programs in 1962, when the average annual rate of economic assistance more than doubled and military assistance rose sevenfold. (Booth, 1982:75)

Luis Somoza died of a coronary in 1967, leaving control in the not so subtle hands of Anastasio. In a manner reminiscent of Shah Pahlavi, "Tachito" Somoza sought to insure the support of the Guardia through creating bonds of personal loyalty. His officers were well paid, as Nicaragua's military spending by 1973 was consistently double that of other Central American countries. However, the classic patterns of uneven development and structural inequality had taken form. In Nicaragua, health and welfare expenditures were at the bottom. Industrialization and capital intensive agriculture concentrated wealth and created a mass of unemployed who migrated to the urban *barrios*. Over the 1960s, while the owning class and some *petit bourgeois* pretenders prospered and consumed, the urban and rural poor were left behind. Slightly over 1/2 of 1 percent of the farms owned over 30 percent of the farmland, while almost 60 percent of the farms had only 3.4 percent of the land. The upper 5 percent had about 30 percent of the national income, compared to 15 percent for the lower 50 percent of the population. Nicaragua's murder, accident, and alcoholism rates led the region, with life expectancy the lowest at 53 years (Booth, 1982: 91–92; 84–85).

All of this did not preserve the Guard. Nepotism, favoritism, and corruption coexisted with Tachito's obsession with conspiracies within the force that insured for him the power of the state. In the aftermath of the devastating Managua earthquake (December 1972), the poorly disciplined Guardia simply disappeared, taking care of their personal concerns and in the case of some, engaging in looting. They also plundered for resale the international relief aid meant for the benefit of all Nicaraguans. In 1974, Nicaragua began a two-year period of martial law. Two years later, Amnesty International provided a detailed account of Guardia violations of human rights. Detentions, torture, and execution coexisted with a war in the countryside. For by now, a counterforce had emerged in the form of a new guerrilla movement, appropriately named the Sandinista National Liberation Front (F.S.L.N.). In characteristic fashion, Somoza's Guard tried to deny the movement new recruits by summary executions of suspected adolescent sympathizers (Booth, 1982: 95).

In the 1960s, the Superior Council of Private Initiative (C.O.S.I.P.) had begun to oppose Somoza's reign, and, with aid from the Alliance for Progress, to fund some reforms to forestall feared revolutionary impulses. The Nicaraguan Development Institute touted free enterprise and democracy as the key to economic growth and prosperity. Other projects included the Nicaraguan Development Foundation, which supported production cooperatives and the Educational Credit Program, which made education loans available to poor families. Thus externally supported organizations of the indigenous elite gained power, and although envisioning the ouster of Somoza, favored the retention of his political party (P.L.N.) and the National Guard. To such powerful opposition rallied other groups for the middle classes, including the small business owners, university and high school students, professionals, and salaried workers (the latter two often belonging to unions). Although reaching critical mass in the 1970s, sporadic opposition on the part of the upper and middle classes had been directed toward the Somozas for forty years. And as the regime depended more and more on terror, that opposition solidified, and in 1978–79 a wave of business and labor general strikes weakened the regime. However, it became clear that it would take more than the disaffection of the privileged to dislodge Somoza (Booth, 1982: 97–114).

From among the student resistance to Somoza came intellectual activists on the left who were to play a fundamental role in the founding of the Sandinista National Liberation Front in 1961. Principal figures included Carlos Fonseca Amador and Tomás Borge, who were both imprisoned and tortured after the assassination of Tacho Somoza in 1956. Active in the Nicaraguan Socialist Party (P.S.N.), these and other early Sandinista ideologists led in the formation of a movement that was more than a reaction to Somoza's corruption. Instead, it was to be a movement grounded in a holistic analysis and rejection of the enduring structures of Nicaraguan society.

Forming strong ties with the peasantry, the Sandinistas had fought the National Guard for eighteen years. When the time came for a final offensive (1978–79), the F.S.L.N. was generally perceived as the vanguard of the Nicaraguan revolution with its ranks growing accordingly.[2] A daring raid on the National Palace (August 1978) in downtown Managua, resulted in the taking of hostages later traded for the release of 59 political prisoners. Anastasio Somoza's "biggest private ranch" in Latin America was on the brink (Bermann, 1986: 267). However, he did not go quietly. In the ensuing National Guard slaughter of September, the Red Cross reported at least 5,000 Nicaraguans killed, some 10,000 missing, and 25,000 homeless. The Human Rights Commission of the Organization of American States noted that: "During the so-called 'mop-up operation,' there was pointed disregard for human life, with the shooting of many people, in some cases children, in their homes or in front of them, in the presence of their parents, brothers, and sisters" (in Lernoux, 1980: 98).

The United States responded by reducing aid and embassy personnel, while encouraging negotiations to replace Somoza with a certified anti-Communist. In May of 1979, a $65.6 million I.M.F. loan for Somoza was given U.S. support, and in June the Carter administration tried unsuccessfully to convince the Organization of American States that it should dispatch a "peacekeeping force;" citing fears that Nicaragua would become a "second Cuba." A final attempt to negotiate a successor government that would eliminate or limit Sandinista representation failed. On July 17, the last of the Somoza dictators departed for Miami. Two days later, the remnants of the Guardia Nacional fell to pieces and victorious rebels took Managua (Bermann, 1987 270). After forty years, the U.S.-backed Somoza dynasty founded in regime terror was ended. But a new surrogate stage was still to come.

## COUNTERREVOLUTION AND SURROGATE TERROR

Given the "loss" of Nicaragua to forces decidedly opposed to the longstanding, multidimensional U.S. intervention in its internal affairs, the moment was ripe for yet another ideological permutation in U.S. hemispheric relations. With the coming of the Reagan administration, the threat of "international communism" (often disguised as "international terrorism") supplanted the human rights focus of the Carter years. The premise was that while "authoritarian" regimes might not be to the liking of the West, the real threat was from Cuban-Soviet expansion (Kirkpatrick, 1979). Although the ends of the policies were quite similar, it would be misleading to equate the means employed by the two administrations. The Carter administration had sought to retain the U.S. special relationship with Nicaragua by using the carrot and stick of aid for the Somoza regime. The Reagan administration decided to roll back the clock. On April Fool's Day, 1981, economic aid to Nicaragua ceased.

On November 16, 1981, at a National Security Council meeting, President Reagan approved a C.I.A. initiative to create an insurgency. On November 23, he implemented the plan by signing National Security Decision 17. The local forces to be used in this redefinition of U.S. surrogacy were experienced in the role. They were former members of the Guardia Nacional, many living in exile or in outlaw bands along the Nicaraguan-Honduras border (Brody, 1988: 111-12). In addition to the initiation of covert paramilitary operations, U.S. policy also called for the increased military aid for El Salvador and Honduras, the mounting of large-scale military exercises by U.S. forces throughout the Caribbean Basin, the development of contingency plans for U.S. military intervention in the region, and the expansion of C.I.A. intelligence-gathering capability (Leogrande, 1985: 431).

It was clear that an insurrection on the part of ex-Somocistas would have little legitimacy inside Nicaragua, but that fact had not mattered greatly from the U.S. side for forty years. However, the appearance of legitimacy for the "counter-revolution" would matter in ensuing battles for funding and credibility. Thus the Reagan administration sought to join the ex-Somocistas with more respectable opponents of the Sandinista-led revolution. According to Conservative party member Edgar Chamorro, who served as a director (1982-84) of the Contra organization known as the Nicaraguan Democratic Force, this merger was realized in August of 1981 in Guatemala City. Both the documents that created the F.D.N., and the meeting to sign them, were prepared by the C.I.A. The name of the organization, as well as the members of its junta and general staff were "all chosen or approved by the C.I.A." (in Brody, 1988: 112).

Agents of the Central Intelligence Agency were later to handle Contra P.R. before their first public appearance in Miami (December, 1982.) Under the Neutrality Act, private citizens are enjoined from using U.S. territory to wage war on another country. Accordingly, the Contra directors were briefed to deny their intention to overthrow the Sandinistas, to evade the source of their funding, and to deny contact with U.S. government officials. They were also instructed that the F.D.N. must have loftier goals than the return of property that might have been lost by the Nicaraguan elite (Chamorro, 1985: 18, 21).

Chamorro, who had at one time defended the guard as professional soldiers doing their job, lost his taste for his new role. Early on he discovered that it was "standard *contra* practice to kill Sandinista prisoners and collaborators."

He complained that the "political dimension" meant nothing to field commanders who believed that "Somoza lost because he had his hands tied by Jimmy Carter and that if he hadn't he could have killed a lot of people and won" (Chamorro, 1985: 22). The C.I.A. was not content to leave the field to U.S. surrogates, however. It organized the bombing in 1983 of petroleum tanks at Punto Corinto (Chamorro, 1985: 22); it prepared a filed manual on "Psychological Operations in Guerilla Warfare" prescribing tactics on "neutralizing" Sandinista officials, creating "martyrs" and hiring criminals (Chamorro in Brody, 1988: 114; Vanderlaan, 1986: 191); and, on January 5, 1984, the C.I.A. instructed the Contras to claim responsibility for the agency's mining of Nicaraguan harbors. The mining ultimately led to the deaths of eight Nicaraguan fishermen and the damaging of nine ships from five nations (Central American Alert, 1986: 107).

Of course, the Guardia practitioners of regime terror needed less in the way of practical experience and instruction. They simply continued their war on the Nicaraguan population under a slightly modified banner and were now called "freedom-fighters" by their sponsors. Indeed, in an historical sense, the Guard had always been a counterrevolutionary force. As many priests and lay pastors trained by the clergy saw no contradiction between Catholicism and national liberation, they became targets of kidnapping, torture, and murder (Lernoux, 1980: 81–107). In their campaign to discredit the Sandinista's ability to defend the population, the Contras routinely assaulted, raped, mutilated, tortured, and murdered unarmed civilians. They engaged in mass as well as individual kidnappings, both as a means of recruitment and to create a hostage population in their Honduran base. And they waged war on both the peasant economy (farms, cooperatives, food storage facilities, coffee harvests), and the new social infrastructure (health centers, schools, food distribution networks) initiated by the Sandinistas (International Human Rights Law Group, 1986: 58). On the ideological front, the Contra cause was also waged with direct Yankee assistance. The U.S. National Endowment for Democracy funded *La Prensa*, whose editorial policy was to "oppose the Sandinista Front." In the meantime, the U.S. embassy in Managua was converted from diplomacy to subversion. On October 12, 1987, it sponsored an anti-Sandinista rally, complete with a sea of American flags, in which former U.S. Ambassador Jeanne Kirkpatrick declared that the Contras were fighting "for the right to live normal lives free of oppression and reprisals" (Wilde, 1987: 957).

This campaign of surrogate terror complemented a program of economic warfare designed to undermine the Sandinista experiment in a mixed economy, with its controls on capital accumulation and absentee domination. U.S. economic destabilization policies toward Nicaragua were not without precedent. Attempts to wreck the Cuban economy are perhaps best known, but Brazil (1964), Bolivia (1971), and Chile (1973) were also victimized by economic aggression in the form of "Communist" containment, directed toward promiscuously defined threats from the left. Under the Reagan administration, bilateral aid to Nicaragua estimated to be $36.4 million from 1981–84 was blocked or cancelled. More importantly, the U.S. used its voting power, veto, and influence to block $422.9 million in multilateral development funds (Inter-American Development Bank and World Bank) over the same period. The objective was an economic assault on Nicaragua's developmental programs; whether agricultural, industrial or social (Vanderlaan, 1986: 171).

On May 1, 1985, Reagan ordered the imposition of economic sanctions including a total trade embargo, termination of its Treaty of Friendship, Commerce, and Navigation, and the closing of the United States to Nicaraguan airlines and flag vessels (U.S. Department of State, 1985b). The familiar rationale turned on allegations of Nicaraguan export of terrorism and subversion, its relationship with Cuba and the U.S.S.R., its arms buildup, which threatened the regional military balance,[3] and the absence of "democratic pluralism." By this point, the Monroe Doctrine had become isomorphic with anticommunism, and terms like Marxist-Leninism used promiscuously as labels of delegitimation.

### The United States and the World Court

In a context of Contra terror, "war games" such as the 1981 joint amphibious assault exercise with Honduras (Leogrande, 1985: 430) and the mine-laying of Nicaraguan harbors, the Sandinistas sought and received an order of "provisional measures of interim protection" from the International Court of Justice (I.C.J.). The U.N. "World Court" issued a two-part finding on May 10, 1984. All 15 judges agreed that the United States should cease restricting access to and from Nicaraguan ports, particularly through the laying of mines. The I.C.J. also found by a 14 to 1 margin (with U.S. Judge Stephen Schwebel casting the lone dissenting vote) that Nicaragua's sovereignty and independence should not be endangered by military or paramilitary activities. The interim order was granted pending a final decision on a Nicaraguan Application (April 9, 1984).

The Nicaraguan Application charged the U.S. with "violation of Nicaragua's sovereignty, territorial integrity and political independence and of the most fundamental and universally accepted principles of international law." It asked the court to call upon the United States to cease its use of force and to pay reparations for the damage to "person, property and the Nicaraguan economy (U.N. Chronicle, 1984: 154–55)." The United States also requested that the case be dismissed on the grounds that the I.C.J. lacked jurisdiction to rule in this case. This too was unanimously rejected. State Department lawyers rushed to provide the Reagan administration with "grounds" for terminating the United States' 40-year acceptance of the compulsory jurisdiction of the I.C.J. (U.S. Department of State, 1985c: 1–4).

One international lawyer argued that the president's decision to terminate usurped the power of the Senate that had recognized the court in 1946, violating its right to advise and consent on all treaties (Boyle, cited in Central America Alert, 1986: 108). But law is ultimately a political product, with the interpretations that matter belonging to the party with power. The Reagan administration declared in its decision not to participate in I.C.J. proceedings leading to a final judgment on the Nicaraguan issue that: "much of the evidence that would establish Nicaragua's aggression against its neighbours is of a highly sensitive intelligence character. We will not risk United States national security by presenting such sensitive material in public or before a Court that includes two judges from Warsaw Pact nations" (U.S. Department of State, 1985a: 64). And, in the grand style of a slighted imperial power, the State Department continued the attack on the United Nations itself.

Whereas in 1945, the United Nations had some 50 members, most of which were aligned with the United States and shared its views regarding world order, there are now 160 members. A great many of these cannot be counted on to share our view of the original constitutional conception of the UN Charter, particularly with regard to the special position of the permanent members of the Security Council in the maintenance of international peace and security. This same majority often opposes the United States on important international questions. (Department of State, 1986: 69)

At least the language is clear. Unable to control the United Nations or the I.C.J., the Reagan administration chose a policy of selective secession. However, the World Court was not so easily disarmed. It heard the case anyway, and in September of 1985 former CIA analyst David MacMichael testified that despite limited Nicaraguan support (late 1980, early 1981) for the rebels opposing the U.S.-supported government by death squad in El Salvador, there was no evidence of further arms shipments (*Time*, 1985: 85). The strategy of the administration according to MacMichael was not to "moderate" the Sandinistas but to force them under conditions of internal war to retrench. "It was hoped the Nicaraguan government would clamp down on civil liberties... arresting its opposition, demonstrating its allegedly inherent totalitarian nature and thus increasing domestic dissent within the country.... it was hoped there would be a reaction against U.S. citizens, particularly against U.S. diplomatic personnel within Nicaragua, thus serving to demonstrate the hostility of Nicaragua toward the United States" (MacMichael, in Ryan, 1988).

On June 27, 1986, the I.C.J. ruled that the United States by activities "in and against Nicaragua" had acted in breach of "customary international law" not to use force, not to violate the sovereignty of another state or intervene in the affairs of another state. The World Court also found that the United States had an obligation to pay reparations to Nicaragua. The decision consisted of a series of 16 separate votes, mostly adopted by large majorities of 12 to 3 or 14 to 1 (U.N. Chronicle, 1986: 110).

## The Doctrine of Low-Intensity Conflict

The campaign to bring down the Sandinistas in Nicaragua cannot be isolated from unconventional forms of warfare, both old and new, constantly developed and redeveloped for intervention in the Third World. The Reagan administration's ideological and strategic conception of state violence took the form of a still-emerging doctrine known as *low-intensity conflict*. It arose from the joint efforts of the State Department, the Pentagon, and the Central Intelligence Agency. Its architects within these institutions sought to establish the threat of "terrorism" and "communist insurgencies" as surging threats requiring new studies, new tactics, and of course, massive funding. Labeled "violent peace" by the navy, low intensity conflict came to be field-tested in Central America, and specifically in Nicaragua during the 1980s. In the "official story," the means of dirty warfare were legitimated by the righteousness of the cause. In the words of former C.I.A. Director William Casey, an architect of the Reagan administration's proxy war in Nicaragua: "I believe the stakes in Central America are huge and historic. The pendulum of history is swinging away from Soviet Marxism as a model for Third World countries, and toward the concepts of democracy and free-market economics. This role reversal could turn out to be one of the great historical turning points of history" (Chardy, 1986).

There are voluminous works that contain a myriad of papers drawn from symposia that bring together military, state department, intelligence, and state consultants on the question of low-intensity conflict. However, a careful review of this literature reveals the thematic structure of this doctrine (U.S. Army Command and General Staff College, 1983).

1. In significant respects, the emergence of L.I.C. is a reaction to the American defeat in Vietnam. A recurring theme in the L.I.C. literature, the Vietnam experience is portrayed as a victory for communism because of: a) unclear U.S. political objectives and b) the limited utility of the doctrines and technologies of conventional military operations. There is little or no serious consideration of the historical forces, including colonialism old and new, that give rise to national liberation movements. Thus descriptions of "what went wrong" are *instrumental, tactical, and ahistorical*.

2. A second theme is that of *nationalist absolutism*. It is assumed that the "national security interests" of the United States have priority, and that what is good for the United States and its allies is good for the Third World.

3. The rationale for L.I.C. is premised on effective resistance to a number of states and ideologies that threaten the "free world." Chief among them is the U.S.S.R., whose hand is seen in most of the insurgencies that threaten Western global order. That national liberation movements come out of Moscow or other states, rather than indigenous conditions, is evidence of a *conspiratorial* theme in L.I.C. literature. However, the theme is not confined to the Soviet Union. According to the Rand Corporation's leading voice on terrorism and frequent contributor to L.I.C. literature, the "patron states of terrorism" include "to varying degrees the entire Arab bloc of nations" (Jenkins, 1983:24).

4. Another theme in L.I.C. doctrine reproduces the common tendency in Western thought to *conceptualize structural contradictions in privatized terms.* Included in L.I.C. proposals are calls for improved "psychological operations" to win the hearts and minds of the indigenous population. Thus "a trial operation recently carried out in a Salvadoran village featured clowns, a Mexican mariachi band and skimpily clad dancers (Chardy, 1986)." Surrogate terrorism not withstanding, counterinsurgency becomes a political theater of the absurd.

5. L.I.C. literature reveals a concern with *image enhancement.* Proposals include granting diplomatic recognition to various "governments in exile" who support U.S. interests; conducting public relations campaigns to gain media support; and stressing "human rights" responsibilities on the part of U.S. allies. Another objective is to convince American public opinion of the need for U.S. involvement in protracted warfare in the Third World. Thus L.I.C. offers another spectrum of conflict, short of nuclear or conventional exchange between the superpowers. Accordingly, the concept of a Third World War acquires a wholly different meaning. It becomes instead a protracted war in the Third World.

6. A final theme explores new *military tactics and hardware* necessary to win in the L.I.C. game. With due regard to interservice rivalry, tactics such as offshore naval bombardment as well as the role of long-range aircraft (including B–52s) and missiles are explored. On the hardware side, new simple weapons suitable for Third World conflicts are called for. However, in the so-called counterinsurgency, counterterrorism game (the terms are virtually interchangeable in L.I.C.), there is a major role for the special forces. The low-intensity conflict literature includes not only glowing historical tribute to the rangers and Green Berets but examines the role of "special forces" in other societies, including the British SAS and Israel's Sayaret Matkal.

L.I.C. policy makers are taken with books like *Terror: The West Fights Back* (Dobson and Payne, 1982), with large excerpts reprinted for use in military courses. Such books assume, of course, that the West only *responds* to terror, never initiating it. And through the political language of the "preemptive strike," it is even possible for the West to respond in advance. The consequence of this closed interpretation is to insulate the West from accusations of terrorism. L.I.C. doctrine, taken as a whole, develops a paranoid conception of geopolitical relations, portraying a grandiose West under attack from persecutory and conspiratorial elements. In this context, the full range of Western institutional and operational violence is defined as self-defense.

Of course, improved capability in unconventional warfare is not confined to Central America, nor to the invention of wholly new strategies of intervention. They involve the bolstering of "war games," some 60 of which are conducted yearly around the world. Under the Reagan administration, the 1983 version of Operation Brightstar in the Middle East involved five times as many troops as the 1980 exercise. The Big Pine series in Honduras was unprecedented in scope and duration for Central America. General Paul Gorman, former chief of the U.S. Southern Command, declared that Big Pine II made both the American people and the congress aware that "exercises send signals," and are "instruments of national policy." Former Secretary of Defense Caspar Weinberger noted in 1984 that Special Operations Forces (Green Berets, Rangers, civil affairs specialists, psych-op troops, Delta Force, Task Force 160, the Navy Seals) had been assigned a high priority as low-level conflict represented the most likely threat to U.S. interests through the remainder of the century. Accordingly, SOF grew from some 10,000 in 1981 to just under 15,000 four years later, with a projected strength of 20,900 active and 38,400 with reserves by 1990 (Morrison, 1985; Goose, 1985).

As an ideological system, the doctrine of low-intensity conflict is the product of those who view themselves as servants of the national interest, of global democracy, and of Western civilization. One of their number includes General Edward C. Meyer of the U.S. Army. His summary remarks on the army's role in low-intensity conflict are instructive.

> These are not unfamiliar responsibilities for the Army. Looking back at our history, we realize that the Army has often been involved in incidents of low-level conflict similar to those we face today: intervention during domestic strikes, riot control, border control, insurrections, civil wars, counterinsurgency activity, and nation-building.... These efforts will not have full utility until we are able to correct some severe limitations. We need a cadre of experts to train U.S. and friendly nations in techniques of insurgency/counterinsurgency, unconventional warfare, and psychological operations. We need improved... human intelligence capabilities. We need material and personnel to bolster our support of international security-assistance programs. We need an enhanced personnel exchange program with the armed forces of friendly nations. We need continued support from multinational schools, such as the School of Americas in Panama. We need a stockpile of low-level conflict weaponry. (Meyers, 1983: 3–4)

According to Meyers, such things are necessary to prevent "our descent into an age of terror." Clearly, this example of L.I.C. ideology, does not question whether by impartial standards, counterterrorism and counterinsurgency are terms that may mask the terrorism of the state. The servants of reified state power do not think to ask why it is appropriate to use the army to suppress workers; do not question the causes of riots and insurrections; do not ask at whose expense "nation-building" is achieved, and do not inquire whether the Latin American military leaders trained at the School of the Americas are engaged in the massive repression of popular resistance. In the closed ideological system of antiterrorism, there is no room for critique.

### The Real Narcoterrorism

In Chapter 2, reference was made to the longstanding attempt of the U.S. right wing to link the enormous U.S. appetite for drugs with the ubiquitous international Communist/terrorist conspiracy, and its specific attempts to link the traffic in Latin America to the Sandinistas. (As evidenced in his radio broadcast to the nation on July 30, 1988, Ronald Reagan continued to make this claim even as very different evidence was taking form.) To the chagrin of an administration that had declared a "war on drugs," evidence began to emerge that it was instead the Contras who were receiving profits from cocaine sales in the United States, and payoffs for allowing drug smugglers the use of contra bases. One key player was convicted trafficker George Morales who claimed to have paid Contra Fernando Chamorro $250,000 quarterly. Another was a National Democratic Force (F.D.N.) organizer, Norwin Meneses-Cantero, whose drug ring had funneled at least $500,000 to Chamorro's Costa Rican organization. Meneses-Cantero, a Nicaraguan expatriate, was the brother of Tachito Somoza's former chief of police in Managua (*Contra Watch*, 1987: 8; *San Francisco Examiner*, 1986a and 1986b).

George Morales claimed that Contra leaders promised that his 1984 U.S. indictment for drug trafficking would be taken care of if he would help set up a smuggling operation. He also claimed (as did one of his pilots, Gary Betzner) that Contra weapons were flown to the ranch of an ardent American anti-Communist, John Hull in northern Costa Rica, where drugs were picked up to be flown to Florida. Another pilot, Michael Tolliver, claimed that he flew some 14 tons of Contra weapons to Aguacate air base in Honduras, and returned with over 12 tons of marijuana in a DC-6, which he flew into Homestead Air Force Base in Florida without being inspected (Cockburn, 1987: 17, 183). Ramon Milian-Rodriquez, tied to the Medellin cartel and the C.I.A., told both C.B.S. news and a Senate Foreign Relations subcommittee that he orchestrated the transfer of $10 million of Columbian drug money to the Contras (Christic Institute, 1987: 3).

Two caveats are in order when considering the "Contra-drug" connection. The first is that the evidence bearing on the international drug trade, as is the case with the murky world of conventionally defined terrorism, is elusive. It often consists of testimonials from convicted drug kingpins and functionaries. Still as noted in the case of Southeast Asia, there is historical precedent for U.S. government complicity in the "anti-Communist drug trade." For those interested in critical sociology, however, there is another level of skepticism. Tails such as these, even when well-founded, may simply weave an *alternative conspiracy theory* that fails to place dramatic events in the historical context of dependency relations.

Conspiracy "theories" are routinely devices of *reactionary* thought, in part because they do not focus on *systems* of domination. Thus the opposition to Communist conspiracies is not based in serious critical study of the logical and ideological properties of Marxist thought (and its varieties ranging from Lenin to Trotsky to Bukharin to Mao Zedong to Cabral to Amin). It is rooted instead in a series of half-myths and half-perversions, complete with atrocity tales and demonology. Conspiratorial thought embodies a false absolutism, which in the case of the "Soviet menace" holds that the only alternative to private ownership is the Archipelago. However, an alternative, left-leaning conspiracy theory may simply substitute the C.I.A. for the K.G.B., and drug gangs for shadowy "cells."

Likewise, a narrow focus on the corruption of the Contras may but distort their membership in a dispossessed elite, who formerly ruled in surrogation a land and a people victimized by regressive development.

## THE NICARAGUAN EXPERIMENT AND HEMISPHERIC HEGEMONY

The significance of the U.S. reaction to the Nicaraguan revolution may be lost if it is understood as a routinely bizarre Reagan administration expression of anticommunism. This is not to say that a particular administration does not shape a specific policy; but policy expressions are rooted in more enduring material forces. The intensity of the reaction would itself suggest that there is more at stake here than the allegiance of a poor country of three million persons, which from the outset of the Sandinista period has sought normal relations with the United States. Again, it may be true that Nicaragua is historically destined to "export" a revolution, not through shipments of arms, but through new forms of economic, social and political development.

The Sandinistas eschewed a narrowly defined political model that confuses a changing of the guard with an authentic social revolution. The transformation of Nicaragua was instead to embody an alternative model of development, together with the holistic change of the state and civil society as well as popular culture. In particular, the Sandinistas argued that there could be no massive industrialization or further uneven urbanization of Nicaraguan society in the short term. Instead, the agrarian economy, small scale-business and manufacturing, and the service sector would be basic. A capitalist class would continue, but through the "popular hegemony" of the state, that class would exercise neither economic or political control. Land reform and rural services in the interest of the peasants called for the judicious break-up of large estates often held by absentee landlords.

The Sandinistas also envisioned the nationalization of foreign trade and the financial system and an end to the transnational reproduction of capital. Once institutionalized, such measures would control the *accumulation* of capital (founded in global, systemic bottom-up redistribution of surplus value), if not negate the capitalist class. Such a transformation would end the traditional conflicts between Liberal and Conservative party elites for whom national sovereignty had only meant the trappings of political office and some measure of cultural pride. Instead, authentic sovereignty could only follow the end of Nicaragua's neocolonial status (Coraggio, 1986: 22–47).

The adoption of the name *Sandinista* is itself ideologically instructive. Sandino was a popular folk hero, but he was more. His was a struggle against external imperialism that did not (or perhaps could not) extend to the transformation of the indigenous relations that follow imperial history. The New Sandinistas were not content to be rid of Somoza and his guard. Nor did they hold a simple conception of "yankee imperialism" that did not address the systemic consequences of hemisperic hegemony *inside* Nicaragua. On another level, Sandinista ideology has proved compatible with liberation theology (certainly more popular with local priests, layworkers, and missionaries than the church hierarchy). In a society where 91 percent of the population is Roman Catholic (*World Almanac*, 1987: 599), it is liberation theology that synthesizes faith and a critique of class domination that addresses the real conditions of many of the most ardent Sandinista supporters.

The importance of Sandinista relations with the peasants is vital in a country where 65 percent of the labor force is in agriculture (*World Almanac*, 1987: 599). The commitment to land reform and rural services also signalled an intention to avoid the plague of uneven development. It was the countryside where the benefits of educational and health programs were most keenly felt. Nicaragua's reading campaign improved the literacy rate from 47 percent to 83 percent and won a U.N.E.S.C.O. prize. A primary health care program became a model for the World Health Organization. By targeting teachers, nurses, and land reform organizers, as well as members of the National Union of Farmers and Ranchers and the National Women's Association, the Contras have waged a brutal war on the Sandinista model of development (Brody, 1988: 116).

Surrogate terror inside Nicaragua during the 1980s drained the resources needed for development, and led to measures of suppression of opposition groups and the expulsion in mid–1988 of U.S. diplomats accused of orchestrating anti-Sandinista demonstrations. (The evidence for official U.S. leadership in counterrevolution is abundant, but its official, late recognition by Speaker of the House Jim Wright in September of 1988 was still embarrassing to the Reagan administration.) It is thus impossible to judge the successes or failures of an unimpeded Nicaraguan revolution in its first decade. However, there have been certain consequences of this conflict that may enhance Sandinista standing in the hemisphere. Despite being marked for overthrow, they survived through two Reagan terms. They were confident enough of their popularity to allow a national election (condemned as unfair by the United States but not by most European observers), and in 1988 entered into negotiations with the Contras, offering amnesty for disarmament.

The Sandinistas also pressed their case with skill in the United Nations and the International Court of Justice. While Nicaragua was demonstrating its confidence in international law, the Reagan administration was reduced to a classic display of imperial arrogance. And finally, the Sandinistas invited numerous groups of U.S. citizens to visit Nicaragua for themselves, thus fashioning a political end run around the forces of the state. Given the historical symbolism of "Yankee imperialism" throughout Latin America, U.S. surrogate terrorism may historically prove only to increase Sandinista credibility as a Central American model of national liberation. In this sense, the basic structures of surrogate terrorism may have planted the seeds of their own negation.

## NOTES

1. This account of ambassadorial complicity is hearsay. Lane felt impelled to rebuke Somoza for violating his pledge not to act against Sandino "without my consent" (cited in Bermann, 1986:222). However, that Somoza would seek legitimacy through identifying himself with U.S. interests is consistent both with the general Nicaraguan history and with the reign to come.

2. Now allied with the Sandinistas in a pragmatic if not ideological sense were members of the elite opposition, including 12 influentials exiled by Somoza.

3. The U.S. had little interest in military imbalance when arming the Somoza regime.

# *Bibliography*

Abdrabboh, Bob. *Libya in the 1980's: Challenges and Changes*. Washington, D.C.: International Economics and Research, 1985.
Abrahamian, Ervand. *Iran between Two Revolutions*. Princeton, N.J.: Princeton University Press, 1982.
Abun-Nasr, Jamil M. *A History of the Maghrib*. Cambridge University Press, 1971.
Adams, Gordon, and Geoff Quinn. "The Iron Triangle: The Politics of Defense Contracting." *Council on Economic Priorities Newsletter* (June 1981): 3.
Afshar, Haleh. "The Army." Pp. 175–98 in Haleh Afshar (ed.), *Iran: A Revolution in Turmoil*. Albany, N.Y.: State University of New York Press, 1985.
Ahmad, Eqbal. "Comprehending Terror." *Middle East Report* (May–June 1986): 3–4.
Al-Abed. "From Dreyfus to Pollard." *The Washington Report on Middle Eastern Affairs* (July 1987): 4.
Alavi, Bahram. "Khomeini's Iran: Israel's Ally." *The Washington Report on Middle East Affairs* (April 1988): 4–6.
Alisky, Marvin. "Our Man in Nicaragua." *The Reporter* (December 22, 1960): 26–27.
Allen, Bem P. "After the Missiles: Sociopsychological Effects of Nuclear War." *American Psychologist* (August 1985): 927–37.
Alnasrawi, Abbas. *OPEC in a Changing World Economy*. Baltimore and London: John Hopkins University Press, 1985.
American University. *Libya, a Country Study*. Washington, D.C.: Foreign Area Studies, 1979.
Amnesty International. *Political Killings by Governments*. London, 1983.
———. *Amnesty International Report*. London, 1985.
Amos, James W. *Palestine Resistance: Organization of a Nationalist Movement*. New York: Pergamon Press, 1980.

Aptheker, Herbert. *American Negro Slave Revolts*. New York: Columbia University Press, 1943.

Arjomand, Said Amir. *From Nationalism to Revolutionary Islam*. Albany, N.Y.: State University of New York, 1984.

Arkin, William M., and Richard W. Fieldhouse. *Nuclear Battle-fields: Global Links in the Arms Race*. Cambridge, Mass.: Ballinger Publishing Co., 1985.

Aroian, Lois A. "A Different View of Libya's Qaddafi." *Christian Science Monitor* (January 18, 1982): 23.

Asmal, Kader. "Apartheid and Terrorism: The Case of Southern Africa." Pp. 127–55 in Hans Koechler (ed.), *Terrorism and National Liberation*. Frankfurt: Peter Lang, 1988.

Awan, Akhtar A. *The Partners, Not Wage Earners Economy*. Tripoli: The World Center, 1983.

Bagdikian, Ben. *The Media Monopoly*. Boston: Beacon Press, 1983.

Bahbah, Bishara. *Israel in Latin America: The Military Connection*. New York: St. Martin's, 1986.

Ball, George. *Error and Betrayal in Lebanon*. Washington, D.C.: Foundation for Middle East Peace, 1984.

Barnet, Richard. *Real Security*. New York: Simon and Schuster, 1981.

Bayat, Mangol. "Islam in Pahlavi and Post-Pahlavi Iran: A Cultural Revolution?" Pp. 87–106 in John L. Esposito (ed.), *Iran and Development*. Syracuse, New York: Syracuse University Press, 1980.

Beaubien, Michael C. "The Cultural Boycott of South Africa." *Africa Today* 29(4) 1982.

Beit-Hallahmi, Benjamin. *The Israeli Connection: Who Arms Israel and Why*. New York: Pantheon, 1987.

Bell, J. Bowyer. *Transnational Terror*. Stanford, Calif.: Hoover Institution on War, Revolution and Peace, 1975.

Benziman, Uzi. *Sharon: An Israeli Caesar*. Adama, 1985.

Beres, Louis Rene. *Terrorism and Global Security: The Nuclear Threat*. Boulder, Colorado: Westview Press, 1979.

Berger, Elena. *Dealing with Libya*. Editorial Research Reports, Vol. 1, No. 10 (1984): 187–204.

Bermann, Karl. *Under the Big Stick*. Boston: South End Press, 1987.

Booth, John A. *The End and the Beginning*. Boulder, Colorado: Westview Press, 1982.

Bowman, Robert M. "The Militarization of Space,." Pp. 355–72 in Hans Koechler (ed.), *The Reagan Administration's Foreign Policy*. Vienna: International Progress Organization, 1984.

———. "63% of Your Income Taxes Go to the Military." *Space and Security News*. Chesapeake Beach, Maryland: Institute for Space and Security Studies (December 1987): 1.

Boyle, K., T. Hadden, and P. Hillyard. *Ten Years on in Northern Ireland: The Legal Control of Political Violence*. London: The Cobden Trust, 1980.

Brandt Commission. *North-South: A Program for Survival*. Report of the Independent Commission on International Development Issues. Cambridge, Mass.: MIT Press, 1980.

Brenner, Levi. *Zionism in the Age of Dictators*. Westport, Conn.: Lawrence Hill, 1983.

Broad, William J. "X-Ray Laser Weapon Gains Favor." *New York Times* (November 15, 1983): 17, 20.

Broder, Jonathan. "Politics of Despair." *Chicago Tribune* (June 23, 1986).
Brody, Reed. "U.S. Sponsored Terrorism Against Nicaragua." Pp. 111–25 in Hans Koechler (ed.), *Terrorism and National Liberation*. Frankfurt: Peter Lang Publishing, 1988.
Brownlie, Ian. *Basic Documents on African Affairs*. London: Oxford University Press, 1971.
Bruce, Steve. *God Save Ulster: The Religion and Politics of Paisleyism*. Oxford: Clarendon, 1986.
Bunting, Brian. *The Rise of the South African Reich*. Harmondsworth, England: Penguin Press, 1964.
Carleton, David. "The New International Division of Labor and Repression in Latin America." In George A. Lopez and Michael Stohl (eds.), *Development, Dependence, and State Repression*. Westport, Conn.: Greenwood, 1988.
Casey, William J. "The International Linkages—What Do We Know?" Pp. 5–15 in Uri Ra'anan, et al., *Hydra of Carnage: International Linkages of Terrorism*. Lexington, Mass.: Lexington Books, 1986.
Central America Alert. "The World Court and Nicaragua's Lawsuit: The Point." Pp. 105–10 in Gary McCuen (ed.), *The Nicaraguan Revolution*. Hudson, Wis.: Gary McCuen Publishers, 1986.
Chamorro, Edgar. "Confessions of a Contra." *The New Republic* (August 5, 1985): 18–23.
Chardy, Alfonso. "U. S. to Test Violent Peace." *Spokane Spokesman-Review*, (October 5, 1986).
Chirot, Daniel. *Social Change in the Twentieth Century*. New York: Harcourt Brace Jovanovich, 1977.
Chomsky, Noam. *The Fateful Triangle: The United States, Israel, and the Palestinians*. Boston: South End Press, 1983.
———. "Libya in U.S. Demonology." *Covert Action* 26 (Summer 1986a): 15–24.
———. *Pirates and Emporers: International Terrorism in the Real World*. New York: Claremont Research and Publications, 1986b.
Chomsky, Noam, and Edward S. Herman. *The Washington Connection and Third World Fascism*. Boston: South End Press, 1977.
Christian, Shirley. *Nicaragua*. New York: Random House, 1985.
Christic Institute. "The Contras Drug Connection." November 1987.
Clark, Kenneth R. "Africans Lack Central Viewpoint." Spokane Spokesman-Review (October 12, 1986): 19.
Claremont Research. *The Beirut Massacre: Press Profile*. 2nd. ed. New York: Claremont Research and Publications, 1984.
Cockburn, Leslie. *Out of Control*. New York: Atlantic Monthly Press, 1987.
Cohen, Stephen F. *Rethinking the Soviet Experience: Politics and History since 1917*. New York: Oxford University Press, 1985.
Cole, G. D. H. "The New Middle Classes and the Rise of Fascism." In William Chambliss (ed.), *Problems of Industrial Society*. Reading, Mass.: Addison-Wesley, 1970.
Collins, Frank. "Beyond the Palestinian Uprising." *The Washington Report on Middle East Affairs* (March 1988): 5–6.
Commission on Integrated Long-Term Strategy. "Discriminate Deterrence." Washington, D.C.: U.S. Government Printing Office (January 1988).

*Contra Watch.* "The Contra conspiracy." No. 4–5 (May–June 1987): 1–12.
Cooley, John. "The Libyan Menace." *Foreign Policy* 42 (spring), 1981.
Copeland, Miles. *The Games of Nations.* London: Weidenfeld and Nicolson, 1969.
Copson, Raymond W. "Libya: U. S. Relations." Issue Brief, Number IB81152. Washington, D. C.: Library of Congress Congressional Research Service, 1982.
Coraggio, Jose Luis. *Nicaragua: Revolution and Democracy*, Boston, Mass.: Allen and Unwin, Inc., 1986.
Curtiss, Richard. "In Toto: Outrageous." Editorial in *The Washington Report on Middle East Affairs* (December, 1986): 2.
———. November 1947 Palestine Partitions Launched 40 Years of Warfare. *The Washington Report on Middle East Affairs*, Vol. 6, No. 7 (November 1987): 3–5.
———. "Palestinians Take a Giant Step," *The Washington Report on Middle East Affairs.* (December, 1988): 3–6.
Dalrymple, Dana. "The Soviet Famine of 1932–34." *Soviet Studies* 15 (January 1964): 250–84.
Danaher, Kevin. *In Whose Interest? A Guide to U.S.-South African Relations.* Washington, D.C.: Institute for Policy Studies, 1984.
Davis, Peter. *Where is Nicaragua?* New York: Simon and Schuster, 1987.
Debt Crisis Network. *From Debt to Development: Alternatives to the International Debt Crisis.* Washington, D. C.: Institute for Policy Analysis, 1985.
Deeb, Marius K., and Mary Jane Deeb. *Libya since the Revolution: Aspects of Social and Political Development.* New York: Praeger, 1982.
Dessouki, Ali E. "The Islamic Resurgence." Pp. 3–31 in Ali E. Dessouki (ed.), *Islamic Resurgence in the Arab World.* New York: Praeger, 1982.
Dobson, Christopher, and Ronald Payne. "Israel: An Eye for an Eye." Pp. 160–72 in *Low Intensity Conflict* (P31) Fort Leavenworth, Kansas: U.S. Army Command and General Staff College, 1983.
Dorfman, Ariel. *The Emperor's Old Clothes.* New York: Pantheon, 1983.
Drucker, Henry M. The Political Uses of Ideology. New York: Harper and Row, 1974.
Dumas, Lloyd J. "The Military Burden on the Economy." *Bulletin of the Atomic Scientists* (October 1986): 22–26.
Editors of the Bulletin of the Atomic Scientists. "Nuclear Winter Report Excerpts." *Bulletin of the Atomic Scientists* (March 1985): 39–40.
Eisenhower, Dwight D. "Farewell Address." Pp. 206–7 in C. W. Pursell (ed.), *The Military Industrial Complex.* New York: Harper and Row, 1972.
Enayat, Hamid. "Iran: Khomeini's Concept of the 'Guardianship of the Jurisconsult.' " Pp. 160–80 in James P. Piscatori (ed.), *Islam in the Political Process.* Cambridge: Cambridge University Press, 1983.
Erickson, Kai. *Everything in Its Path.* New York: Touchstone Books, 1978.
Europa Yearbook. "Libya." Vol. 2: 1945–54. London: Europa Publications Limited, 1984.
Ezwai, Mohammed Bel Kasem. *Al Fatah Revolution in Ten Years.* Tripoli: Ministry of Information, 1980.
Fallows, James. *National Defense.* New York: Random House, 1982.
Fanon, Frantz. *The Wretched of the Earth.* New York: Grove Press, 1963.
———. *A Dying Colonialism.* Tr. by Haakon Chevalier. Intro. by Adolfo Gilly. New York: Grove Press, 1965.
Farrell, Michael. "A Permanent State of Emergency: The Suppression of the Irish Na-

tionalist Revolt in Northern Ireland." Pp. 171–84 in Hans Koechler (ed.), *Terrorism and National Liberation*. Frankfurt: Peter Lang, 1988.

Finnema, M. *International Networks of Banks and Industry*. The Hague: Martinus Nijhoff Publishers, 1982.

Fisher, Dan. "Israel Junks Lavi Jet in Dramatic Vote." *Los Angeles Times*—Washington Post Service (August 31, 1987).

Fitzgibbon, Constantine. "Red Hand: The Ulster Colony." Pp. 8–37 in Jonathan Bartlett (ed.), *Northern Ireland*. New York: H. W. Wilson, 1983.

Frederickson, George. *White Supremacy: A Comparative Study in American and South African History*. New York: Oxford University Press, 1981.

Freidman, Robert I. "Who Killed Alex Odeh?" *The Washington Report on Middle East Affairs*. Vol. 6, No. 9 (January 1988): 20.

Fulbright, J. W. "National Security and the Reagan Arms Buildup." Pp. 69–77 in R. Dellum (ed.), *Defense Sense*. Cambridge, Mass.: Ballinger, 1983.

Galtung, Johan. "On the Causes of Terrorism and Their Removal." Paper presented at the International Progress Organization Conference on the Question of Terrorism. Geneva, March 19–21, 1987.

Gans, Herbert. *Deciding What's News*. New York: Vintage, 1979.

George, Susan. *Ill Fares the Land: Essays on Food, Hunger, and Power*. Washington, D.C.: Institute for Policy Studies, 1984.

Gibson, Richard. *Contemporary Struggles Agaisnt White Minority Rule*. New York and London: Oxford Univeristy Press, 1972.

Giddens, Anthony. *The Nation-State and Violence*. Berkeley and Los Angeles: University of California Press, 1985.

Goose, Stephan D. "The Dirty Job Specialists." *South* (October 1985): 40.

Gottfried, Kurt, and Bruce A. Blair (eds.) *Crisis Stability and Nuclear War*. New York: Oxford University Press, 1988.

Grant, Lawrence. *Civil Liberty: The NCCL Guide to Your Rights*. Third Edition. Harmondsworth, Eng.: Penguin, 1978.

Greisman, H. C. *Social Meanings of Terrorism: Reification, Violence and Social Control*. Contemporary Crisis, Vol. 1, No. 3 (July 1977): 303–18.

Gresh, Alain. *The PLO: The Struggle within; Towards an Independent Palestinian State*. London: Zed, 1985.

Greenway, H. D. S. "Schultz's Action Switched." *Spokane Spokesman-Review* (December 15, 1988): A6.

Gurr, Ted Robert. "Some Characteristics of Political Terrorism in the 1960's." Pp. 31–58 in Michael Stohl (ed.), *The Politics of Terrorism*. New York and Basel: Marcel Dekker, 1988.

Habermas, Juergen. *Legitimation Crisis*. Boston: Beacon Press, 1975.

Habib, Henri. *Libya: Past and Present*. Malta: Aedam Publications, 1979.

Haley, P. Edward. *Qaddafi and the United States since 1969*. New York: Praeger, 1984.

Halliday, F. *Iran: Dictatorship and Development*. Penguin Books, 1979.

Hammond, Saad Qasem. "The New International Information Order: Why and How?" Pp. 29–46 in Hans Koechler (ed.), *The New International Information and Communication Order*. Vienna: Wilhelm Braumuller, 1985.

Hansen, G. H. *Militant Islam*. New York: Harper and Row, 1979.

Hazo, Robert. "The Palestinian Uprising." *The Washington Report on Middle East Affairs*, Vol. 6, No. 10, (February 1988): 3.

Herman, Edward S. *The Real Terror Network*. Boston: South End Press, 1982.
Hersh, Seymour. "Target Qaddafi." *New York Times Magazine*, February 27, 1987.
Hirson, Baruch. *Year of Fire, Year of Ash: The Soweto Revolt, Roots of a Revolution?* London: Zed Press, 1979.
Hoffman, Bruce. "Terrorism in the United States and the Potential Threat to Nuclear Facilities." Santa Monica, Calif.: Rand Corporation, 1986.
Horowitz, Irving Louis. *Three Worlds of Development: The Theory and Practice of International Stratification*. New York: Oxford University Press. 1966.
Hough, Jerry F., and Merle Fainsod. *How the Soviet Union is Governed*. Cambridge, Mass.: Harvard University Press, 1979.
Humphreys, R. Stephan. "The Contemporary Resurgence in the Context of Modern Islam." Pp. 67–83 in Ali E. Hillal Dessouki (ed.), *Islamic Resurgence in the Arab World*. New York: Praeger, 1982.
Hunt, Harry. *Texas Rich: The Hunt Dynasty*. New York: W. W. Norton, 1981.
Hutchinson, Martha Crensaw. *Revolutionary Terrorism: The FLN in Algeria, 1954–1962*. Stanford, Calif.: Hoover Institution Press, 1978.
International Defense and Aid Fund. "Removals and Apartheid." Briefing Paper No. 5. July, 1982.
International Human Rights Laws Group. "Contra Terror, Torture and Murder." Pp. 56–64 in Gary McCuen (ed.), *The Nicaraguan Revolution*. Hudson, Wis.: Gary McCuen Publications, 1986.
Ishmael, Taureq. *The Middle East and World Politics*. Syracuse, N.Y.: Syracuse University Press, 1974.
———. *Iraq and Iran*. Syracuse, N.Y.: Syracuse University Press, 1982.
*Israel Defense Forces Spokesman*. "International Terror July 1968–July 1986." Consulate General of Israel, San Francisco.
———. "Terrorist Attacks in Israel with Casualties. June 1967–October 1985." Consulate General of Israel, San Francisco.
Jamail, Milton, and Margo Gutierrez. *It's No Secret: Israel's Military Involvement in Central America*. Belmont, Mass.: AAUG Press, 1986.
Jamahiriya News. *Eighteen Years of the Revolution*. September 1, 1987.
Jenkins, Brian. *Terrorism and Beyond*. An International Conference on Terrorism and Low-Intensity Conflict. Santa Monica, Calif.: The Rand Corporation, 1982.
———. "New Modes of Conflict." Pp. 5–31 in *Low Intensity Conflict: Selected Readings* (R B 100–39), Fort Leavenworth, Kan.: U. S. Army Command General Staff College, 1983.
Jenkins, Loren. "All Things Considered." An NPR interview in FBIS, *The Beirut Massacre*. New York: Claremont, 1982.
Karis, Thomas. Pp. 471–616 in Gwendolyn Carter (ed.), *Five African States: Responses to Adversity*. Ithaca, New York: Cornell University Press, 1963.
Khalidi, Rashid. "The Palestinians in Lebanon: Social Repercussions of Israel's Invasion." *Middle East Journal*, Vol. 38 (Spring 1984): 255–66.
Khomeini, Imam. "Selected Messages and Speeches of Imam Khomeini." Tehran: Ministry of Islamic Guidance of the Islamic Republic of Iran, 1982.
Khrushchev, Nikita. *Khrushchev Remembers: The Last Testament*. Boston: Little, Brown and Co., 1974.
Kifner, John. "Israeli-backed Arab Chiefs Forced to Resign and Repent." *New York Times*, March 27, 1988.

Kirkpatrick, Jeane. "Dictatorships and Double Standards." *Commentary* (November 1979): 34–35.
Knapp, Wilfrid. *Northwest Africa: A Political and Economic Survey*. London: Oxford University Press, 1977.
Krieger, David M. "What Happens If? Terrorists, Revolutionaries, and Nuclear Weapons." *The Annals of the American Academy of Political and Social Sciences*, 430 (March 1977): 44–57.
Kurtz, Lester. *The Nuclear Cage*. Englewood Cliffs, N.J.: Prentice-Hall, 1988.
Laqueur, Walter. *The Age of Terrorism*. Boston: Little Brown, 1987.
Laroui, Abdullah. *The History of the Maghrib*. Princeton, N.J.: Princeton University Press, 1977.
Laurence, John C. *Race Propaganda and South Africa*. London: Victor Gollancz Ltd., 1979.
Lee, Alfred McClung. *Terrorism in Northern Ireland*. Bayside, N.Y.: General Hall, Inc., 1983.
Lefebvre, G. *The French Revolution*. Vols. 1 and 2. London: Routledge and Kegan Paul, 1962–64.
Legassick, M. "South Africa: Capital Accumulation and Violence." *Economy and Society*, Vol. 3, No. 3. 1974.
Lenin, V. I. *The State and Revolution*. Peking: Foreign Languages Press, (1917), 1970.
Leogrande, William M. "The United States and Nicaragua." Pp. 425–46 in Thomas W. Walken (ed.), *Nicaragua: The First Five Years*. New York: Praeger, 1985.
Leontief, Wassily and Faye Duchin. *Military Spending: Facts and Figures, Worldwide Implications and Future Outlook*. New York and Oxford: Oxford University Press, 1983.
Lernoux, Penny. *Cry of the People: United States Involvement in the Rise of Fascism, Torture and Murder and the Persecution of the Catholic Church in Latin America*. Garden City, N.Y.: Doubleday, 1980.
Lewis, Anthony. "Israel's Future Character at Stake Unless Present Trends Reversed." *New York Times*, April 19, 1988(a).
———. "Occupation Brutalizing Israel." *New York Times*, May 17, 1988(b).
Lewis, Bernard. *Islam in History*. New York: The Library Press, 1973.
Lifton, Robert. *Death in Life: Survivors of Hiroshima*. New York: Random House, 1967.
Linz, Juan. "Some Notes Toward a Comparative Study of Fascism in Sociological Historical Perspective." In Walter Laqueur (ed.), *Fascism: A Reader's Guide*. Berkeley and Los Angeles: University of California Press, 1976.
Lipton, Merle. *Capitalism and Apartheid*. Towata, New Jersey: Roman and Allanheld, 1985.
Lodge, James. *Terrorism: A Challenge to the State*. Oxford: Martin Robertson, 1981.
Lucas, Noah. *The Modern History of Israel*. London: Weidenfeld and Nicolson, 1974.
Lukács, Georg. *History and Class Consciousness*. Cambridge, Mass.: MIT Press (1923) 1971.
Lukas, J. Anthony. "Class Reunion: Kennedy's Men Relive the Cuban Missile Crisis." *New York Times Magazine*. August 30, 1987: 23–27, 51, 58, 61.
McBride, Sean. "Nuclear Terrorism." Pp. 35–40 in Hans Koechler (ed.), *Terrorism and National Liberation*. Frankfurt: Peter Lang, 1988.

McClintock, Michael. *The American Connection: State Terror and Popular Resistance in Guatemala*. Boston: Zed Press, 1985.

McCoy, Alfred W. *The Politics of Heroin in Southeast Asia*. New York: Harper and Row, 1972.

McFadden, Dave, and Jim Wake (eds.) *The Freeze Economy*. Mountainview, California: Mid-Peninsula Conversion Project, 1983.

Magdoff, Harry. "Militarism and Imperialism." Pp. 127–138 in K. T. Fann and Donald C. Hodges (eds.), *Readings in U.S. Imperialism*. Boston: Porter Sargent, 1971.

Mandel, Neville. "Turks, Arabs and Jewish Immigration into Palestine, 1882–1914." Pp. 77–108 in *St. Anthony's Papers*, No. 17 (Middle Eastern Affairs, No. 4). London: Oxford University Press, 1965.

Mannheim, Karl. *Ideology and Utopia: An Introduction to the Sociology of Knowledge*. Translated by Louis Wirth and Edward Shils. New York: Harcourt, Brace and World (1936) 1968.

Marger, Martin N. *Race and Ethnic Relations: America and Global Perspectives*. Belmont, Calif.: Wadsworth, 1985.

Mark, Clyde R., E. Laipson, and R. Copson. *Libya-U.S. Relations*. Foreign Affairs and National Defense Division, Congressional Research Service. May 8: IB86040, 1986.

Marx, Karl and Friedrich Engels. *The German Ideology*. New York: International Publishers (1845–1846), 1967.

Masmoudi, Mustapha. "The Liberty of the Press and Its Responsibility in Accordance with the New International Information and Communication Order." Pp. 9–22 in Hans Koechler (ed.), *The New International Information and Communication Order*. Vienna: Wilhelm Braumuller, 1985.

May, Robert. *The Southern Dream of a Caribbean Empire*. Baton Rouge, LA.: Louisiana State University Press, 1973.

Mazrui, Ali. *The Africans: A Triple Heritage*. Boston: Little, Brown and Company, 1986.

Medvedev, Roy. *Let History Judge*. New York: Vintage Books, 1971.

Merad, Ali. "The Ideologisation of Islam in the Contemporary Muslim World." Pp. 37–48 in Alexander Cudsi and Ali Dessouki (eds.), *Islam and Power*. Baltimore and London: John Hopkins University Press, 1981.

Metrowich, F. R. *South Africa's New Frontiers*. Sandton, S.A.: Valiant Publishers, 1977.

Meyers, Edward C. "Low Level Conflict: An Overview." Pp. 1–4 in *Low Intensity Conflict: Selected Readings* (RB 100–39). Fort Leavenworth, Kansas: U. S. Army Command and General Staff College, 1983.

Meyrowitz, Elliot. "Nuclear Weapons are Illegal Threats." *Bulletin of the Atomic Scientists* (May 1985): 35–37.

Michalak, Laurence. *Cruel and Unusual: Negative Images of Arabs in Popular American Culture*. Washington, D.C.: American-Arab Anti-Discrimination Committee (January 1984).

Mills, C. Wright. *The Power Elite*. New York: Oxford University Press (1956) 1959.

Misra, K. P. "The New International and Communication Order: An Overview." Pp. 23–28 in Hans Koechler (ed.), *The New Inter-national Information and Communication Order*. Vienna: Wilhelm Braumuller, 1985.

Moleah, Alfred. "Zionism and Apartheid: The Negation of Human Rights." *The International Journal of World Studies*, Vol. 1, No. 1 (Winter 1984): 67–88.

*Moody's Industrial Manual.* Vols. 1 and 2. New York: Moody's Investor Service, Inc., 1986 and 1988.

Morrison, David C. "Reagan's Secret Soldiers." *South* (October 1985): 37–40.

National Rifle Association. "What Should the Rules Be?" *Parade* (February 1988): 7.

Neel, James V., Gilbert W. Beebe, and Robert W. Miller. "Delayed Biomedical Effects of the Bombs." *Bulletin of the Atomic Scientists* (August 1985): 73–75.

Nemko, Ned. "The Pillars of Apartheid." *Christian Science Monitor* in *The Oregonian* (June 25, 26, 27, 1986).

Netanyahu, Benjamin (ed.). *Terrorism: How the West Can Win.* New York: Farrar, Straus, Giroux, 1986.

Newman, David. *Jewish Settlement in the West Bank: The Role of Gush Emunim.* Durham, U.K.: Centre for Middle Eastern and Islamic Studies, 1982.

*New Statesman.* "Think of Britain" (115 (3), April 8, 1988).

*Newsweek.* "The West Bank Boils Over" (April 1982): 34–46.

———. "A View from the Bullseye." (April 28, 1986): 30.

*New York Times.* "U.N. Council Votes to Condemn Killing of Top PLO Aide," April 26, 1988.

———. "U. S. Protests Move by Israelis to Deport Non-Violent Resister," May 7, 1988.

Noer, Thomas J. *Britain, Boer and Yankee: The United States and South Africa, 1870–1914.* Kent, Ohio: Kent State University Press, 1978.

Norris, Robert S., Thomas B. Cochran, and William M. Arkin. "History of the Nuclear Stockpile." *Bulletin of the Atomic Scientists* (August 1985): 106–9.

Nuclear Weapons Databook (Working Paper No. 87–1). "U. S. Soviet Strategic Nuclear Forces (1946–1986)." *Bulletin of the Atomic Scientists,* May, 1987.

Offe, Claus. *Structural Problems of the Capitalist State.* London: Macmillan (1972), 1982.

Othman, Haroub and Judith Kiss. "The Destabilizing Role of the Apartheid Regime." *Enfoques* (12) Havana: Centro de Estudios de Africa y Medio Oriente, 1986.

Palestine Human Rights Campaign. *Israeli Settler Violence in the Occupied Territories (1980–84).* Chicago, Ill., 1986.

Panofsky, Wolfang, K. H. "Arms Control: Necessary Process." *Bulletin of the Atomic Scientists* (March 1986): 35–38.

Parenti, Michael. *Inventing Reality: The Politics of the Mass Media.* New York: St. Martin's Press, 1986.

Parry, Albert. *Terrorism from Robespierre to Arafat:* New York: Vanguard, 1976.

Pasti, Nino. Personal correspondence to author. Rome, February 12, 1987.

Paterson, Thomas G. *American Foreign Policy: A History.* New York: D. C. Heath, 1977.

Perdue, William D. "Ideology and the Third Universal Theory." *The International Journal of World Studies* (Winter 1984): 89–106.

———. "The Ideology of Terrorism." Pp. 27–55 in T. Sono (ed.), *Libya: The Vilified Revolution.* Langley Park, Md. Progress Press, 1985.

———. *Sociological Theory: Explanation, Paradigm, and Ideology.* Palo Alto, Calif.: Mayfield Publishers, 1986.

Perkins, Raymond K. "Deterrence is Immoral." *Bulletin of the Atomic Scientists* (February 1985): 32–34.

Pesaran, M. H. "Economic Development and Revolutionary Upheavals in Iran." Pp. 15–

50 in Haleh Afshar (ed.), *Iran: A Revolution in Turmoil*. Albany, N.Y.: State University of New York Press, 1985.

Pfohl, Stephen. *Images of Deviance and Social Control: A Sociological History*. New York: McGraw-Hill, 1985.

Pion-Berlin, David. *Ideas as Predictors: A Comparative Study of Coercion In Peru and Argentina*. Ph.D. Dissertation, University of Denver, 1984.

Poland, James, *Understanding Terrorism*. Englewood Cliffs, N.J.: Prentice-Hall, 1988.

*Public Report of the Vice President's Task Force on Combatting Terrorism*. Washington, D.C.: U.S. Government Printing Office, February, 1986.

Qaddafi, Muammar. *The Green Book*. Tripoli: Secretariat of Information, 1976.

Ramazani, Rouhollah. *Iran's Foreign Policy (1941–1973): A Study of Foreign Policy in Modernizing Nations*. Charlottesville, Va.: University Press of Virginia, 1975.

Rangel, Domingo Alberto. "Ronald Reagan's Policy in Central America and the Violation of Human Rights, International Law and the Sovereignty of the Nations of This Region." Pp. 57–70 in Hans Koechler (ed), *The Reagan Administration's Foreign Policy*. Vienna: IPO Press, 1984.

Reagan, Ronald. "The New Network of Terrorist States." Current Policy No. 721. United States Department of State. Washington, D. C.: U. S. Government Printing Office, 1985.

———. "Libyan Sanctions." Current Policy No. 780. United States Department of State. Washington, D. C.: U. S. Government Printing Office (January 7) 1986.

Reasons, Charles, and William D. Perdue. *The Ideology of Social Problems*. Sherman Oaks, Calif.: Alfred, 1981.

Reifel, Stuart. "Children Living with the Nuclear Threat." *Young Children* (July 1984): 74–80.

Republic of South Africa. Department of Foreign Affairs and Information. *South Africa 1983: Official Yearbook of the Republic of South Africa*, 9th Edition. Pretoria: D.F.A.I., 1983.

Reston, James. "A President Who's Not in Charge." *Spokane Spokesman-Review* (November 28 1986): 4.

Robertson, Ian and Phillip Whitten. "Introduction." Pp. xi–xx in Ian Robertson and Phillip Whitten (eds.), *Race and Politics in South Africa*. New Brunswick, N.J.: Transaction, 1978.

Rodinson, Maxime. *Israel: A Colonial Settler State?* New York: Monad Press, (1967) 1973.

Rodney, Walter. *How Europe Underdeveloped Africa*. Washington, D.C.: Howard University Press, 1974.

Rokach, Livia. *Israel's Sacred Terrorism*. Third Edition. Belmont, Mass.: AAUG Press, 1986.

Roosevelt, Kermit. *Counter-coup: The Struggle for the Control of Iran*. New York: McGraw-Hill, 1979.

Rosenberg, Howard L. *Atomic Soldiers: American Victims of Nuclear Experiments*. Boston: Beacon Press, 1980.

Roy, Sara. *The Gaza Strip Survey*. Jerusalem: The West Bank Data Base Project, 1986.

Rubenberg, Cheryl. *The Palestine Liberation Organization: Its Institutional Infrastructure*. Belmont, Mass.: Institute of Arab Studies, 1983.

Ryan, Paul B. *The Iranian Rescue Mission: Why it Failed*. Annapolis, Maryland: Naval Institute Press, 1985.

Ryan, Randolph. "Reagan vs. Nicaragua: Thwarting Peace Efforts, Destabilizing the Country." *Boston Globe*, July 26, 1988.
Sabri, Jiryis. *The Arabs in Israel*. Monthly Review Press, 1976.
Sagan, Carl. "Nuclear War and Climatic Catastrophe: Some Policy Implications." *Foreign Affairs* 62(2) 1983/84: 257–92.
———. "Billions and Billions." *Parade* (May 31, 1987): 8–9.
Said, Edward. *Orientalism*. New York: Pantheon, 1978.
———. *The Question of Palestine*. New York: Times Books, 1979.
———. *Covering Islam*. New York: Pantheon, 1981.
*San Francisco Examiner*. "Big Bay Area Cocaine Ring Tied to Contras." March 16, 1986a.
———. "Nicaraguan Exile's Cocaine-Contra Connection." June 23, 1986(b).
Sartori, Leo. "When the Bomb Falls." *Bulletin of the Atomic Scientists* (June/July 1983): 40–47.
Scarry, Elaine. *The Body in Pain: The Making and Unmaking of the World*. New York and Oxford: Oxford University Press, 1985.
Scheer, Robert. *With Enough Shovels: Reagan, Bush and Nuclear War*. New York: Random House, 1982.
Schmidt, Elizabeth. *Decoding Corporate Camouflage: U. S. Business Support for Apartheid*. Washington, D. C.: Institute for Policy Studies, 1985.
Schoenbaum, David. *Hitler's Social Revolution*. New York: Doubleday, 1967.
Segev, Tom. 1949: *The First Israelis*. New York: The Free Press, 1986.
Selser, Gregorio. *Sandino*. Tr. by Cedric Belfrage. New York and London: Monthly Review Press, 1981.
Shaheen, Jack A. "Media Coverage of the Middle East: Perception and Foreign Policy." *The Annals of the American Academy of Political and Social Science*, Vol. 482 (November 1985): 160–75.
Shemesh, Moshe. "The founding of the PLO, 1964." *Middle Eastern Studies*, vol. 20, No. 4 (October 1984): 105–41.
Shirer, William. *The Rise and Fall of the Third Reich*. New York: Simon and Schuster, 1960.
Sick, Gary. *All Fall Down*. New York: Random House, 1985.
Silberner, Joanne. "Psychological A-Bomb Worlds." *Science News* (November 7, 1981):296–98.
Sinai, Ruth. "U.S. Officials Say Habre Planning Final Push." *Spokane Spokesman-Review* (August 27, 1987): B6.
Sivard, R. L. "Arms or Alms." *National Catholic Reporter* 24 (April 8, 1977): 8.
Sizwe, No (Pseudonym). *One Azania, One Nation: The National Question in South Africa*. London: Zed, 1979.
Skocpol, Theda. *States and Social Revolutions*. Cambridge, U.K.: Cambridge University Press, 1979.
Sono, Themba. *Reaganism over Libya: Politics of Aggression*. Langley Park, Md.: International Center for Democracy, 1984.
———. *Libya: The Vilified Revolution*. Langley Park, Md.: Progress, 1985a.
———. "Why the Need for a New International Information Order?" Pp. 47–49 in Hans Koechler (ed.), *The New International Information and Communication Order*. Vienna: Wilhelm Braumuller, 1985b.
———. "State Terrorism and Liberation Movements: The Case of South Africa." Paper

presented at the International Progress Organization (Vienna) Conference on the Question of Terrorism. March 18–20, Geneva, Switzerland, 1987.

Sorokin, Pitirim. *Contemporary Sociological Theories*. New York: Harper and Row, 1964.

*Spokane Spokesman-Review*. "Soviet N-Subs Sail off U.S. Shores" (May 21, 1984): 1.

———. "Democrat Claims Reagan Not Measuring Up to FDR" (August 2, 1984): 3.

———. "South Africa's Economy Not Hurt by Curtailment" (October 22, 1987): B6.

———. "PLO Office Closed Down" (September 16, 1987): D4.

———. "Noriega: Find Origin of Charges" (February 8, 1988): A2.

———. "PLO 'Ship of Return' Ripped by Explosion" (February 16, 1988): A2.

———. "U.N. Condemns U.S." (March 24, 1988): A2.

———. "Israelis Accused of Rampage" (April 10, 1988): A3.

———. "Guerrillas Shoot Down Plane with 29 Aboard" (April 11, 1988): A3.

———. "Assassination of Wazir Reunites Arafat, Syria" (April 25, 1988): A8.

———. "World Court Rebukes U.S." (April 27, 1988): A3.

———. "Arab Students Return to West Bank Schools (May 24, 1988): A2.

Sterling, Claire. "Qaddafi Spells Chaos." *The New Republic*. March 7, 1981a.

———. *The Terror Network*. New York: Holt, Rinehart and Winston, 1981b.

Stimson, Henry. *American Policy in Nicaragua*. New York: Arno Press (1927), 1970.

Stork, Joe. "Mad Dogs and Presidents." *Middle East Report* (May–June 1986): 6–10.

Sumner, William Graham. *Social Darwinism: Selected Essays of William Graham Sumner*. Englewood Cliffs, N.J.: Prentice-Hall, 1963.

Sutherland, D. M. G. *France 1789–1815: Revolution and Counterrevolution*. New York and Oxford: Oxford University Press, 1986.

Tatum, Lyle (ed.). *South Africa: Challenge and Hope*. New York: Hill and Wang, 1987.

Temko, Ned. "Afrikaner 'Glue' Beginning to Come Unstuck." *The Oregonian* (June 27, 1986): A2.

Thompson, John M. "Allied and American Intervention in Russia, 1918–1921." Pp. 319–80 in Cyril Black (ed.), *Rewriting Russian History*. 2nd edition. New York: Vintage, 1962.

Thompson, Leonard M. "The South African Dilemma." Pp. 178–218 in Louis Hartz (ed.), *The Founding of New Societies*. New York: Harcourt, Brace and World, 1964.

Thompson, Mark. "U. S. Warship Downs Jetliner; 290 on Board." *Spokane Spokesman-Review* (July 4, 1986): A1.

Thornton, A. P. *Imperialism in the Twentieth Century*. Minneapolis, Minn.: The University of Minnesota Press, 1977.

Thornton, Thomas. "Terror as a Weapon of Political Agitation." Pp. 71–99 in H. Eckstein (ed.) Internal War, 1964.

*Time*. "Two Teeth for a Tooth." (June 16, 1980): 32–33.

———. "Shootout over the Med." (August 31, 1981): 14–18.

———. "U.S. Policy Goes on Trial" (September 30, 1985): 85–86.

———. "Hitting the Source." (April 28, 1986): 17–33.

*Tower Commission Report*. New York: Bantam, 1987.

Townshend, Charles. *Political Violence in Ireland: Government and Resistance Since 1848*. Oxford: Clarendon Press, 1983.

Tuchman, Gaye. *The T.V. Establishment: Programming for Power and Profit*. Englewood Cliffs, N.J.: Prentice-Hall, 1974.

Tully, Andrew. *CIA: The Inside Story*. New York: William Morrow, 1962.
U.N. Chronicle. "Nicaragua's Sovereignty and Indpendence Should Not Be Jeopardized by Military Activities." Pp. 154–78 in Andrew C. Kimmens (ed.), *Nicaragua and the United States*. New York: H. W. Wilson (1984), 1987.
———. "International Court Rules United States' Actions Towards Nicaragua 'breach of international law,' " Vol. 23, 1986: 110.
U.S. Arms Control and Disarmament Agency. *World Military Expenditures and Arms Transfers 1972–1982*. Washington, D.C.: U.S. Government Printing Office, 1984.
U.S. Army Command and General Staff College. *Low Intensity Conflict*. Fort Leavenworth, Kan. U.S. Army Command and General Staff College, 1983.
U.S. Arms Control and Disarmament Agency. *World Military Expenditures and Arms Transfers 1972–1982*. Washington, D.C.: U.S. Government Printing Office, 1984.
U.S. Army Command and General Staff College. *Low Intensity Conflict*. Fort Leavenworth, Kan. U.S. Army Command and General Staff College, 1983.
U.S. Bureau of Census. *Statistical Abstract of the United States: 100th Edition*. Washington, D.C.: U.S. Government Printing Office, 1979.
ities." July 8. Washington, D.C.: U.S. Government Printing Office, 1981.
U.S. Congress, Committee on Internal Security, House of Representatives. Terrorism, Parts 1, 2, 3, and 4. Washington, D.C.: U.S. Government Printing Office, 1974.
U.S. Congress, Committee on Labor and Human Resources, United States Senate. *Drugs and Terrorism*. Washington, D.C.: U.S. Government Printing Office, 1984.
U.S. Congress, Committee on the Judiciary, United States Senate. *Trotskyite Terrorist International*. Washington, D.C.: U.S. Government Printing Office, 1975.
U.S. Congress, Congressional Budget Office. "Trident II Missiles: Capability, Costs and Alternatives." Washington, D.C.: U.S. Government Printing Office, 1986.
U.S. Congress, Subcommittee on Europe and the Middle East, Committee on Foreign Affairs, House of Representatives Hearing on "The Media, Diplomacy and Terrorism, in the Middle East." July 30. Washington, D.C.: U.S. Government Printing Office, 1985.
U.S. Congress, Subcommittee on Security and Terrorism, United States Senate. "Soviet, East German and Cuban Involvement in Fomenting Terrorism in South Africa." Washington, D.C.: U.S. Government Printing Office, 1982.
U.S. Congress, U.S. Senate. Executive Report No. 97–8, *Nomination of Chester A. Crocker*. Washington, D.C.: U.S. Government Printing Office, 1981.
U.S. Department of Defense. Directorate for Information Operations and Reports. "100 Companies Receiving the Largest Dollar Volume of Prime Contract Awards." Washington, D.C.: U.S. Government Printing Office, 1985.
———. "National Defense and Total Military-Related Spending by the U.S. from 1981 to 1988." Cited in *Spokane Spokesman-Review*, A–13, June 26, 1988.
U.S. Department of State. "U.S. Withdrawal From the Proceedings Initiated by Nicaragua in the ICJ." *Department of State Bulletin* (March 1985(a)): 64–65.
———. "Economic Sanctions against Nicaragua." *Department of State Bulletin* (July 1985(b)): 74–77.
———. "Statement by Abraham D. Sofaer on the United States and the World Court." *Department of State Bulletin* (December 1985(c)):1–4.
———. "Libya Under Qadaffi: A Pattern of Aggression." *Special Report No. 138*, January, 1986.
———. Office of Media Services, Bureau of Public Affairs. *Viet Cong Terror Tactics*

*in South Vietnam* (No. 7). Washington, D.C.: U.S. Government Printing Office, 1968.

U.S. Department of the Treasury. "Monthly Statement of the Public Debt of the United States, November 30, 1988." Washington, D.C.: U.S. Government Printing Office, 1988.

*U.S. News and World Report.* "New Sellers in Arms Bazaar." (February 3, 1986): 37–39.

Utley, Robert. *Lessons of Ulster.* London: J. M. Dent and Sons, 1975.

Vanderlaan, Mary B. *Revolution and Foreign Policy in Nicaragua.* Boulder and London: Westview, 1986.

Vatin, Jean-Claude. "Popular Puritanism Versus State Reformism: Islam in Algeria." Pp. 98–121 in James P. Piscatori (ed.), *Islam in Political Process.* Cambridge: Cambridge University Press, 1983.

Von Lave, Theodore H. *Why Lenin? Why Stalin?* Philadelphia: J. B. Lippincott, 1964.

Waggoner, Fred E. *Dragon Rouge: The Rescue of Hostages in the Congo.* Washington, D.C.: U.S. Government Printing Office, 1980.

Walker, Tony. "Debt Service Problems in Egypt." *The Banker* 135 (December 1985): 101–2.

Wallerstein, Immanuel. *The Modern World-System: Capitalist Agriculture and the Origins of the European World Economy in the 16th Century.* New York: Academic Press, 1974.

———. *The Capitalist World Economy.* London: Cambridge University Press, 1979.

———. *The Modern World System II: Mercantilism and the Consolidation of the European World-Economy, 1600–1750.* New York: Academic Press, 1980.

Walter, Eugene Victor. *Terror and Resistance: A Study of Political Violence.* London: Oxford Press, 1969.

Wardlaw, Grant. *Political Terrorism: Theory, Tactics and Countermeasures.* Cambridge: Cambridge University Press, 1982.

*Washington Report on Middle East Affairs.* "The Full Cost of Israel" (September 8, 1986): 2–3.

Wax, Murray L. *Indian Americans: Unity and Diversity.* Englewood Cliffs, N.J.: Prentice-Hall, 1971.

Weber, Max. *Theory of Social and Economic Organization.* Translated and edited by A. M. Henderson and Talcott Parsons. Glencoe, Illinois: The Free Press (1922), 1957.

Weisman, John. "Why American TV is so Vulnerable to Foreign Disinformation." *TV Guide* (June 12, 1982): 5–16.

Weitzman, Chaim. *Trial and Error.* New York: Harper and Row, 1949.

Whited, Charles. "A Quarter-Century Ago, World was at the Brink." *Spokane Spokesman-Review* (October 23, 1987): 5.

Wilber, D. *Riza Shah Pahlavi: The Resurrection and Reconstruction of Iran.* New York: Exposition Press, 1975.

Wilde, Margaret. "Fighting the Sandinistas With Dollars." *The Christian Century* (November 4, 1987): 957–58.

Wilkinson, Paul. *Terrorism and the Liberal State.* London: Macmillan, 1977.

Wilson, Monila and Leonard Thompson. *The Oxford History of South Africa.* New York: Oxford University Press, 1969.

Wish, Harvey. "American Slave Insurrections Before 1861." *Journal of Negro History* 22 (July 1937): 299–320.
Woodward, Bob. *VEIL: The Secret Wars of the CIA, 1981–1987*. New York: Simon and Schuster, 1987.
Woodward, Ralph. *Central America: A Nation Divided*. New York: Oxford University Press, 1976.
*World Almanac*. New York: Pharos, 1987.
World Health Organization. *World Health Statistics*. Geneva, Switzerland, 1986.
Wright, Robin. *Sacred Rage: The Wrath of Militant Islam*. New York: Simon and Schuster, 1986.

# Index

Abbas, Abul, 139
Abdel-Wahhab, Muhammad Ibn, 166
ABM (Anti-Ballistic Missile) treaty, 84
Abrams, Elliot, 182
Abu-Nidal (Sabri Al Banni), 13, 55, 139
Achille Lauro, 139
Adelman, Kenneth, 78
Adler, Alfred, 77
African National Congress (ANC), 3, 92, 94–95, 106, 107; Freedom Charter of, 108. *See also* apartheid
*Africans, The*, 115
Afrikaner, 97. *See also* apartheid
Age of Imperialism, 141
Ahmad, Eqbal, 140
Ahmad, Muhammad (Al-Mahdi), 166
Ajax, Operation, 172–73. *See also* Iranian reaction, imperialism and
ALF (Arab Liberation Front), 139
Al Fatah, 138
Al-Ghazzali, Muhammad, 164
*Al-Kiyan Al-Filastini*, 140
*Al-Saiqa*, 139
Al-Sanusi, Muhammad Ibn Ali, 166
Amador, Carlos Fonseca, 193
Amal, 169

Amin, Idi, 117
Amini, Ali, 175
Amnesty International, 31, 49
Anderson, Jack, 53
Anglo-Irish Agreement (1985), 32
anticommunism, ideology of, 11–12, 15, 85, 90–92, 120–21, 136
Aouzou Strip, 116. *See also* Libya
apartheid, xi, 90, 108; Afrikaner *Broederbond* and, 100; Afrikaner Nationalist Party and, 98, 100; caste capitalism and, 99–103, 105; Comprehensive Anti-Apartheid Act (1986) and, 96; constructive engagement, Reagan Administration policy and, 95–96, 104; divestment movement and, 106; Dutch Reformed Church and, 100; Global, xi, 103–7; grand, 98–99, 102; "Great Trek" and, 99; ideology of, 97–99, 101; institutional terror of, 96–97; International Convention on the Suppression and Punishment of the Crime of Apartheid (1973), 95; Israeli ties and, 106–7; Land Act of 1913 and, 105; Langa Massacre and, 96; National Security Management System and, 92–

94; Ossewabrandwag and, 101; petit, 103; second Anglo-Boer War and, 100; Sharpeville massacre and, 96; South African Defence Force and, 92; South African National Emergency State and, 92–94; Soweto rebellion and, 97; Stellenbosh and, 100
Arafat, Yassir, 138, 139
Arbenz, Jacobo, 190
Arens, Moshe, 135
Arguello, Leonardo, 190
Article 51 (U.N. Charter), 137
Aryan myth, 5
*Ashkenazim*, 134
"Atomic Soldiers," 80. *See also* nuclear terrorism
Auschwitz, 36–37
*Auto-Emancipation*, 141
Avineri, Shlomo, 133
Awad, Mubarak E., 152
Awan, Akhtar A., 130

Balfour, Arthur (Balfour Declaration), 141–42
Bani-Sadr, Abolhassan, 179
Bantustans. *See* apartheid, grand
Barbarossa, 119
Battle of the Boyne, 27. *See also* Northern Ireland
Begin, Menachim, 145, 146
Beita, 151
Ben-Gurion, David, 143, 146, 147
Berri, Nabih, 169
Betzner, Gary, 201
Biko, Steve, 89, 96
Blacks and Tans, 28
Black September, 138, 139
Blood River, Battle of, 99. *See also* apartheid
Bloody Friday, 31. *See also* Northern Ireland
Bloody Sunday, 31. *See also* Northern Ireland
Blum, Yehuda, 136, 137
Borge, Tomas, 193
Botha, Pieter W., 103
Bretton Woods, New Hampshire (1944), 143; General Agreement on Tariffs and Trade and, 143; International Monetary Fund and, 143; World Bank and, 143
Broederbond, Afrikaner, 100
Buchenwald, 36, 41
Bukharin, Nikolai, 41
Bundy, McGeorge, 78
Burntollet Bridge, 30
Bush report, the (*Public Report of the Vice President's Task Force on Combatting Terrorism*), 2–4

Calvinism. *See* apartheid, ideology of
Camp David accords, 145
Carter, Jimmy, 145, 160, 163
Casey, William, 54, 161, 198
Castro, Fidel, 70
Central Intelligence Agency (CIA), *xi*; blunders and, 122; Chad and, 116; Cuban Bay of Pigs and, 191; Guatemala and, 191; Iran and, 173, 175 (*see also* Ajax, Operation); Lebanon and, 46; Libya and, 53–54, 116; Neutrality Act and, 194; Nicaragua and, 194–95, 195–96
Chamberlain, H. S., 5
Chamorro, Edgar, 194
Chamorro, Emiliano, 186, 189
Chamorro, Fernando, 201
Chauvin, Nicolas, 25
chauvinism, 25–26
Chichester-Clark, Major James, 30
Chipman, William, 81
Chomsky, Noam, 55
Clark, Ramsey, 43n
Cline, Ray S., 53
colonialism, 5–6, 10, 23–26, 118–21; apartheid and, 90. *See also* imperialism; internal colonialism; neocolonialism
Connolly, James, 28
Consulate, the, 36
Contras. *See* surrogate terrorism, Contras and
Convention, the, 34
Copson, Raymond, 52
counterterrorism, *ix*
crackpot realism, 2
Cranston, Alan, 135

Crocker, Chester, 90, 91, 104, 113–14
Cromwell, Oliver, 27
Cuadra, Abelardo, 188
Cuban Missile Crisis, 78–79. *See also* nuclear terrorism

Dachau, 36
Dail Eireann (Irish Constituent Assembly), 28
Danaher, Kevin, 101
Danton, George Jacques, 34
Davis, Peter, 181
Dayan, Moshe, 147
death squads, *xi*, 48
Delta Force, 47, 59, 160
dependency relations, 26
Dessouki, Ali, 161
development: for dependency, 15, 174–75; growth and distribution models of, 41. *See also* modernization, ideology of
Diaspora, the, 134
Diaz, Adolfo, 186, 189
Direct Action (French), 2
Directory, 35. *See also* French Revolution

Edwards, James B., 81
Eisenhower, Dwight D., 77, 78
Elizabeth I, 27
Engels, Friedrich, 7
Erikson, Kai, 74
*Estates-General*, 34
European Convention for the Protection of Human Rights and Fundamental Freedoms, 32
*Everything in its Path*, 74
existentialism, 80

Faisal, Emir, 142
Fanon, Frantz, 12, 24
*faqih*, 164; guardianship of the jurisconsult (*wilayat-i-faqih*) and, 164–65
Fedlallah, Sheikh, 46
Fenian Brotherhood, 28
Fermi, Enrico, 80
Fikentscher, Wolfgang, 136

final solution *xi*, 36–38. *See also* global market disjunction; Nazi Germany
Free Presbyterians, 29
French Revolution, the: British commercial ascendance and, 33; Committee of Public Safety and, 34, 35; the Convention and, 34–35; First Republic, 34; ideology and, 34–35; National Constituent Assembly and, 34; Revolutionary Tribunal and, 35; *Sans-coulotte* and, 34. *See also* global market, disjunction; Jacobins; Terror, the
*Front de la Liberation Nationale* (Algeria), 10

Garrison, Cornelius, 183
George V, 28
Giuffrida, Louis, 81
global market disjunction, 33
Gobineau, Arthur de, 5
Gordon, Charles, 167
Gorman, Paul, 199
Government of Ireland Act (1920), 28
Gralnick, Jeff, 53
Great Depression, 37
Great Patriotic War, 38
Great Satan, the, 163, 166
Guardianship of the Jurisconsult. *See Faqih*

Habermas, Juergen, 8
Habre, Hissene, 116
Haig, Alexander, 54, 90, 91, 113
Hanna, Matthew, 188
Hatfield, G. D., 188
Hawatmeh, Nayaf, 139
Hawkins, Paula, 11
Henry II, 27
Henry VIII, 27
Hersh, Seymour, 53, 56
Hertzl, Theodor, 141, 142
Hertzog, J.B.M., 100
*Hizbollah*, 46, 169. *See also* Iranian reaction, the
holy terror, 161–63, 166–69. *See also* Iranian reaction, the
Hoover, Herbert, 189
Hull, John, 201

Hunt, Nelson Bunker, 121
Hussein, Saddem, 160
Hussein, Sharif, 142

ideology: defined, 6–8; domination and, 4–6; modernization and, 41–42; particular, 7; terrorism and, *x*; total, 6–8, 60. *See also* terrorism, dominant and utopian ideologies of
imperialism, 23–26; Age of, 6; Britain and Ireland, *xi*, 26–33
Inkatha, 107
internal colonialism: Israel and, 155–56; South Africa and, 97–103
International Court of Justice (World Court), 57. *See also* Nicaragua
International Economic Order, 4, 8. *See also* world system
International Monetary Fund, 174
*Intifadah*, 151–53
Iran-Contra Affair (Irangate), 18, 161, 176–77
Iranian reaction, the: cultural purification and, 162–63; imperialism and, 162, 169–72; *Jihad* and, 166, 167, 168; *Mahdi* (*Intizar*) and, 165; Movement ideology and, 164–69; Mujaheddin Khalq and, 176, 179n; Theocratic state, the, 164–66; U.S. Embassy takeover in Tehran, 159–60
Iran-Iraq War, 160–61; *Ba'ath* Arab socialism and, 160; Israeli support of, 176–77; Shatt al-Arab waterway and, 160
*Irgun Tsvai Leumi*, 145
Irish Free State, 29
Irish National Liberation Army, 43n
Irish Republican Army, 29–32
Irish Republican Brotherhood, 28
Islam: ideological structure of, 162–63; social movements (*Mahdist, Sanusi, Wahhabism*), and, 166–69. *See also Shi'ite; Sunni*
Israel: arms exports and expenditures, 144, 156–57; Peace Now Movement, 156; South African connection, 144, 154–57 (*see also* apartheid); U.S. aid to, 144. *See also* sacred terrorism; settler terrorism, Israeli; Zionism

Jabril, Ahmed, 139
Jacobins, 15, 34–36
*Jewish State, The*, 140–44
Johnson, Lyndon, 65
Johnson, Paul, 135
Jonathan Institute, The, 135
Jones, Phil, 53
Jones, T. K., 82

Kalb, Bernard, 57
Kennedy, John F., 78, 79
Khaldun, Ibn, 9
Khan, Reza (Pahlavi), 170–72
Khomeini, Ayatollah Ruhollah, 159, 160, 161, 164–66, 175, 178; *Asala* and, 165; Twelfth or Hidden *Imam* and, 165. *See also faqih*; Iran; *Shi'ite*
Khrushchev, Nikita, 38, 41
King, Martin Luther, Jr., 47
Kirkpatrick, Jeane, 135, 195
Kissinger, Henry, 175
kneecappings, 31
Krohn, Robert, 80
Kupperman, Charles, 82

Lane, Arthur Bliss, 188, 204n
Laxalt, Paul, 135
Ledeen, Michael, 11
legitimation, 18
legitimation crisis, 8
Lenin, V. I., 39, 41, 201
liberation theology, 162, 203
Libya: agricultural synthesis, 129–30; Chadian intervention, 116–17; colonial history of, 118–21; conventional terror, 114–15; counterrevolution, U.S. policy of, 114, 120–21; disinformation and, 53–57, 114; Draper Committee, 120; *El Fatah* Revolution, 113, 121–23; Free Officers Movement, 121; "great artificial river, 129–30; hit team story, 52–54; Israel, opposition to, 117–18, 122; Italian colonization, 119–20; LaBelle discothèque bombing, 56; *Lijan Thawriya* (revolutionary committees),

131; material transformation of, 127–31; media coverage, 51–57; National liberation movements, support of, 116; OPEC and, 124–25; Operation El Dorado Canyon, 50–51, 56; Operation Prairie Fire, 55–56; Petrocorporations and, 120–21, 124–25; Reagan Administration allegations, 51–53, 113–14; Sirte (Gulf of) shootout, 51–52; Third Universalism, ideology of, 113, 126–27, 131–32; Ugandan policy, 117–18; women in, 127–28; zonal revolution, 112, 131–32
Louis XV, 33
Louis XVI, 33
low-intensity conflict, 198–99
Luken, Thomas, 47

McBride, Sean, 71
McCloughlin, Father James, 47
Machiavelli, Niccolò, 18
McMichael, David, 197
McNamara, Robert, 78
Maghrib, The, 118
Malan, D. F., 101, 107
Mandela, Nelson, 96
Manifest Destiny, 182–83, 184
Mannheim, Karl, 7–8
Marat, Jean-Paul, 34
Marshall, Ruth, 56
Marshall Plan, 143. *See also* world-system
Marx, Karl, 7, 159
Masmoudi, Mustapha (media paradigm), 61
Matanzima, George, 107
Maududi, Abulala, 164
Mau-Mau, 10
Mauthausen, 36
Maze Prison, 31
Mazrui, Ali, 115
Medellin Cartel, 201
media (the selling of international terrorism): "beholding the mote," 49; commodification of terrorism, 48–50, 61–62, 65–66; corporate structure of, 62–65; "counterfeit balance," 49; merger-mania and, 63; "struggling for democracy" myth, 49; UNESCO, the need for a new international information order and, 66; Western international domination, 60–61
mediaspeak, 45, 48–49
Medvedev, Roy, 40
Meese, Edwin, 135
Meneses-Cantero, Norwin, 201
Merad, Ali, 165
Merton, Thomas, 72
Meyer, Edward C., 200
Milian-Rodriquez, Ramon, 201
Mills, C. Wright, 1. *See also* crackpot realism
Millspaugh, Arthur, 170
*Mission Civilisee*, 154
modernization, ideology of, 41–42. *See also* development
Moncada, Jose, 187
Monroe Doctrine, The, 183, 185
Morales, George, 201
MOSSAD, 145, 178
Mossadeq, Mohammed, 172–73
Moynahan, Daniel P., 135
Mukhtar, Umar El (Lion of the Desert), 119–20
"Murder Incorporated," 10
Mussolini, Benito, 119–20

*Nadelstichtaktik*, 137
Namibia, 91, 94, 95. *See also* apartheid; RSA; SWAPO
Napoleon (Bonaparte), 25, 35–36
narcoterrorism, 11, 200–202. *See also* Medellin Cartel; Nicaragua
Nasser, Gamal Abdul, 121, 122
National Jewish Agency, 56
national liberation movements, 10, 26, 94–96, 112, 116
National Security Council, 54, 57, 181, 194
National Security State, 16, 20–23, 42
Native Americans, 3, 23, 25
Nazi Germany, 36; Great Depression and, 37; ideology of nation-race and, 37–38; new middle classes and, 37. *See also* global market disjunction
neocolonialism, 24–26, 119–21

Netanyahu, Benjamin, 135, 136
Netanyahu, Jonathan, 135
New Economic Policy (Lenin), 41
New Global Security Economy, 16, 20–23, 83
New International Information and Communication Order (UNESCO), 61, 66
Nicaragua: Alliance for Progress and, 191, 192; authentic development and, 202–3; "big stick" and, 185, 190; *Camisas Azules* and, 189; Conservative and Liberal Parties in, 184–91; Dawson Pact and, 185; "dollar diplomacy" and, 185; Educational Credit Program and, 192; "Good Neighbor" policy and, 189–90; *Guardia Nacional* and, 188–93; International Court of Justice and, 196–97; *La Prensa* and, 195; National Endowment for Democracy and, 195; Nicaraguan Development Foundation and, 192; Nicaraguan Socialist Party (PSN) and, 193; Organization of American States (OAS) and, 193; Sandinista National Liberation Front (FSLN) and, 191–93; Superior Council of Private Initiative and (*C.O.S.I.P.*), 192; U.S. economic destabilization and, 193–96. *See also* Iran-Contra; Manifest Destiny; Monroe Doctrine, The; Sandinistas; surrogate terrorism, Contras and
Nixon, Richard, 65, 78, 169, 175
North, Oliver, 161, 181
Northern Ireland, 26–33, 116; Campaign for Social Justice, 30; Civil Rights Association, 30; Royal Ulster Constabulary, 30; Ulster Special Constabulary, 30. *See also* imperialism; I.R.A.; P.I.R.A.
*Nuclear Hostages*, 70
nuclear terrorism: bomber gap and, 77–78; consequentialist argument and, 85–86; discriminate deterrance and, 72, 84; *Hibakusha* and, 75; ideology of nuclear deterrence, and, 80–82; *in utero* victims in Japan and, 74; Manhattan Project and, 82; "missile gap" and, 78; Multiple Independently Targeted Reentry Vehicle (M.I.R.V.) and, 77, 81; Mutually Assured Destruction (M.A.D.) and, 72; nuclear battlefields, and, 83; nuclear warfare state and, 82–83; nuclear winter and, 72, 76; the official story and, 70–71; SALT II (Strategic Arms Limitations Treaty), Soviet compliance and, 79–80; superpower strategic forces and, 79; terrorism unlimited (the real nuclear terrorism) and, 71–72; U.S. nuclear stockpile, history and cost of, 82–83, 87–88; window of vulnerability and, 78–79

Obote, Milton, 117
O'Connell, Daniel, 28
Offe, Claus, 49
Ogburn, W. F., 77
O'Keefe, Bernard, 69, 70
O'Neal, Terence, 30
Oppenheimer, Robert, 80
Organization of African Unity (OAU), 107, 116, 117, 132
Ottoman Turks, 119
Oueddei, Goukouni, 116

Pahlavi, Shah Mohammed Reza, 160, 161, 163, 171–76
Paisley, Ian, 29, 30
Palestine Liberation Organization, 3, 46, 135, 137–40; PLO National Council, 139. *See also* ALF; *AL Fatah*; *Al Saiga*; PDFLP; PFLP; PFLP-GC; PLA; PLF; PNF; Zionism
Panofsy, Wolfgang, 79
Parnell, Charles Stewart, 28
PDFLP (Popular Democratic Front for the Liberation of Palestine), 139
Pearson, Karl, 5
People's Democracy Movement, 30. *See also* Northern Ireland
Peres, Shimon, 146
Perez, Rigoberto, 191
PFLP (Popular Front for the Liberation of Palestine), 138, 139
PFLP-GC (Popular Front for the Liberation of Palestine-General Command), 139

Pinsker, Leo, 141
PLA (Palestine Liberation Army), 138
Platt Amendment, 185
PLF (Popular Liberation Front), 139
PNF (Palestine National Front), 139
Poindexter, John, 57
Pollard, Jonathan, 157
Poret, Tirza, 157
Poseidon Submarine, 81
potato famine (Irish), 27–28
*Prensa Latini*, 88
Prevention of Terrorism Acts (U.K.), 31
Price, Raymond, 1
Proudhon, Pierre-Joseph, 77
Provisional Irish Republican Army, 3, 30–33

Qaddafi, Muammar, 50, 51, 53, 54, 55, 56, 57, 70, 113–17, 122, 124–31. See also Libya
Qadir, Abdel, 168
Qumsaya, Bicharra, 155

Rabin, Yitzhak, 135, 149
racial terrorism. *See* Apartheid
*Raison d'état*: nuclear state terror and, 87–88; preemptive strikes and, 137
*Raison du monde* and nuclear disarmament, 87–88
Rand Corporation, 14
Rather, Dan, 47, 53
Rational-Legal Authority, 17–18
Reagan, Ronald, 10, 46, 52–57, 66, 95, 113, 114, 181, 194, 196
Red Army Faction, 2–3
Red Brigade, 2
reification, 18–19
RENAMO, 109n
Republic of South Africa (RSA), *x*, 10; occupation of Namibia and, 94; regional invasions, 91, 94–96; "resource war," 90. *See also* African National Congress; apartheid
Reynolds, Frank, 53
Rhodes, Cecil, 99
Rida, Rashid, 164
Robespierre, Maximilien Marie Isidore de, 33, 34, 35. *See also* French Revolution, the
Rockefeller, David, 175
Rockefeller, Nelson, 175
Rodinson, Maxime, 134, 142
Roosevelt, Franklin, 169, 189, 190
Roosevelt, Theodore, 23, 25, 185
Rousseau, Jean-Jacques: on contractualism, 34; on the peace of dungeons, 86

Sabra and Shatila. *See* sacred terrorism
Sacasa, Juan, 188, 189
Sachsenhausen, 36
sacred terrorism, 144–50; iron fist and, 147–48, 152–53, 156; Qibya and, 146–47; Sabra and Shatila and, 13, 148; *Sayaret Matkal* and, 149, 153, 199. *See also* Israel; settler terrorism, Israeli; Zionism
Sadat, Anwar, 145
St. Augustine, 15
Saint-Just, de, Louis, 35
Sandinistas, 116, 191–93; ideology of, 202–3. *See also* Nicaragua; surrogate terrorism, Contras and
Sandino, Augusto Nicolas Calderon, 187–89
Sands, Bobby, 31
Sartre, Jean Paul, 80
SAVAK, 164, 173–76. *See also* Iranian reaction, the
Scheer, Robert, 81
School of the Americas, The, 200
Segev, Tom, 146
self-determination, 137
"selling of the Pentagon," 23
separate development. *See* apartheid, grand
*Sephardim*, 32, 134, 155
settler state. *See* Zionism
settler terrorism, Israeli, 150–51; Deir Yassin and, 145; *Gush Emunim* and, 150; *Irgun Tsvai Leumi* and, 145; King David Hotel, bombing of, 145; *Lehi* (Stern Gang) and, 145
Shamgar, Meir, 135
Shamir, Yitzhak, 133, 145, 152
Shaka, 15

Sharett, Moshe, 144, 147
Shariati, Ali, 178
Sharon, Ariel, 146, 147, 148
Shi'ite, 3, 53, 159, 166–67; *Imam* and, 164–65; *Ulama* and, 164
Shultz, George, 54, 135, 136
Simba, 10
*Sinn Fein*, 28, 29
slave trade, the, 5
Smuts, General J. C., 107
Social and Democratic and Labour Party, 32. *See also* Northern Ireland
Social Darwinism, 5–6
Somoza, Anastasio ("Tachito"), 191–93, 201
Somoza, Anastasio ("Tacho"), 188–91
Somoza, Luis, 191
Southern African Development Coordination Conference, 94. *See also* apartheid; RSA
Special Air Service, British (SAS), 31, 199. *See also* Northern Ireland
Special Operations Forces, U.S., 200
Spencer, Herbert, 5
Stalin, Joseph, 38, 39, 40, 41
Stalinism, 38–41; Great Purge, 40; historical antecedents of, 39–41; *Kulaks* under, 40; Leninist state and, 39; modernization and, 39–40
Star Wars (Strategic Defense Initiative), 83–84
*State and Revolution, The*, 39
statespeak, 1, 20
stereotypes: Arab, 57–59; Islamic, 59; movies and, 59
Sterling, Claire, 9, 48, 135
Stern Gang (Lehi), 145
Stethem, Robert, 46
Stimson, Henry, 187
Sumner, William Graham, 5
Sunni, 168
"Supergrasses," 32
surrogate terrorism, Contras (Nicaraguan Democratic Force or FDN) and, 136, 181, 193–96. *See also* Sandinistas
SWAPO (Southwest Africa People's Organization), 94, 95. *See also* Namibia

Teller, Edward, 80
Terror, the, *x*, 33, 35. *See also* French Revolution, the
terrorism: dominant ideology of, 2–3, 8–12, 135–37, 200; higher, 19; hunger and, 4; institutional, *x*, 15–16; media prism and, 57; "one man's terrorist...," *ix*, *x*; political economy of, *x*, 15–16, 23–26, 33; power relations and, 3–4; privitization of, 112; psychologizing of, 9; revisionist definitions of, 41–43; "selling of," *xi*, 48–50; state (defined), *x*, 17–19; stereotypes and, 3; utopian ideology of, 12–14; vendetta terror, 13–14; war games and, 199; Western academic construction of, 14–16. *See also* holy terror; nuclear terrorism; settler terrorism, Israeli; surrogate terrorism, Contras and
*Terrorism: How the West Can Win*, 135
*Terror Network, The*, 9, 48
terrornoia, 113
Thatcher, Margaret, 105, 137
*Tohor Haneshek*, 146
Tolliver, Michael, 201
Trident Submarine, 81
Trident II Missiles, 81
Trotsky, Leon, 41
Trujillo, Rafael, 189
Truman Doctrine, 15
Tudeh Party, 172, 173. *See also* Iranian reaction, the
Turkamni, Hanza, 155
TWA Flight 847, 45–47; Amal and, 46; Bir al Abed and, 46

Ulster, 27, 29. *See also* Northern Ireland
Unequal Exchange, 16n, 155
Uneven Development, 127, 129
UNITA, 109n
United Nations, and Reagan Administration rejectionism, 196–97
United Nations Centre Against Apartheid, 94
United Nations International Covenant on Civil and Political Rights, 32

Vanderbilt, Cornelius, 183, 184
Verwoerd, H. F., 101

Viet Cong, 10
Villa, Pancho, 3, 189
Vorster, 101

Walker, William, 183, 184
Wallerstein, Immanuel, 24
warfare state, the, *xi*, 20–23. *See also* New Global Security Economy, the
Wazir, Khalil, 149
Weber, Max, 17–18
Webster, William H., 135
*Wehrmacht*, 38
Weinberger, Caspar, 200
Weisman, John, 53
Weizman, Chaim, 142
*Weltanschauung*, 60
Whelan, Thomas, 191
Will, George, 135
William of Orange, 27. *See also* Northern Ireland
Wilson, Woodrow, 185
Woodward, Bob, 57

world-system, the, 24–25
Wright, Jim, 203

x-ray laser. *See* Star Wars

ZANU (Zimbabwe African National Union), 10, 95
Zapata, Emiliano, 3, 189
ZAPU (Zimbabwe African Peoples Union), 10, 95
Zelaya, Jose Santos, 185
Zionism: Balfour Declaration and, 141–42; Congress of Basel and, 141; European colonialism and, 134, 140–44; Greater Israel and, 147, 150; Law of Return and, 150; Maximal variety of, 156–57; politico-religious ideology of, 134, 140–41; world-system and, 142–44. *See also* Israel
Ziya, Sayyid, 172
Zulu, 15, 25, 99, 107. *See also* apartheid; Inkatha

## ABOUT THE AUTHOR

WILLIAM D. PERDUE is Professor and Chair of the Department of Sociology and director of the Contemporary World Studies program at Eastern Washington University. He received his Ph.D. from Washington State University. His other books are *Sociological Theory: Explanation, Paradigm and Ideology* (1986) and *The Ideology of Social Problems* (1981) (with Charles Reasons). Recent articles include "The Ideology of Terrorism," "Crackpot Democracy: Reification and Ideology," "Settler State Terrorism," and "The Selling of International Terrorism." A frequent organizer and contributor to UNESCO Non-Governmental Organization conferences on conflict resolution, he is an affiliate of the International Progress Organization (Vienna), the Nomura Center (Tokyo), the Centro De Estudios De Africa Y Medio Oriente (Havana), Concern International (Manila), the World Centre (Tripoli), the Comité Permanent International de Juristes sur la Palestine et la Paix au Moyen-Orient (Brussels), and a founding member of the Comité International Pour la Paix en Mediterranée (Besançon). He is a member of numerous professional and honorary organizations in the United States and abroad. He is currently at work on *The Genesis Zone: Africa and the Middle East in the 21st Century.*